The Journey of the Stone Man

A Novel by

Edward Mooney, Jr.

Stone Man Press

California USA

This is the Second Book of the "Stone Man Trilogy"

Book 1 - **The Pearls of the Stone Man**
Book 2 – **The Journey of the Stone Man**
Book 3 – **The Hope of the Stone Man**

This book is
© 2002-2016 Edward Mooney, Jr.

Stone Man Press
is the imprint of the author,
Edward Mooney, Jr.

Prologue

A mountain peak is a lonely place. It's impossible to stay there for long without protection and sustenance. Men and women may come for a short visit, but it's a place where nature comes to play for long hours each day. Pine Mountain is an artist's palette, and many great artists come to express themselves there.

Appearing at regular intervals are the seasonal winds, which wistfully push the grains of sand back and forth. They bounce from rock to boulder, seeking refuge from their powerful playmate. Just below the summit the little grains find their shelter. The winds are the sculptors of the summit.

Contributing only now and then, for this is Southern California, the clouds enjoy adding shadows to the paths and ledges. They blur lines between different type of rocks, and the crevasses that create the summit. The clouds are the painters of the peaks.

A rare visitor to the mountain, water occasionally joins in the play of creation. Droplets decide which aspects of the wind's sculpting need to be changed.

All of these artists shape and play with Pine Mountain, but only one makes its home there. For untold centuries, sunlight has claimed ownership of the palette. It heats the rock, the sand, the water and the air itself. Sunlight provides the energy for the wind, and it moves the waters. It brings the water and air together in the clouds, but there comes a time when it must leave the mountain to still another set of artists. These are the shadows of night, and they appear in the late afternoons, working steadily to steal the slopes from the daytime artists.

Late afternoon sunlight in spring reaches only one side of the rocky valley below Pine Mountain. Sometimes the darker side of the valley proves to be very deceptive. While the bright sky and warmth of the day is enjoyed by many, the coldness of the shadows surprises all but the most experienced mountain dweller.

There are those who spend a great deal of time and energy moving away from the late afternoon shadows, trying to absorb the last of the day's warm rays. It may be easier to simply climb into the family car, with its comfortable heater, but, oftentimes, there are many reasons why chasing the last of the day's sunlight is preferable. Many visitors hate to return to the world of work and responsibilities that the car represents. There is an escape in the shadows of Pine Mountain.

For some, however, neither sunlight nor car heater is necessary for warmth. There was a young couple, with children in tow, one spring afternoon who happened to stumble upon an answer to a gnawing question from their past, and they were comforted by the warm glow of understanding that this afforded.

Tim and Shannon had driven many times up to Pine Mountain over the years. A few cryptic words spoken before an old man's death a dozen years before this trip had changed their lives, and the lives of their children. Many, many times they had scoured the mountain for the meaning a phrase that old man muttered, "Remember the stone". On this particular afternoon they had found "the stone". It was a simple rock, scratched with the words of a lonely widower. It was a sign of love.

But now the shadows were growing longer, and there weren't many hours of sunshine left. It was time to go.

"I'm really sorry, Paul. We've messed up your afternoon looking for that stone! You had a lot of work you wanted to get done here!" Tim said with a twinge of guilt in his voice and a sweep of his arm. He almost struck a pretty young woman in the top of the head as he moved his arm.

"Tim! Watch it!" Shannon ducked, as if she's done it a hundred times before. She was carrying a load of sticks and dead leaves, and was headed for the trash bin in the back of the yard. There was no animosity in her voice, just the resignation of someone who has had to endure absentmindedness many times before.

"Oops...sorry!" Tim pulled his arm in.

"Don't worry about it, Tim. You paid for it already. What you told me about my father's last few months helped me more than I can tell you. I can't think of a better way to spend the afternoon. Besides, we can just stay over one more night." An older man, Paul, responded. Another woman, apparently older than Shannon, spoke up.

"Hey, wait. I have to be at church in the morning, remember? My solo with the choir?" Merrie interrupted Paul.

"Oh, man, that's right. And we have a realtor showing the place in the morning." Paul frowned as he scratched behind his ear.

"How long is the drive to San Diego?" Tim asked.

"If we miss traffic, about four hours. Sometimes it's five." Paul responded.

"Oh, no. You'll never make it. Maybe we could help out." Shannon said, staring at Tim. She had a way of using eye communication with her husband. She looked first at Tim and flashed toward Paul, then looked back at her husband. Tim knew from experience that this particular look said, "Say something - offer to help him". There was a certain expression in the shape of her mouth as well. One corner was higher than the other. Yep, he thought, he knew what she's getting at.

"Hey, that's a great idea, Paul. Four pair of hands are quicker than two! What'ya think?" Tim smiled at Paul, and then quickly glanced at Shannon.

"That would be great, but only if you'll let me buy dinner!" Paul smiled.

"I've never been known to turn down a free meal, Paul."

Tim answered.

"He has a habit of mooching off of the owner of this house, Paul!" Shannon interjected. Paul laughed as he scratched his chin.

* * *

"Why don't Tim and I conquer what's left in the garage, and you and Shannon go through the kitchen, Merrie?" Paul pointed toward the house.

"Works for me. Just the thought of going through that garage makes me tired!" Merrie was already turning toward the house. Shannon turned and called for the children playing by the stone wall.

"Joey! Annie!"

"What?" They said in unison.

"Mom will be in the house, and Dad'll be in the garage. Don't go past the stone wall, and don't go into the creek."

"Ahh, Mom! We wanna see the water down there." Joey answered with a whine as he pointed into the trees. The sound of a creek can prove irresistible to someone who is twelve years old.

"Absolutely not! You are responsible for your sister, do you understand? There is a lot of mud, and a ton of slippery rocks that are dangerous." Shannon scolded. Tim shook his head.

"Did you ever think you'd be standing here, saying that, Shan?" Tim smiled.

"I didn't sound like my mother, did I?" Shannon looked worried.

"I don't think that's possible!" Tim smiled. Tim smiled, and Shannon shook her head and started toward the house. Tim watched the kids for a moment. It was obvious to Tim that Annie had noticed that he had stayed outside near the garage. She had been watching him, and Tim knew it.

"Dad! Can we go to the creek?" She whined, tilting her head with a smile that she used whenever she wanted to manipulate her father. Kids always seem to think that if one parent doesn't give you the answer you want to hear you can always try the other one. They also always seem to know how to turn on the right measure of charm with the right parent.

"Let's see. Your mother said no. I guess that settles it, then." Tim responded as he shrugged his shoulders and shook his head. It was work for him to turn his daughter down, and he knew it. It had taken him years of arguing with Shannon before he had been able to admit to himself that little Annie regularly wrapped him around her little finger with her smiles and gestures.

He turned toward the garage.

* * *

As they surveyed the piles of boxes in the dusty old garage at the back of the cabin, Tim found it amazing how many possessions Joseph and Annie had accumulated over the years. There seemed to him to be as many knick-knacks and furniture items to go through as there were rocks on the property.

"Wow! The stuff they collected!" Tim whistled after he spoke.

"Yep. Strange. My father warned me about all of this." Paul rubbed his chin.

"He did? The last time you saw him?" Tim asked.

"Hah! Nope. But it was in a garage as messy as this one, only in another state. That was a long time ago." Paul squinted as he thought he spotted a familiar object.

"I don't get it." Tim frowned.

"I didn't expect you would. Don't worry about it. I was just remembering something from when I was a kid." Paul smiled and waved his hand. He stepped toward the wall on the opposite side of Tim. He was still squinting.

"Do you recognize something?" Tim asked as he looked around.

"Maybe. On the wall, it looks like a key chain." Paul pointed.

"Here, I can reach it." Tim leaned over and grabbed it.

"Yep, it's a key chain. Some of those keys are pretty ancient." Paul nodded.

"Hey, this one's got the Chevy bow tie logo on it. But this is some old key. Pretty rusted. How about I start the clean up by tossing it?" Tim pulled his arm back, ready to throw the chain toward the trashcan.

"Whoa! Wait a minute! I think that's a keeper." Paul reached out and pulled the keys out of Tim's hand. Paul's eyebrows were high on his forehead.

"I'm not sure how to help here, Paul." Tim said with great hesitancy in his voice. He had thought the rusted keys were worthless.

"I'm not sure how I can help here, either, Tim." Paul whispered as he lovingly touched each key on the chain. Tim counted two old Chevy keys. Both were rusted.

"How about if we just go through and move things that are obviously valuable toward the front of the garage, and then we'll be able to make sure those things aren't thrown out?" Tim suggested.

"If I can tell if something is valuable or not. That's the real problem. I guess that's really the only way to go. Well, you take the left side, and I'll sort through the right side." Paul pointed. Tim picked up an unidentifiable wooden object.

"So, what sort of things would you call valuable, Paul?" Tim realized that this wasn't going to be as easy as he had thought.

"Well, if neither of us can identify what it is, then it's not valuable, I guess." Paul was staring at what Tim was holding;

it appeared to be a carved, dried out old branch.

"Well, this fits that description. What in the heck could this be?"

"God only knows. My father had a hard time throwing all sorts of things out. He seemed to attach a lot of sentiment to material things." Paul shrugged. He kept looking at the stick. It appeared that there was something familiar about it to Paul, Tim thought. It was in his look.

"So, you have no idea?" Tim asked as he pulled his arm back, preparing to throw the stick on a pile of debris just outside the door of the garage.

"Wait! Let me see it." Paul grabbed Tim's arm. He carefully took it from his young assistant and turned it over slowly. He ran his right index finger over some lettering.

"Look, here are my parent's names! 'Joey + Annie'. It was written in a style that's like my father's printing. He was so young when he did it. The lines are so straight." Paul traced each letter.

"It doesn't look like it's from any of the trees around here." Tim added. He was leaning over, trying to see the letters inscribed.

"It's from Maine. They grew up there. Huh! I remember now! It's their Chocolate Chip Creek stick." Paul shook his head and lovingly caressed the piece of wood.

"Say, Paul, do you have any garbage bags out here?" Merrie stepped into the garage. Paul turned quickly toward her, dropping the stick on a nearby wooden chair

"Uh, no. They're, well, I think..." Paul stammered.
Merrie stared at all of the debris surrounding the two men.

"Paul? You haven't made much progress out here."
She said in a monotone.

"Uh, yeah. You're right."

"So?" Merrie asked.

"We'll get moving!" With a guilty glance toward Tim,
and a nod of his head, Paul quickly grabbed a few old rags
and tossed them out of the garage. Paul looked at Tim, who
then reached for a different pile.

"Paul?" Merrie hadn't moved.

"Huh? What?" Paul stopped.

"The garbage bags?" Merrie frowned and put her hand
out.

"Oh! Yeah! Ummm, check the front porch. I think I left
the package there." Paul answered as Merrie turned and
headed for the house.

* * *

The pile of items to be thrown out grew outside the little
garage. Tim and Paul developed a system of sorting through
things. If Tim were not sure he'd hold the object up for Paul to
make a judgment. Their conversation over the value of items
evolved into single words. It went on for over an hour like that.

"Paul?" Tim would start. He'd hold some object up. There was a long piece of black cloth, and, in Tim's other hand, a jar of broken window glass.

"Wow! I can't believe he saved THAT!" Paul pointed at the broken glass.

"Why would anyone save some old broken glass?" Tim shook his head.

"You'd be surprised, Tim. Really. But go ahead and throw that out. I don't ever want to see that again."

"Something personal, huh?" Tim asked.

"Oh, yeah. Something personal and embarrassing." Paul raised his eyebrows.

"Well, I won't ask then." Tim threw it in the large trashcan outside the door.

More yearbooks, old boxes of newspapers and things from every phase of Joseph and Annie's life would be sorted through. Every now and then this dialogue would be repeated. If the item were a discard, Tim and Paul would toss them on a pile. Each item protested in a different way, depending on its size and weight. Large bulky things such as a broken chair hit the pile with a thud, followed by a slow slide down, and then the creaking of wood. Small lighter objects, such as an old red and gray worker shirt that Joseph kept in the garage, made fluttering sounds in the air, and slid with little fanfare to the side.

"You know, Paul, I have a few old work shirts that are

overdue for the dumpster, but that's gotta be one of the shabbiest shirts I've ever seen!" Tim exclaimed.

"I'm not sure where the heck that thing came from. I never saw my father wear it. I do remember he got it in the mail one fall afternoon. I have a feeling his mother sent it to him. Who knows? Get rid of it anyway." Paul shrugged.

They got used to the rhythmic sounds of items being thrown. They made a game of sorts out of the sounds that each item made when it hit the growing pile. Tim threw a heavy item and asked Paul, who was looking the other way, what it was.

"Let me guess, a wooden lamp, broken at the base." Paul asked.

"Right! Five points for identifying the lamp, and a ten point bonus for knowing it was cracked! How did you know it was cracked?" Tim replied.

"Who do you think made the crack in the base?" Paul smiled sheepishly. "My mother couldn't bear to throw the old thing out, so I guess it sat here the rest of their lives in this garage!"

"There must be some sort of story behind that!" Tim smiled.

"There's a story behind everything in this garage, unfortunately. That's why it's taken me years to get it cleaned this far!" Paul shook his head as he pulled a handkerchief from his rear pocket to wipe his forehead. Just then Tim heard his wife call from the house.

"Tim! Can you see the kids? It's getting dark, and I'm not sure they're by the stone wall!" Shannon sounded worried.

"I'll check!" Tim struggled to step over a pile in the middle of the garage as he made his way to the garage door. He walked down the stone path toward the wall

"Joey! Annie" Tim called, his hands cupped around his mouth. There was no answer.

"Do you see them?" Shannon shouted from the porch of the cabin. Tim turned his head over his shoulder.

"No. I'll see if they're over by that clump of trees." Tim pointed to his right. As he turned back toward the stone wall something unusual caught his eye. Part of the stone wall had fallen into the yard, leaving a small "U" shaped depression.

"Hey, Shan, it looks like Isaiah's been here!" Tim chuckled, remembering a similar scene from years ago.

"Huh? What do you mean?" Shannon moved closer to the railing of the porch.

"Some of the stones of the wall were knocked off the top. The kids were playing here, so I can guess who's responsible." Tm shook his head, and then called their names again. He picked up a stone and replaced it on the wall. He knew he remembered that particular stone. He recognized the marks of the hammer on the bottom, where he had chipped off a protrusion.

"You'd better go over the wall and look below."
Shannon shouted.

"Just what I was thinking." Tim responded. Paul
arrived form the garage and offered to go down the path with
him.

"Being that I've raised a couple of kids myself, I would
be willing to bet good money that your two are in the creek
bottom." Paul offered.

"I wouldn't bet against that, Paul." Tim frowned as the
two of them climbed over the wall.

The shadows were growing as they walked the path
toward the creek. As they descended the gurgling of the
creek increased in volume. A new sound competed with the
water, the sound of children talking and laughing.

"Gee, Tim, who could that be?" Paul said sarcastically.

"There they are...in the water!" Tim stopped quickly in
the middle of the trail. He could feel hot anger rising up.

"Oh, damn! They'll be a mess!" Paul shook his head.
He called out to Tim's children. Standing there, like deer
looking into the headlights of a car, were Joey and Annie.
They had mud all over their clothes.

"HEY! JOEY! ANNIE! GET OVER HERE! I MEAN
NOW!" Tim shouted, not trying to disguise his anger. He
started kicking the leaves beside the trail. There could be no
doubt that the two children heard their father's command.
They immediately splashed their way to the bank. Paul

walked down the trail a bit and pointed the way back up. The shadows were now dark enough that the children would not be able to get up the slope to the cabin without a guide.

"They'll be okay, Tim. Don't worry. We can get them cleaned up inside." Paul was trying to calm Tim down.

"You bet they'll get cleaned up. And wait until Shannon sees them. She'll blow a gasket for sure!"

* * *

"Well, it'll take Shannon a bit to get those two cleaned up, Tim. Let's go back out to the garage and throw all of that pile sitting in the driveway into the dumpster." Paul suggested as he opened the screen door in the kitchen. He reached for the porch light switch and flipped it up.

"I don't know. Shannon's pretty steamed. Maybe I should hang around in case her temper kicks up." Tim rubbed his knee. He had stumbled on the path up to the kitchen while bringing the children in.

"She's doing fine, Tim. I'll help dry them off when they get out of the shower. Their clothes are just about done. It wasn't much to clean up." Merrie added.

"I just don't get it. I thought we were really clear about the creek." Tim shook his head.

"Come on, Tim. Kids are like this. They listen only when it's convenient. That's the way I was. This time it wasn't convenient for them, and." Paul paused and smiled, "besides, we had the same problem with our two years ago."

"Maybe you're right. I guess throwing junk into a dumpster would be good therapy!" Tim stepped toward the back door.

"Besides, I want to get to Edie's before the Saturday night dinner rush hits!" Paul grinned.

"Oh, Edie's! Why didn't you say so! That makes all the difference! Hey, wait a minute. The restaurant's still there?" Tim's eyebrows went up.

"Yep. We ate there last night. Sat at the same table my parents used to eat at." Paul smiled gently.

"Let's get at it! I'm hungrier than a bear that's been in hibernation all winter!" Tim licked his lips. Shannon's voice echoed from the hallway.

"Aren't you always?"

* * *

"You know, Paul, I've been a father for a dozen years now, and I still haven't figured out how to deal with kids." Tim said as he threw a load of old newspapers into the dumpster.

"Hey, I've been doing it for almost twice as long and I'm in the same situation!" Paul replied as he handed Tim a stack of old magazines. "As soon as I figure out one stage of child development, the kid moves into the next stage. Here, grab this wire." Paul tossed a wire to Tim.

"Got it. Do you want me to just hold it?"

"Pull gently. It seems to be stuck under that board. Huh. That board seems familiar. Whoa. It looks like a piece of siding from my grandparent's garage!" Paul smiled.

"There it goes...watch out!" Tim jumped aside as the wire harmlessly flopped against the side of the garage.

"I think we have it all, Tim"

"Yeah, just an odd piece here and there. I guess we just had to outlast the garbage" Tim coiled the wire and tossed it into the dumpster.

"I think that's the solution with a lot of other things, too."

"Other things?" Tim asked.

"Things like kids! We sometimes just have to scratch our heads and wait until a kid grows out of one weird phase or another." Paul replied.

"That seems to describe my view of parenthood. Waiting until the kid stops pooping in his pants, so he can start writing on the walls." Tim smiled.

"That's usually followed by fart jokes and gross objects in the pockets." Paul chuckled.

"Grab that old pair of glasses, Paul."

"Hah! I guess it lasts into old age." Paul laughed as he looked over the old, dusty glasses.

"Old age? What do you mean?" Tim asked as he wiped his hands on an old rag.

"My father's collection of sentimental junk. What we're doing right now! Look at this! These glasses are ridiculous! They're rose colored! They aren't for reading or driving!"

"Hah! I guess you're right!" Tim smiled.

"Anything else around, Tim?"

"I'll just give that old carburetor the old heave-ho and we'll..." Tim reached for the old car part.

"NO! Wait! Stop! Did you say a carburetor?" Paul shouted as beat Tim to the device.

"Yeah. But, hey, it's just an old carburetor. It looks like it's from a '69 Chevy. It's no good anymore. It looks like it's been bent up." Tim was confused.

"'68. It's from a '68 Chevy." Paul whispered. He was staring at the gray and black hunk of metal.

"We've thrown out a lot of stuff from this garage, Paul. What's so special about this old thing?" Tim picked up an old rag to wipe his hands on.

"Think about it, Tim. He kept this piece of crap for more than twenty-five years." Paul sounded angry.

"I can see that this 'piece of crap' hit a nerve." Tim shook his head as he handed the carburetor to Paul.

"Yeah, I guess so, but you have to understand. It ruined a relationship." Paul's voice faded as he took hold of the old car part.

"Hey, whatever you want. It's an old '68 Chevy carburetor," Tim put his hands up, "and I'm not here to rob you of anything, Paul. I'm just trying to earn a meal! If you want to keep it, then, hey, keep it!"

"What?" Paul looked up at Tim, "Oh, I'm...I mean, I'm sorry...I didn't mean to snap at you, Tim." Paul gently put the old car part on the pile of items to be kept.

"There's an awful lot of emotional baggage packed into that dual-barreled carb, Paul." Tim pointed.

"It's the reason I left home years ago. Well, that and what happened to an old nineteen forty-eight Chevy Woody. All of the distance between my father and I was created by the attitude that thing represents, and, well, and by other things." Paul mumbled off. He picked the old part up again.

"Other things?" Tim started to pull the garage door down.

"Yeah. Other things. I guess the troubles with those two cars that year didn't cause the problem, but it sure made the keg blow." Paul was almost whispering as he stared at the carburetor.

"Paul! Are you ready?" Merrie asked from the house.

"Yeah, we're just shutting the door now!" Paul shouted back. He wrapped the carburetor in the old rag that Tim had wiped his hands with and walked out of the garage.

"You're going to take it with you, Paul?" Tim gingerly asked.

"You can't possibly understand, Tim. The story about why this piece of junk is sitting in this old garage in Pine

Mountain is the story of why my father and I fought for years. The attitude that forced him to keep this piece of metal defined our relationship." Paul was shaking.

"A carburetor?" Tim shook his head.

"Think about it. He moved it here to Pine Mountain, from where we used to live. He had to purposely make sure it was brought here. Why? Why would he hang on to this piece of debris from that...that accident?" Paul grumbled.

"An accident? What happened?" Tim asked.

"Well, it wasn't an accident like you're thinking, Tim. But I didn't do it on purpose. But he never believed me! It happened back in 1971, just after school let out."

Paul started painting the story of a journey taken years ago. Slowly the years dissolved.

PART ONE

Midday in America

Chapter 1

"Joseph, it's almost lunch. Time to wash up!" The sound of his wife's voice calling from inside the house prompted Joseph to look out from under the hood of the car he called his "toy". He winced as he noticed that the shadows from the ash tree in the front yard were reaching far down the sidewalk, almost touching the old water meter at the end of the yard. He hadn't realized how late it had become. Joseph reached up to run his right hand through his thinning, gray-peppered hair and stopped as he realized it was covered by what must amount to three ounces of grease.

"So, what're we having?" Joseph shouted toward the open door that led from the garage into the house. He thought he had caught a whiff of the smell of tomato sauce as it worked its way from the house, through the garage, and out toward the street. He craned his neck, waiting for a reply, as he moved toward the workbench on the other side of the garage. He gently returned the carburetor he had been working on to the cleaning pan, and picked up an old rag. Slowly he began wiping the oily residue from between his fingers. He started scanning the tool-covered bench for his glasses.

"Will my answer be the deciding factor on how quickly you'll make it to the table?" Joseph's wife, Anne, answered.

"Definitely, Anne! Say it's spaghetti and meatballs and I won't even clean my hands first." Joseph smiled while licking his lips lightly. It was an old game between them; Joseph could eat Italian food every day, while Anne preferred Chinese or Mexican food. It was his way of reminding her that an Italian meal every other day wasn't enough. He didn't hate Chinese or Mexican food; it's just that he really liked Italian food. Joseph shuffled a few papers on the workbench, still looking for his glasses.

"Sorry, not today. Come on, Joseph. You'll be holding things up if you don't get moving. You should have been finished washing up by now." Anne said in a tired monotone.

"Are my glasses in there, Anne?" Joseph rubbed the stubble on his chin, not really hearing Anne's answer.

"Your glasses? I don't see them." Anne answered. Joseph noticed that she sounded tired.

"Darn. Where did I put them?" Joseph glanced over to the roof of the car. "Hey, Anne! Did you say no spaghetti tonight? The smell sure says it's tonight!" Joseph answered. Just by chance he noticed the glasses peeking out from under the sports pages scattered across the roof of the car...the pages from last Wednesday.

"Found the glasses!" Joseph announced as he reached over the fender.

"Good. Now get washed up. Sarah's setting the table now."

"You never answered my question. So, what smells like spaghetti and meatballs, but isn't? What's for lunch?" Joseph realized he was hungry, and started wiping his hands more quickly.

"Meatloaf, Joseph. Just meatloaf." Anne's voice trailed off.

"Meatloaf. Ugh". Joseph muttered. His hand cleaning slowed noticeably. Anne had tried to make non-Italian meals taste like they were Italian, but Joseph never had the heart to tell her that they never quite made it. Take the meatloaf, for example. She often cooked it in tomato sauce. It wasn't the same. It tasted like hamburgers with burnt tomato sauce on them.

"Joseph! Lunch! It's ready, and you're not! Would you please get in here? We're late as it is!" Anne was definitely angry.

"I'm on my way in now." Joseph answered as he strode toward the door. There was something in her voice, he thought. He'd heard this tone a few times before. You can't be married for over twenty years to someone without learning how to recognize that other person's moods from the garage. He stopped in the doorway leading form the garage to the house. Down the hall, Joseph could see that Paul was sitting at the kitchen table, but not in his usual seat near the back door. Paul was sitting in Joseph's seat at the head of the table.

"Damn." Joseph whispered under his breath as he shook his head. He'd dealt with this before. Even though he'd been a high school teacher for years, he still struggled with how to cope with the rebellion of his own teens. Paul liked to play a game Joseph called "let's confront Dad at dinnertime". It was the same every time. Every so often, when Paul thought his father wasn't paying him enough attention, he'd "accidentally" sit at Joseph's place at the table.

Joseph noticed that this always seemed to happen whenever Joseph had a major job to accomplish, like repairing the carburetor on the '68 Chevy. Of course, Joseph thought, Paul didn't understand how things were more stressful now. Paul couldn't comprehend how tough it is to deal with an aging father's illness, especially when that aging parent was almost three thousand miles away, in Maine.

Now Joseph understood why Anne sounded the way she did. This scene unfolds this way every time. Anne got stressed out just thinking about the impending fight. Joseph really tried to avoid the fight. Anne didn't believe it, but he really didn't want a fight. Anne just didn't understand that Paul would keep poking until a fight erupted. That's what Joseph called the "First Fight". The follow up bout usually erupted about two hours later, in the master bedroom.

"Hey, Paul. I don't feel much like having a fight over where we sit at the table tonight. Can you just move on over to your chair and allow us to have a nice Saturday meal in peace?" Joseph tried to sound conciliatory. He even smiled. He knew it wasn't a real smile, but, hey, he thought, Anne would at least see that he was trying to be reasonable.

"Joseph, let's just leave it alone this afternoon. It's been a hard day. Don't start anything." Anne interjected.

"I'm not starting 'anything', Anne. I'm trying to avoid 'anything'." Joseph emphasized. He rubbed the back of his left wrist with his right hand.

"Yeah...like you never start anything," Paul added. Paul was slumped in the chair, looking out the window. Sarah, Paul's sister, got up from the table and quickly left the room. Anne slowly put the plate she was carrying down, and turned toward Joseph.

Joseph glared at his son. He could feel the anger rushing up from deep inside. He knew what he wanted to say. He knew he could say it very clearly, and very loudly. He remembered what Anne had told him what must have been a hundred times. Count to ten, consider what you should say and then speak. He knew that he'd have to count much higher than ten this time; ten would only bring his anger down from "terrible" to "raging". Slowly he counted...one...two...

"Err...Joseph? Are you feeling all-right?" Anne had moved up next to him. Joseph wasn't sure if he should speak. He knew he couldn't really control his tongue at that point. Joseph opened his mouth slowly.

"Fine. Just trying to stop from exploding in HIS

29

direction!" Joseph pointed as he replied with an overbearing acidic tone in his voice.

"Paul! Get upstairs and wash up for dinner!" Anne intervened. She always seemed to know when the two men in her life were beyond reason, and she knew that this time Joseph had been pushed too far.

"But I already did," Paul said in a lackadaisical manner. He started inspecting his fingernails.

"PAUL! I said NOW! Get upstairs NOW!" Anne said in something a bit more than just a raised voice. Her arm was outstretched, pointing toward the living room, beyond the refrigerator.

Joseph was surprised by his wife's outburst; he turned to look at her. Anne's face was very red, especially her neck. Paul sat up suddenly, and looked at his parents. He quickly rose and ran out of the kitchen. Joseph nodded. At least Paul knew how to act when he was surrounded, Joseph thought.

Anne brought her hand up to her eyes, and Joseph noticed a tear flowing down her cheek. Joseph stood by the table looking at her for what seemed to be an hour to him. It always seemed that way; he never quite knew what to do when she was crying like this and he was part of the problem that made her cry.

"Annie..." Joseph began.

"Stop! Please!" Anne put her hand up in a familiar command gesture.

"But..." Joseph tried to continue. Anne continued to hold her hand in front of her face.

"Joseph Marino, right now I don't want your sympathy. I don't want your explanations. I don't want one of your attempts to smooth over a really rough situation. You can't, so don't even try!" Anne almost sounded like she was growling.

Joseph was stunned. He found himself slowly closing his mouth, and without much to say. But he felt he had to try something.

"Anne, please. I don't want this to come between us. Let's not do this. We can find a way to work through it."

Anne didn't reply. She continued staring down at the tile floor, her eyes covered with her hand.

"Annie? Are you OK?" Joseph stretched out his arm, and tried to touch her shoulder. She pulled away.

"Leave me alone." Anne replied.

"Don't do that. Please. Tell me what's going on." Joseph pleaded. He hated when this happened. It wasn't the first time in their twenty-five years of marriage that he had seen her like this, but it was one of the strongest reactions he had seen. Then she did some things that she had never done before.

Anne opened her mouth, but not her eyes. It seemed like no matter how much she tried to speak, she couldn't do it. She dropped her hand from her face, revealing reddened eyes and a very wrinkled brow. Joseph felt a tremendous wave of sadness, and he looked down at the earth-toned tiles below his feet. Anne started walking, which turned to stomping, toward the kitchen cabinets.

The stomping turned to storming as she moved over to the cabinets. She flung the door to the right of the refrigerator open, and pulled out a handful of old brown paper shopping bags, the kind one brings home groceries in. The door slammed against the side of the refrigerator, and Joseph winced as he heard the wood crack. She then stormed over to the kitchen drawer next to where they kept the forks and spoons. This is where Anne kept things like screwdrivers, pens and wrapping tape. After slashing around in the drawer for one or two minutes she pulled out a large permanent ink marking pen.

"Anne? What are you doing?" Joseph said quietly. Anne stopped and stared at him for a moment and shook her head. She wasn't speaking, but she was glaring.

Anne quickly went to the kitchen table, and then pushed aside the lunch dishes. She slammed the stack of grocery bags down at her place at the table. Two of the plates she had pushed aside fell to the floor when the bags hit the tabletop. One broke. Joseph stepped over to pick them up. Anne spoke.

"No! LEAVE them where they ARE!" She stared at her husband as she screamed and pointed. Joseph stepped back, raising his hands up to his shoulders to show that he would offer no resistance. He discovered that he was shaking. He had seldom seen Anne like this.

"Let them sit there on the floor...no problem," he whispered as he stepped back. Anne pulled the cap off of the top of the marking pen and leaned over the stack of bags. She started writing. Well, writing is a mild way of describing what she did. She tore at the paper bags, slashing out letters and words, as if the anger itself was writing. Every letter was a very large capital. Joseph watched as she wrote, reading each word as she slashed it out. He wondered why she couldn't just say the words, but he knew that yelling and screaming in the house of her parents was reserved only for the father. Everyone else was forbidden to carry on in loud anger.

WHEN DOES THIS CRAP END? I'M TIRED OF BEING CAUGHT IN THE MIDDLE OF TWO MOODY, ANGRY, STUBBORN MEN WHO CAN'T FIND A WAY TO UNDERSTAND EACH OTHER!

"Anne...please. I feel the way you do. Can we just talk...?" Joseph started, but his wife's angry writing interrupted.

SHUT UP, WILL YOU? YOU ALWAYS HATE IT WHEN I INTERRUPT YOU! CAN'T YOU GIVE ME THE SAME RESPECT?

I'M SICK AND TIRED OF BEING SEEN AS A PIECE OF THE FURNITURE!

"I'll just be quiet now... " Joseph mumbled as he slowly

sat down at his place at the table. He ran his fingers through his thinning hair.

Anne violently slid the first bag she had written on off of the table. She immediately went right on to the next bag in the pile.

I KNOW HOW PRESSURED YOU FEEL ABOUT YOUR FATHER AND HOW HE DOESN'T HAVE MUCH TIME TO LIVE. BUT, DAMN IT, WE HAVE TO LIVE OUR LIVES RIGHT NOW, AND RIGHT NOW OUR LIVES ARE CRAP! WHAT WILL OUR KIDS REMEMBER ABOUT 1971? THIS????

Anne quickly slid the second bag off of the table. It flew further than the first one. It slammed into the phone table, barely missing Joseph's picture of his mother and father.

I DON'T WANT TO HEAR ANY MORE ABOUT YOUR STUPID CAR. I DON'T WANT TO HEAR ANY MORE ABOUT HOW RUDE YOUR STUDENTS ARE TO YOU. I DON'T WANT TO HEAR ABOUT HOW PAUL SITS IN YOUR CHAIR! CAN'T YOU JUST FIND ANOTHER STUPID CHAIR! WE HAVE FIVE OTHER ONES! PICK ANY ONE! I REALLY DON'T CARE! PICK MY STUPID CHAIR! PLEASE! I'LL SIT ON THE DAMNED FLOOR IF IT WILL ALLOW US TO HAVE JUST ONE PEACEFUL MEAL IN THIS HOUSE!

Anne was slowing down, Joseph noticed. She was getting more words on to each bag now. Each letter was getting smaller. An idea grew on him: he believed that she needed to do this, in this way. He guessed that she felt safe expressing herself in writing. But he was positive that she was slowing down. Joseph noticed that instead of throwing the used-up bag, Anne slowly slid the third one across the table. Anne stopped to take a deep breath as she calmly started on the fourth bag. Joseph noticed that she was crying again, and shaking.

NOW, CAN I JUST PUT THE LUNCH ON THE TABLE? CAN WE JUST EAT THE MEATLOAF WHILE IT IS STILL WARM? CAN WE JUST HAVE SOME PEACE?

Anne stopped writing, put the pen down, and turned to look at her husband. Joseph opened his mouth to answer in the affirmative, but decided to nod his head instead.

The phone rang. Joseph decided that the call could not possibly be worth answering. He decided that Anne needed his full attention. Anne continued to stare at her husband. The phone stopped ringing in the middle of the fourth ring, and Joseph sighed in relief. One of the kids must have answered it upstairs, he thought. Probably Paul.

"Well? Can we just eat a meal in peace?" Anne whispered. Joseph was startled to hear her voice. She was still shaking, and she was still grabbing the permanent marker. Joseph quietly nodded. He watched his wife, waiting for a sign of what to do next. She slowly laid down the pen, and rose from the table. She walked to the window and looked out at her crepe myrtle tree. A minute, then two, passed quietly.

"Anne..." Joseph started. He wasn't quite sure what he should say, but he wanted to say something. He just didn't know what words would be right. Saying 'sorry' seemed so trite and hollow. He waited, and tried to find some words. Fortunately, Anne decided to say something.

"I'm sorry. I was having a tantrum. Writing all over those bags was stupid..." Anne whispered.

"No. You needed to say what you felt, and it was the only way you could do it and feel safe, Annie," Joseph said quietly. He called her 'Annie' the same way he did back in sixth grade, so many years ago, on the other side of the continent. It was how she had introduced herself to him when they met back on Chocolate Chip Creek. He was the only one now who called her 'Annie', but he only did it when he wanted to touch that place in her heart that remembered when they were twelve years old.

He slowly stood up and walked over and stood behind her. Slowly he put his arm around her waist. It was then that he noticed again that she was crying.

"I didn't have to act like a child, Joey..." Anne cried. Joseph was awed about how when he called her 'Annie' after they fought she would call him by his childhood nickname. It was like clockwork.

"Let it go. We have so many other things to worry about right now." Joseph comforted her.

"Yeah, like how the meatloaf is getting cold."

"Here. I'll help." Joseph volunteered. As they turned to go toward the stove they noticed Paul and Sarah sitting in the doorway to the living room. They were both quietly crying. Anne spoke first as she walked over to them. Sarah got up and hugged her mother. Paul reached out and grabbed her upper left arm.

"It's all going to be fine, you two. I'm sorry. I had a tantrum." Anne apologized.

"Mom...it's so hard..." Sarah cried. Paul just looked down at the floor.

Joseph looked at his two children, and something bothered him. It didn't seem as if they were crying over the fight they must have just witnessed. Paul was staring at his old teddy bear, long ago hung in a shadow box on the wall. It was a small one, and its eyes were missing. A companion shadow box hanging nearby held Sarah's first baby doll, which she had appropriately named "Baby". It had been a long time since Joseph had seen Paul paying attention to that old bear.

"Paul? Is something wrong? I mean, beside our little fight here?" Joseph asked. Anne turned toward her husband, looking confused.

Paul nodded, and said nothing.

"Paul? What's going on?" Anne asked her son.

"The phone." Paul answered. Joseph quickly turned toward the phone table. He remembered that the phone had rung during the fight.

"What about it?" Joseph asked.

"Pick it up. It's Grandma. She wants to talk only to you, Dad," Paul answered in a child-like voice. Joseph felt a cold chill in his back as he walked slowly across the room. His mother had called and had been waiting all this time to talk to him?

"Grandma? She's OK?" Joseph whispered.

"She's crying..." Paul started to cry softly, to himself.

Joseph reached for the phone, and slowly brought it to his ear.

Chapter 2

There are telephone calls that one receives in life that seem to last forever; such was the case for Joseph that blustery, sunny afternoon in June. He noticed that his mother was very upset, but he couldn't quite understand what she was saying. So many phone calls from her were like this over the years. He found her conversations tough to follow; she wandered so much. He found himself distracted by the sight of the breeze blowing through the trees in the back yard. He noticed how the wooden fenced needed to have a few boards replaced. So much work to be done, he thought, and there was so little time. He was vaguely aware that his mother was crying over the phone. It was always so hard to hear his mother cry.

"What's she saying, Joseph?" Anne whispered. Joseph was jarred back to the urgency of the phone call. He gently slid his hand over the mouthpiece as he turned toward Anne.

"Uh, she's crying. I'm not sure what to say, or do. I'm never sure what the right thing to do is. I can't even make out what is really wrong, except that it has something to do with my father." Joseph shook his head, and cleared his throat. It always bothered him that his throat made it tough to talk when someone he loved was crying. It was then that he noticed that his hand was shaking gently. He knew he was afraid to ask what was really the matter.

"Maybe just listening is the right thing, honey." Anne rubbed her husband's arm.

"Well, it must be, because that's all I can do." Joseph replied, almost in a whisper. He looked down as he let his hand fall from the mouthpiece.

"Can you tell what's wrong?" Anne mouthed the words, with very little sound, and pointed at the receiver. Anne was always sensitive to interfering with someone else's call. Joseph returned his hand to the mouthpiece and whispered.

"All I can make out is that things have gotten worse for my father. She's not really clear."

"Maybe you have to calm her down, Joey." Anne used the name he was called during his childhood days back in Maine. He felt a smile inch onto his lips as he remembered their early days on what he used to call "Chocolate Chip Creek".

"I'll see what I can do." Joseph whispered as he dropped his hand from the phone again.

"Mom...?" He asked quietly. His mother had not stopped crying and mumbling since he had picked the phone up, and he found it difficult to interrupt.

"...but his car is in the garage under the tarp. I don't know why he kept that old thing all these years. I don't really know if it runs anymore at all." The voice on the other end of the phone line continued.

"Mom? Please...I'm trying to help..." Joseph spoke up a bit more.

"...then the shed in the back yard hasn't been cleaned out. We usually do that in early June, as the flowers are starting to really look nice. I needed to get a new light fixture in that old thing, but I didn't know what account at the bank to take the money out of! Oh, I can't even figure out how to deal with the bank, Joey! You know your father always dealt with the bank." The words turned to crying; Joseph could tell that his mother almost dropped the phone. He felt a cold chill in his back when he realized that his mother used the past tense 'dealt' instead of the present tense 'deals'. What did that mean, he wondered? He didn't want to know the answer, but he knew he'd have to hear it.

"Mom! Please hear what I'm trying to say!" Joseph

was louder still.

"Should I call someone, Joey? All I thought to do was to call you...and I had a hard time finding your number out there in Colorado..."

"Mom! I live in California! I lived in Colorado for a little while a long time ago! You need to slow down, Mom! Please! You talk like this whenever you're really upset. Take a deep breath and listen to me! Do you hear me?" Joseph was working hard to control his anger, but understood that his mother was really upset. He also knew that he had to get her to focus and tell him clearly what was going on.

"What? What did you say?" The old woman on the phone seemed to break out of her confusion.

"Mom, you need to listen to me. You're really hard to follow. I'm not sure what, but something's wrong. What has happened?" Joseph asked, but not with any enthusiasm.

It didn't seem to help. There was more crying from his mother.

"Mom! Stop! Listen!" Joseph said loudly, as he felt Anne squeeze his arm. He turned to see her frowning.

"Yes, Joey" His mother was whimpering. Joseph took a deep breath.

"Good. Now, listen, I know something is wrong. I gather it has to do with Dad. Now, very calmly tell me what exactly has happened." Joseph's words were very deliberate, and very carefully chosen.

"It's so hard...Joey...it happened about an hour ago..."
Joseph's mother trailed off into silence. All Joseph heard was
the sound of an old woman breathing, far away.

"Ok. What happened to Dad about an hour ago?"
Joseph asked, slowly. He rubbed his forehead. He was
feeling very tired. He turned back toward Anne, who was
sitting in the chair at the end of the kitchen table; she was
staring at Joseph.

"Oh, Joey! Your father...oh...Joey, he's gone!" The
crying from the earpiece continued. Joseph noticed that the
time was one forty on the kitchen clock. Joseph took a deep
breath.

"Mom...Mom! Dad! Is he...did he...?" Joseph always
dreaded this type of situation. He didn't know what phrase or
words to use. He flipped through his mental file of
euphemisms, but was unsure which one to use. After all, this
was his mother, and they were discussing his father.
Fortunately he was interrupted, and the message became
very clear.

"I found him, Joey. He was cold, in his bed. I called for
the ambulance. It was horrible, Joey!" His mother was
fighting the tears, he could tell.

"I understand, Mom." Joseph whispered as he turned
to look out the back window again. He felt the tears well up.
His expression must have said enough. Anne covered her
mouth and shook her head. Her eyebrows were up high, and

42

he could see a tear forming in her eye.

"The ambulance person was so heartless, Joey! He just said 'he's dead' and said I needed to sign some papers. Did I do the right thing, Joey? He seemed responsible and all...but it was your father! I know he had a job to do, but, oh, Joey..." His mother started crying again.

"Hold on...please. Take a deep breath again. I'm sure you did the right thing, Mom. Paperwork...the little things are a little hard to deal with at a time like this. It will be all right." Joseph tried his best to soothe her, even though he was struggling to keep calm himself. He had a fleeting thought; he wanted to chew out the ambulance driver for being so callous around an old lady at a time like this. He just shook his head as he realized that it wouldn't do any good now.

"I don't know what to do, Joey. I'm not sure whom to call. Oh, Joey, I don't want to be alone in the house tonight. It's getting dark. What should I do?" His mother's tears flowed again - he could hear her low sobs.

"I'm going to help, Mom. Let's work this out together. Now, who can you call that lives near you? What about Aunt Kate? Can you call her?"

"Oh, my sister is busy on Saturday nights. She has her bridge club, you know. I wouldn't want to trouble her. Besides, Alice has been bedridden with the flu and Kate has to go over there every other day to check on her. You know, it's not easy being eighty-four and sick with the flu. You feel

every ache a hundred times more than you used to..."
Joseph's mother started rambling again.

"Mom! Please! Wait! Now, this is an unusual event.
Aunt Kate is a kind and caring woman. She would help. I
know how much you like her." Joseph tried to sound
reassuring.

"Oh, yes, she has always been close. As close as the
letters "J" and "K", we used to say! I remember how my
mother used to say that she could never call us in for dinner
without saying both names at once! She used to call out 'Julie
and Katie, time for dinner!'" Joseph's mother started
reminiscing again.

"It's Ok, Mom. I know...I'll tell you what. I'll call her,
and I'm sure she'll get right over there. I know she will."

"But I don't want to be a bother. I'm always a bother..."
Joseph's mother whimpered.

"Mom, you're not a bother. This is a very tough
moment in life; I'm sure it would be for anyone. You need to
have someone near. I'll call her and then call you back. Is that
all right with you?" Joseph was finding it easier to be kind to
his mother. He was actually surprised at how well she was
doing, all things considered.

"As long as you'll call me right back, then. Yes." She
replied.

"I will. I promise. I'll call back in not more
than...ummm...say, ten minutes? Is that all right?" Joseph

asked.

"That would be fine." His mother almost sounded relieved, like she felt things in her life were, once again, in control. Joseph told her that he loved her and that all would be fine. They said good bye, after he reassured her again that he would call back in no more than ten or fifteen minutes.

For a minute or two Joseph continued staring out the back window. So much needed to be done out there, in the back yard. He looked down, at the terra cotta tile floor, the tiles his father helped him place on the only trip his parents ever made to California. He could still tell the difference between the tiles he put on the floor and the ones his father had put down. He guessed it was just how it was among professional tile people. They could always tell which person on the crew did what, even though no one else could. No one else could tell which tiles were put down by him, or by his father.

Joseph dreaded the day his father would die. Of course, there was so much unfinished business between his father and him. The two of them never quite got along. It was probably how the two of them were so much alike. They had the same personality, it seemed. Even though it was Joseph's house, his father insisted on doing it his way when they prepared the grout. That's just the way they were. Joseph shook his head.

Something else troubled him, however. His father had been a "manly man". He insisted in handling all of the money, in dealing with the banks. Joseph's father hired contractors and workers. Joseph guessed that this was the way it was done in the old days. He shook his head as he realized that he and Anne had fights over similar problems. What troubled him even more was what would happen to his mother now. Who would she 'lean' on now that her husband was gone? She wasn't young anymore, almost eighty, so he knew she wouldn't change. Joseph realized that he would have to deal with this. He was his mother's only son. Joseph shook his head. The woman his father married would now be his responsibility.

"Joey?" Anne's voice startled him; she was standing behind him like she often did. She had an uncanny way of doing that in many things. She surprised him with gifts that he didn't know that she knew he wanted. And she always seemed to say the right thing, even in tough times.

"Huh? Joseph turned toward his wife.

"Your father? He's...?" Anne couldn't finish the question.

"I guess he passed away sometime this morning. My mother couldn't wake him up from a nap." Joseph took a deep breath and looked at the ceiling.

"Oh, Joey, I'm so sorry...I don't know what to say..." Anne wiped the corner of her eye. Joseph struggled to speak, and Anne just waited.

"I don't know what to say either, honey. It's strange. I'm

46

not sure how I feel. I feel a lot of emotions crashing in all at once. Huh! It's so weird. I never thought it would feel like this. I guess you never can predict how you'll feel. My Dad died! Oh...I'm not sure what to do, or feel. It happens only once in a lifetime; you lose your father only once. This is my time, but what's the right way to feel? I don't know. I want to cry, but that's pushed aside by the anger over so many unresolved problems and differences." Joseph wiped tears from his eye.

"It's OK, Joey, dear..." Anne whispered as she stroked his arm. Her eyes gave him permission to talk about how he felt, so he continued.

"Yeah, I suppose it is, but I don't know. I really don't know how I feel. I feel a gaping pain, but it's because I now know that I'll never have the father I always wanted. Hah! Like I didn't figure that out decades ago. I guess this shows how much we hold out hope. I'm scared, too. What will happen with my mother? What has to be done back there in Maine?" Joseph felt the frown of crying grow on his face.

"Do you have to call her back?" Anne asked, interrupting his thoughts.

"Oh, gosh! Yes! I have to call my Aunt Kate and then get back to Mom!" Joseph walked across the kitchen, opened the drawer near the oven and scrounged through it, looking for the address book.

"Are you looking for this?" Anne handed Joseph the

book.

"Yeah, great! Where was it?" Joseph opened the book to the 'N' section, for Norton.

"Where it's been for ten years now, in the drawer right next to the phone." Anne said patiently. Joseph felt a bit embarrassed. It must have shown on his face.

"That' all right, honey. You're having a rough day." Anne said with a soothing tone in her voice. Joseph was already dialing his Aunt Kate's number. He waited for an answer, and was relieved when he heard an old, familiar voice with a New England accent answer.

"Hi! Aunt Kate?" Joseph's voice trembled.

"Hello! Who is this?

"It's me, Joseph Marino. Your nephew." Joseph replied.

"Who? You don't sound like my Joey. You're one of those telephonic salesmen! I'm not buying anything, I tell you. I'm on to you! You telephone salesmen, or whatever you call yourselves nowadays, pretend to know the person you're calling and then you sell them hundreds of dollars of goods they don't need. I'm not one of those easy sales, I'll have you know!" The old lady on the other end of the phone line answered.

"No, it's me, Aunt Kate...Joseph, err, Joey Marino, from California!" Joseph had forgotten how difficult his Aunt had become over the phone. She had always told him that she never trusted the 'darned electric voice box'. Now it seems she really didn't.

"Hah! Trying hard to fool me! I know for a fact that my nephew Joey and his family live in Colorado. My sister told me she once flew out there and visited him! You voice box salesmen are getting slicker, I tell you!"

"Aunt Kate! It is me! I can prove it! You used to have the boy who became my best friend over to your house for lunch on Saturdays when I was a kid. That's how we met. You used to watch him when his mother went to clean Mister King's house on Saturdays." Joseph ran his right hand through his thinning hair, wishing she would just listen.

"Well, the story sounds right. But maybe you've just done your homework, salesman! Answer me a question: what was that boy's name?" Aunt Kate sounded smug.

"Petey Barnes. I went over to your house every Saturday that summer to play with him."

"Really good, salesman. But only my real nephew would know what I fed to old Petey when he came over. So, what was it?" Aunt Kate's voice grew quiet, almost to a whisper.

"Oh, that's easy! It's the real reason I came over! You baked a special Angel food cake every Saturday and Petey and I loved every bite of it! You put lemon in the cake, and lemon frosting on top of it!" Joseph had to smile. He still loved lemon cookies, lemonade, and even lemon in his soda.

It all started in Aunt Kate's house in Maine.

"Oh, it is you, Joey! Only Joey would remember how I would put lemon in the cake! You used to remind me if I forgot the lemon!" Aunt Kate mellowed.

"Yep. I still like lemon cake, Aunt Kate! Anne just doesn't make it enough!" Joseph looked over at Anne, who was cleaning up the remains of dinner. She smiled gently, but tears stained her cheeks. That image brought Joseph back to the chore at hand.

"Hah! Come over to my house. I'll fix you another lemon cake!" Aunt Kate laughed.

"Well, I may be there soon, Aunt Kate. I've called with some bad news, unfortunately." Joseph found it hard to shift gears from the lightness of lemon cake to the burden of death.

"Bad news? Not someone in our family? Someone who's a close friend?" Aunt Kate was quieter. There was a long silence as Joseph cleared his throat. He still hadn't figured out what the best phrase was in the situation.

"Umm...yeah..." Joseph replied.

"This is hard for you, Joey. I can tell. Let me help. I know your friend Petey wasn't feeling well recently. I saw him just last Thursday, but he didn't look too..." Aunt Kate was interrupted. Joey was getting more nervous as Aunt Kate described Petey and his health problems.

"My father. He passed away this morning, I'm sorry to have to tell you." Joseph decided the direct approach was best. He couldn't bear to think of Petey being ill. It's unsettling to hear people talking of friends in your age group in this way.

"Oh, no! Julie must be hurting something fierce! Oh, no!" Aunt Kate started crying.

"Please, Aunt Kate...I wanted to ask..." Joseph began.

"Oh, no! I have to go right over there now! I have to see that she is all right! Oh, Joey! I have to get ready. I have to see if Nancy can drive me over there! I know how she must feel!" Joseph could tell that Aunt Kate had stood up and was pacing.

"If you could go see how..." Joseph tried again.

"She can't stay in that house alone...oh, no! She must come over here! I'll clear a space in the closet!"

"Uh...I knew I could count on you, Aunt Kate." Joseph gave up trying to ask her for help. Besides, he thought, she volunteered.

"Of course I can help. Why didn't you ask? That was always one of your weak points, Joseph Marino. There are times when you can't just come right out and say what you mean. You know, you need to work on that!" Aunt Kate lectured.

"Yes, ma'am. I'll let you get ready to go," Joseph shook his head and rolled his eyes. "What time should I tell my mother you'll be at her house?" Joseph thanked her and gently hung the phone up.

"So, the Norton curse strikes again, huh?" Anne was smiling a bit wider now.

"Yep. Aunt Kate hasn't changed a bit! Now to reconnect with my mother. It's been almost twenty minutes. She's probably frantic!" Joseph picked up the phone and dialed. The line in Maine was busy. Joseph waited about three minutes and dialed again. Still busy. About ten minutes later the phone on the other end rang, and his mother answered.

"Mom? I've been trying to..." Joseph started.

"Oh, Joey! My sister just called! She'll be here in about ten minutes. She said she talked to you. Joey, Joey! What am I going to do with you! Why didn't you just tell her that I was all right? Now she's all worried. She told me that you wanted to talk about lemon cakes, and she had to pry what happened to your father out of you." Joseph's mother chided him.

"Yes, Mom. As long as you're all right, then." Joseph was resigned to the situation. In fact, he knew it would end up this way. She was able to scold him only because she felt some safety now, knowing her sister was on the way.

That's the way things ran in his crazy family. Nobody just came right out and dealt with anything real. Everybody just fought over surface things. Nobody wanted to talk about what was really wrong. Joseph and Anne had made it a pledge early in their marriage to do things differently. He wasn't sure how well they were doing, but, well, they've been trying. Joseph hung up the phone, knowing that the immediate emergency with his mother was solved, even if he looked foolish while working on it.

As he turned to look down the hall he spotted Paul looking back at him. He had a sullen, depressed look on his face. Joseph realized that he had another "situation" to deal with.

Maybe just dealing with superficial issues was better, like how much lemon to put into a cake mix.

Chapter 3

Joseph wasn't sure how to break the news to his son, but he was pretty sure Paul had figured out what was going on. Still, he knew it was the right thing to do. He had to see how Paul was doing, and he had to make sure he fully understood the situation. He knew Anne was doing the same for their daughter. As Joseph took a moment to study the outline of his son, he slowly came to realize that he was feeling some degree of empathy for the boy, in spite of all of the conflicts the two had shared in recent years. Paul's facial expressions became easier for Joseph to read; they spoke of grief and fear.

But how could he tell his son? Joseph knew that Paul would not be taking this easily.

Paul had spent the better part of the last two summers visiting his grandparents in Maine, and Joseph was aware that some sort of emotional connection had developed between Joseph's father and Paul. The last time Joseph and Anne had dropped Paul off at the airport, almost a year ago, Paul seemed quite happy, in fact almost gleeful, to be on his way to visit Joseph's parents. When he returned he could speak of nothing but what he and his grandfather had done.

Joseph remembered how he felt when he saw Paul walk off of the plane wearing a Boston Red Sox hat. All Paul could talk about was how he had watched Carl Yastrzemski hit a home run over the Big Green Monster in Fenway Park. Joseph had only been to a Red Sox game once in his life with his father; he was always told the drive to Boston was too expensive for poor Maine folk. That moment seemed to be the highlight of Paul's young life, and Joseph felt quite a conflict. Of course he wanted the boy to have great experiences, and to be close to Joseph's father, but he also felt the loss of his own relationship with his now-deceased father. Joseph felt the shaking again, as he remembered that it was now over, for good. He knew he could never have another outing at Fenway Park with his father.

"How're you doing, son? I suppose you've figured out what's going on..." Joseph trailed off.

"Yeah. I guess grandpa's, well, he's...I dunno..." Paul quickly glanced at his father.

"It's hard to say, I know. It's strange that we can't seem to find a way to say this. I think that we find it tough because the mere fact that we say it makes it real. Maybe we hope that if we don't mention the words then it won't be true. Unfortunately, our words can't help him now. Words seem pretty cheap for those of us who are left behind, too. We have a gaping hole in our lives that wasn't there when we woke up this morning." Joseph walked up in front of the memory boxes that Anne had hung on the wall, one by one, over the years. These boxes were their lives, really. They held the mementoes and photographic images that chronicled all that they had been through.

Yeah. I didn't feel like this when I woke up." Paul whispered.

Joseph watched the pattern of Paul's eyes as they scanned the boxes. He was almost staring at the box that contained the old, yellowed pictures of Joseph's father when he was a young man. In the middle was a picture of Paul's grandfather wearing an old-style New York Yankees baseball uniform.

"I was always proud that my Dad played for a year with the Yankees, Paul. No other kid in my school could say that their Dad had played major league baseball. Of course, it wasn't until later on that I found out he had played not for the Red Sox, but for the Yankees."

"Yeah," Paul smiled, "he told me how mad you were

when you finally discovered that."

"Boy was I!" Joseph grinned. He looked hard into the face of the man in the old picture. He felt tears welling up as he realized how hard it was to see his face, either in the picture or in his mind. Why was that, he thought? Why is it so hard to see the faces of people close to you? Gosh, he can remember the face of the kid who always tormented him in his classroom at school. Why not his own father?

"So, Dad. He's really gone?" Paul whispered.

"I'm sorry, Paul. I've been trying to find a way to say it to you, but I don't even know what to call it. I guess I could just say it straight. He died this morning." Joseph felt bad, but knew there was no easy, or pretty, way to break this kind of news to anyone. He looked down at the carpet; he wished there was something else that he could deal with at the moment. He remembered something Anne had said to him years ago. She had told him that he had a habit of running away from difficult issues, and finding something to do with his hands instead. Joseph had to acknowledge that this was true, but he wished Anne would realize that he had come to a place in his life where he knew which issues he could actually make a difference in, and which ones he knew were hopeless. Joseph felt a real urge at that very moment to find something to fix or take apart. After a long silence, Paul replied.

"Yeah, I know. I was afraid about how to say it myself." Paul nodded.

"I know how much he meant to you, son." Joseph offered an invitation to talk.

"It doesn't seem fair. I only got two summers with him, and now he's gone. No more baseball games. No more rides in his old car. No more stories of whaling ships and of trenches in France in World War One."

"Life is like that, Paul. No one is guaranteed any more than this very time, this very hour. We like to push this aside in our thoughts, but it's still the truth."
Joseph put his hand on Paul's shoulder. Paul turned toward his father, and Joseph saw the lines of tears on his son's smooth, lightly creased face. He remembered a little boy who had come to him with a broken tricycle. That little boy was crying a lot like this husky teenager. Joseph felt a large wave of sadness rush over him. It was so easy to fix that tricycle a dozen years ago. It wasn't so easy to deal with this boy's broken heart.

"But we had no time at all, Dad. Two years ago I had only heard his voice and seen his pictures. Then I had some weeks with him, and now I can never hear his voice again."
Paul wiped his eyes.

"I understand." Joseph whispered. He knew the right thing to do was just listen.

"I have nothing to remember him by." Paul sobbed.

"Oh, not true, son. You carry something every single day of your life, and he will always be a part of your life because of it." Joseph smiled, even though it was full of pain, and was thankful that he had listened to Anne at least once in his life.

"What do you mean?" Paul turned toward his father.

"Your name. Paul Edward Marino. You have his name. You have his eyes. You have so many things that made him who he is. Of all my father's grandchildren and nephews, you are the only one who carries the one thing that set him apart for his entire life. His name." Joseph smiled. He repeated his son's name two or three times in his mind. It was hard for him to come to grips with the idea that there was only one person in his family with that name now. The urge to do something with his hands was strong, stronger than ever.

"Yeah, I guess so." Paul shrugged.

"Hey, I've got to clean up in the garage. I almost have that new carburetor working. Wanna help?" Joseph gingerly asked. Paul shrugged again.

"I guess so. After all, I'm the reason you have to work on it." Paul turned his head toward the pictures.

"Listen, I know you want to help. Just remember to think things through before you start working on a problem." Joseph reached out and squeezed his son's arm. Joseph turned toward the garage and Paul followed.

"I'm sorry. I thought Mike knew everything there was to know about carburetors. I just followed his directions." Paul said in a matter-of-fact tone. Joseph felt the anger rise, and consciously tightened his lips. He forced himself to concentrate solely on opening the door to the garage. It was a strange thing, to consciously walk through the ritual of turning a door handle. Joseph did this because he knew that whatever he would say would not be productive. Anne had taught him how to do this years before. Joseph realized that the situation back then had been very similar; Anne's brother was a lot like Paul's friend Mike.

Joseph had a difficult time dealing with Mike; he found the boy's know-it-all demeanor to be nauseating. There were too many times that Joseph had caught Mike offering an explanation that was completely ridiculous, false, full of half-truths and, often, downright destructive. Unfortunately, this time Joseph had to pay for one of Mike's little experiments.

"Well, next time ask, or check things out. Those little nozzles in a carburetor are really touchy; taking a pair of pliers to them is never a great idea. Anyway, I got the new carb just about done and the car'll be running any time now, so let's just forget it." Joseph walked over to the workbench and picked up a screwdriver.

"So, what can I do to help?" Paul asked, running his finger along the front left fender of the 1968 Camaro.

"How about cleaning the grease off of the top of the manifold? Here's a rag..." Joseph reached across the workbench and grabbed a relatively clean rag; it took him two tries, there was a failed attempt because he misjudged the distance.

"Are you all right, Dad?" Paul asked.

"Sure. Why?" Joseph reached for a can of WD-40.

"You missed the rag the first time you reached for it."

"Just tired, that's all. Nothing to worry about." Joseph was a bit gruff.

"And he needs new glasses, Paul." Anne added. She was standing in the doorway to the house.

"I'm fine, Anne. I got new glasses two years ago." Joseph pointed at the grease smear in the engine compartment of the car.

"That's the grease, Paul. Just get that wiped up." Joseph turned toward his son.

"Sure, two years ago you were fine. Of course there is the nasty 'p' word that the doctor mentioned." Anne had a smirk on her face.

"'P' word? What 'p' word?" Joseph continued to point out the grease spots as Paul wiped.

"Presbyopia, Joseph, and you know it." Anne shot back.

"Ah, come on, Anne. Give it a rest. So I can't focus as well as I used to?" Joseph was feeling uncomfortable. Any time the discussion moved to the subject of vision or the eyes he started squirming. When he was a kid he had rubbed his eye while he was getting a tooth filled; his fingernail had accidentally cut the outer layer of his eye. Ever since then he generally tried to avoid the subject entirely. Of course, Anne knew this. She hadn't let him run away from this topic often over the last year or two. Or many other topics that Joseph hated to deal with.

"Ok, I'll change the subject. There is a more pressing matter. Your father's passing. There's going to be a funeral. We have to deal with this, Joseph." Anne was obviously trying to keep her tone friendly.

"Anne, I think I need to finish the carburetor with my son first. I'll be honest. I can't cope with that right now. I'm just trying to swallow the idea that he's gone, and I'm not doing well with that." Joseph said in a very gruff voice. He turned back toward Paul as Anne walked back into the house.

"Thanks for saying that, Dad. I feel the same way. It's strange that I'd rather deal with the mess I left in the Camaro. It seems easier." Paul whispered, obviously not wanting his mother to hear.

"It is, Paul. Dealing with a piece of metal is always a lot less emotional than dealing with a death, and sometimes a man just needs to keep his hands busy when he's hurting. Remember that. That idea may help you someday. Keep this piece of advice with you always: when the emotions get too thick, go clean out the garage, and move some boxes." Joseph pointed toward a stack of boxes that looked quite out of place, and disorganized.

"I've noticed that you do that sort of thing a lot. I

remember how you dug that trench in the back yard the night I broke your high school football trophy." Paul's eyebrows went up quickly, and an expression of fear splashed onto his face. Joseph didn't have much trouble reading his son's emotions.

"Don't worry, Paul. It's long forgotten. Besides, it was an old dust-collecting paperweight with a dent in the side. Hey, the old brass plaque looks great in that shadow memory box your mother made." Joseph squirted a bit of liquid from the can into the hinge of the car's hood. Paul looked confused.

"Did I mess up the hinges, too?" He asked his father.

"Nah. It's always a good idea to do a little lubricating when you're under the hood. Another lesson for you! Try to prevent problems from happening." Joseph missed with the squirt aimed at the hinge on the right side of the engine compartment.

"Darn. Maybe your mother is right. I hate to admit it, but maybe I need new glasses."

"So what's wrong with getting new glasses?" Paul asked as he dug some oil out from under his fingernail.

"Nothing, except these will be bifocals, probably." Joseph replied.

"Bifocals?"

"Yeah. Bifocals. You know, in my class at school I teach a lesson on the Latin and Greek root words of our language. I am ashamed to admit that this year I skipped two of the roots: 'bi' and 'focus'." Joseph shook his head as he wiped the errant spray off of the side of the engine compartment.

"What do they mean?" Paul asked.

"Oh, that's right! You were in Mister Davidson's World History class, not mine! You missed one of my specialties!" Joseph stared at his son over the top of his glasses. There was a twinge of resentment in his statement. The choice his son had made to not be in his father's class last year still stung.

"Come on, Dad. You have to understand." Paul threw the rag onto the workbench.

"Forget it, Paul. I'll get over it."

"I don't know. You don't get over things like that really easy."

"You're right, but I will get over it in time." Joseph softened his tone.

"I guess you will. I just hope I'm not forty six when you do."

"Thirty years? Nah, I will have forgotten that by then!" Joseph smiled. A rare thing happened as he did. Paul smiled in return.

"So, are you going to tell me what 'bi' and 'focus' mean?" Paul asked.

"Simple. 'Bi' means two. 'Focus' means, well, I think you know what it means. I guess the best way to explain it is 'seeing things clearly'. You see, at your age your lenses are flexible and can focus back and forth easily. When you get to be my age, the lenses start to stiffen a bit. It takes longer to see things far away and then switch to looking at something close up. When I reached for that rag on the counter I rushed it too much. I had been looking at you, and you were closer. Most of the time I can only see things clearly that are near my eyes, but the reverse is true when I've been looking far away for a long time."

"Oh, like how you look over the top of your glasses sometimes. You do better not seeing through them, I guess?" Paul asked.

"Um, yeah. I didn't know you had noticed..." Joseph was very uncomfortable.

"Dad! You do it all the time!" Paul smiled, and then wiped the smile off of his face.

"Time to go to the eye doctor, I guess." Joseph shook his head. At that moment Anne opened the door from the house.

"Joseph...your Aunt Kate just called. They want your help with the arrangements for your father." It was quite apparent that Anne was nervous.

"Could you let her know that I'll call her back in an hour or two? I guess we should talk about how we're going to deal with this. I was afraid of this, being the only son and all." Joseph glanced over at Paul.

"I think that's a good plan." Anne nodded as she went back into the house.

"I guess were in the same boat, huh, Dad? Both of us are the only sons."

"Yep. I hope you won't be stuck with my mess, and that it's not the same kind of mess that I expect to see in Maine." Joseph felt a new rush of sadness.

"What d you expect to find?" Paul asked.

"My father was a pack rat. He never threw anything out. I just hope we don't have to clean out his garage. I know some of the things that are still in that rat's nest."

"Like what?" Paul seemed definitely interested.

"One time I took one of his new golf clubs out into the back yard. I thought I was the next great golfer, and I wanted to try swinging a club." Joseph sounded sheepish, mainly because he felt that way.

"Oh, no...you didn't lose it!" Paul had a funny smile on his face.

"I wish I had. That would have been easier." Joseph's eyebrows went up. He paused a long time while he pulled down on the hood of the car.

"So...?" Paul wanted to hear more.

"Well, ever see a cartoon in which the stupid rabbit wraps a golf club around the tree and it looks like a pretzel?"

"Yeah, there's a good one like that!"

"They don't bend like a pretzel. They break." Joseph

smiled a painful smile.

"Oh...ouch!" Paul smiled.

"Shall we see if the old Camaro will start?" Joseph gestured toward the driver side door.

"Let's crank it up!" Paul smiled.

Father and son shook hands as they never had when they heard that big Chevy six-cylinder engine come to life. Joseph felt a deep sense of accomplishment. It was good to repair something that you cared about that had been broken.

Chapter 4

Joseph felt a little better about how his relationship with Paul as he walked slowly down the hall toward his bedroom. Ever since Paul had hit adolescence their relationship had varied from a high one week to the depths of despair and anger the next. Joseph understood all that Anne had told him about puberty, hormones and the uncertainty of growing up, but it didn't make Paul's behavior any easier to deal with. Well, at least this week things were on the upswing. He needed that, since he was fighting a large emotional drop into the proverbial black hole of depression because of his father's passing. Death always brought him to the edge of that dreaded place.

There was that phrase again. Everyone used the word "passing" when they discussed a death. He wondered why people couldn't just say the words "died" or "death". The word was used as if someone had just driven in front of another car on the freeway, or had completed third grade. Then it hit him. Death was so final, so unchangeable, so full of fear and dread. The closer the person is to one who has died, the harder it is to use the word "death".

Joseph felt his heart race as he confronted the forbidden topic in his own mind: the end of his own life. Of course, this was the ultimate cold shiver up his back. This happened every time he had to acknowledge someone's passing. He started obsessing on how it would end for him. It had been so easy for his father; he had fallen asleep in the chair in the living room and will never awaken. Joseph was surprised that he was feeling anger when he considered this. For some reason, he felt his father should have suffered more. He took a deep breath as he remembered those many years when his father drank too much. Nah, he thought, it was better that he left this life this way.

But how would his own life end? In a chair in the living room? Maybe when he was on vacation, or camping or something? Would it happen in his classroom, as he often feared? Joseph was haunted by the idea of never being able to retire; old man Hamer died that way. One day Joseph walked into the teacher's lounge, sat down next to Mr. Hamer, and started chatting about the new attendance taking procedure they were now using in class. It was only after two or three minutes that he noticed that the older teacher wasn't nodding as he usually did. Joseph shook his head as he remembered how Mr. Hamer's face had looked. Joseph had always thought that people shut their eyes when they died. Now he knew it wasn't always true.

A strange thought passed through his mind. Was his father's eyes closed when his mother had found him? Joseph shook his head and muttered about how obsessive he could get. He also decided that he had to find a way to retire, even if monthly checks and benefits for retired teachers were garbage. Anne and he had talked many times about building a cabin on their small piece of land in Pine Mountain. Maybe they should start now. Maybe, he thought, Anne was right. Maybe they could afford to retire if they simplified their lifestyle.

He began to understand why the word "passing" worked better. It just was. There was so much one had to deal with when one uses the word "death". "Passing" sounds so much easier somehow. God, how he didn't want to talk to his mother, or go back to Maine, or deal with caskets and burials. He'd rather rebuild his Camaro from front to back, even if he didn't have a clue about how to do it. He felt a little anger; he wanted to be able to savor the fleeting moment in which he and Paul had found a way to connect to each other. It was so rare anymore. Joseph didn't want to have that special feeling ruined by the harsh reality of a funeral crashing in.

Joseph rubbed his hands as he slowed down considerably. As he approached the doorway he heard Anne's voice, and she sounded like she was on the phone. He decided to linger for a minute or two and listen; he was worried about Anne's tone of voice.

Considering his father's death, and all that had just gone on with the various phone calls, Joseph wanted to make sure he knew what he was getting into before he went into the room.

"...I understand, Mom. I'm sure Joseph will understand as well." That was all Anne said for quite a long time. Joseph felt his eyebrows press down over his eyes.

"No. I'm not sure what our plans are. We..." Anne said. It seemed to Joseph as if Anne had been cut off again. There was another long silence.

"I can probably call you tonight if..." The pattern of Anne speaking and then being cut off had repeated itself. Joseph nodded with understanding. This was the way phone calls between Joseph's mother and Anne had always sounded.

"I already spoke with him, I'm just waiting..." Anne sighed deeply as she went silent. Joseph decided that maybe she needed him to interfere. He stepped toward the door.

"Oh. He's here right now, Mom! Would you like to talk to him this time?" Anne's eyes moved from Joseph's eyes to the phone receiver, and back again. She was obviously asking him to jump in and take over. Joseph reached out for the receiver with hesitation; he just stared at the phone for a long time.

"Joey?" Anne whispered. He noticed that she was gently rubbing his arm.

"Huh?" Joseph turned to look at Anne.

"It's your mother. She needs to talk to you. There are so many arrangements to be made..." Anne trailed off. Joseph nodded as he lifted the receiver to his ear.

"Mom? What can we do to help?" Joseph looked down at the floor. He really didn't want to offer any help, but he knew that he had to. Anne would have been upset with him if he had simply mouthed the words "I'll call back later" to her. Over the half-century of his life he had learned that he couldn't avoid the difficult issues by just running away from them. He knew he would be better off confronting them earlier. Issues got tougher as they got older. This was a good example of this idea.

"I need you here, Joseph. I can't arrange all of this myself, son. You know I can't drive anymore, and so many errands need to be done. I will pay for a plane flight. Anne said she understands." Joseph's mother stated.

"I need to talk to her; we have to decide how to handle this, Mom. The kids, well, they may want to go back also." Joseph looked at Anne, who nodded.

"I can't afford to pay for the whole family, Joseph, and

you know that." Joseph's mother answered. She sounded like she was getting irritated. Joseph knew this tone of voice well. It was the same tone that he had heard while he was in his teens and trying to get out of Saturday chores. Back then she had used the expression "I'm not going to come out there to the garden and do your job for you", but the emotional tone dripping from each word was the same.

"Mom, I'm not saying you should. All I'm saying is that my wife and I need to make a joint decision on how to do this, that's all." Joseph explained, in a resigned voice. He knew he could not communicate with his mother about his relationship with Anne. He had never been sure if his mother had liked Anne, or how she felt about his children. A thought dawned on him - he may never know.

"Well, you do what you have to. You know what is important right now." His mother replied, each word strongly tainted with sarcasm. Joseph felt the muscles in his jaw tense up, and started squeezing his fist tighter.

"Mom. Listen. I'll be there. We will call you back this evening and let you know our plans. We will be there." Joseph said, using all of his energy to restrain himself.

"Ok, but just remember that we are a couple of hours ahead of you. Colorado time is about six-fifteen right now, but we're at eight-fifteen here in Maine. We're in the middle of our evening here, and I have to get to bed before ten."

"Mom, for heaven's sake! How many times do I have to

explain that we live in California? And I will call you in about an hour!" Joseph was losing his patience, and he knew it. His emotions were raw, and he was always on the edge with his mother anyway. He had to get off the phone. Joseph looked at Anne and stretched out the phone cord toward her, offering the receiver Anne nodded and took the phone. Joseph walked heavily and slowly into the master bathroom.

"Mom? It's Anne. Joseph wasn't...um...feeling too well and he went into the bathroom." Anne knew she had to stretch the truth a bit. She also knew when to just do as Joseph asked. The silence returned. Anne nodded, and it seemed as if the receiver was the pivot point of her movement.

"I do understand. Yes, I know Colorado is where we moved twenty years ago. Yes, Colorado is two hours behind Maine." Anne just went with the flow. Joseph stood in the doorway and shook his head. He had figured out Anne's secret in dealing with his mother. She didn't argue. She just nodded and went along, even if the words coming through the earpiece were senseless.

"Ok. Yes, Mom. I promise. We'll call you back before your bedtime. No problem." Anne smiled a pained, forced smile. The silence once again filled the room. Joseph took a deep breath, and felt grateful for the strength Anne brought to a situation like this one.

"Everything will be fine, Mom. I know it's hard, but we'll

get through this together. I know we will." Anne reached out with her left arm, as if to comfort the distant woman on the shoulder. Joseph felt a pang of guilt. He had dumped the problem of his mother on to Anne's shoulders.

"We'll be talking to you in an hour or so. Yes. We love you. Bye, Mom!" Anne smiled as she hung up the phone. Joseph thought it strange how she would erase the smile the instant the phone was hung up, as if the far away person could no longer see her.

"Thanks, honey." Joseph said in a soft, quiet tone.

"For what?" Anne looked confused.

"For handling her when I couldn't. It wasn't right of me to dump her on you like that." Joseph pushed a stray sock on the floor toward the wall.

"It wasn't wrong, either, Joey." Joseph looked up when she used his boyhood name. He had recognized years before that she used it whenever she wanted to shut the rest of the world out, and find a way to touch emotionally. He saw that she was crying.

"Was she hard on you, honey?" Joseph stepped over to his wife's side.

"Oh, no, that's not it...not that. I'm used to her wandering. I'm used to her attitude, too. After twenty years you learn how to deal with someone like her." Anne wiped her tears away with one of her small, thin handkerchiefs.

"Well, I know I'm struggling with my dad's death, so I

understand." Joseph put his arm around his wife

"Oh, no, that's not it...I was..." Anne quickly stopped in mid-sentence. Joseph was confused.

"It doesn't bother you?" Joseph asked.

"No. I mean, yes it does bother me. That's not what I mean. Of course your father's death is hard." Anne stepped back and gestured.

"I'm really confused. What's going on?" Joseph rubbed his day-old beard.

"It's just that...well, something hit me." Anne struggled with words.

"Hit you?" Joseph responded.

"Not 'hit me' like a stick or something. Emotionally I was hit."

"Go on..." Joseph sat on the edge of the bed.

"I never saw your mother separately from your father. She's alone now." Anne started crying again.

"Yes...I know that's hard. It's hard seeing her apart from my father. I'm worried about how she'll do. He's always taken care of so many things for her." Joseph nodded.

"No. Well, that's hard, too. What I mean is that, well, this isn't about them." Anne pointed to her tears.

"So, who's it for?" Joseph said quietly.

"Us. One day one of us will be left behind. One of us will pass away first, leaving the other alone." Anne cried as she sat next to her husband on the bed. Joseph didn't know what to say. He hadn't thought of that angle on all of this. He turned and looked at her side of the bed. It was hard to imagine an empty space there.

"Um...oh, Anne. I...um...don't think I can...um...deal with that idea right now." Joseph found the words difficult in coming. There was a lump in his throat. Anne had caught him off-guard. He had struggled with the idea of his own death, but dealing with Anne's would be something he'd have to face in the far-distant future. He had to. He had nothing inside left to be able to cope with it today.

"You're right, Joseph. It just hit me. Someday I might be in her shoes. Where would it happen? What would I do? Someday I'd have to..." Anne trailed off. Joseph rubbed her back and pulled his lips together. He raised his index finger to his lips.

"Well, let's not go there, Anne. I can't. It's a strange idea. One of us will understand. One will never know where or when." Joseph placed his right index finger in front of her mouth as he hugged his wife.

"We have a lot to deal with today, Joey. I guess you're right. We have to figure out what to do, and call your mother back. We'll just have to let the future take care of itself." Anne took a deep breath and straightened her shirt.

"And it will, Anne. Right now all that matters is that we're here, sitting on our bed, and safe." Joseph feigned a smile as he pulled Anne close to himself.

75

"You're right. It's our place, where we can feel safe."
Anne smiled weakly.

Chapter 5

"Paul! Sarah!" Joseph called downstairs. There was
no response.

"Can anyone down there hear me?" Joseph continued.
Anne walked up behind him.

"Nobody home?" She asked.

"There doesn't seem to be." Joseph picked up his
baseball hat from the rack in the hall and headed downstairs
to find his two children.

"Relax, Joseph. Don't be too hard on them. They're
having a hard day, too. They lost their grandfather,
remember." Anne whispered.

"Yeah, but they don't have to make things tougher on
us by disappearing when we have to make some important
family decisions. They've been around long enough to realize
that we need a family meeting at a time like this. Besides,
after dealing with my mother four times today I need a break!
This isn't the 'break' I hoped for!" Joseph shook his head.

The late afternoon sun was harsh as Joseph stepped
outside and scanned up and down the street. He squinted as
he look west, directly into the setting sun. Paul and Sarah
weren't hanging out in the cul-de-sac with their friends as they

usually do on a Saturday in the late afternoon. Joseph shook his head as he whispered to himself.

"Gotta go search house to house."

He believed that the two were either at Jonathan's house, hanging out and watching television, or at the backyard pool of Mrs. Howland. Joseph winced, and hoped Paul and Sarah were at Jonathan's house. A visit to Mrs. Howland's house was a torment. She was the "unusual" woman on the block. The wives on the street called her the "home wrecker". She'd been married three times, and was without a husband at the moment. Two of her former husbands, numbers two and three, had been neighbors on the block who had left their wives and kids to move in with her. It was strange, Joseph thought, that he still thought of her as 'Mrs. Howland' when she had changed names twice since she moved into the neighborhood. Her name was, legally, 'Mrs. Anderson', since she was still in the divorce process with Garret Anderson, but Joseph still thought of Cheryl Anderson, two doors down on the other side of the street, as the 'real' Mrs. Anderson. It was sad, Joseph thought. Cheryl was one of the nicest, kindest, and patient women on the block. A distinctly lewd voice interrupted Joseph's mental meanderings.

"Hey, Joe! Check it out! The suit is in the yard!" Bob Granger said, almost under his breath, as he lifted his rake up. Bob lived next door to Mrs. Howland. That fact caused many fights between Bob and his wife Emily. Joseph stopped and glanced in the direction of the Howland house.

Anyone in the neighborhood could tell when Judy Howland had split up with a man; she would start wearing her tight bikini (or the "suit" as most women around called it) around the yard while picking weeds or raking leaves. She'd been taking out the trash in the "suit". Joseph hated to admit it, but he caught himself a time or two wandering out of the garage to have a peak at the way she did her yard work. It was strange to see the number of men that chose that time of day to do their front yard chores. Joseph usually just shook his head and turned back inside the garage.

"Yep. Have you seen my two kids?" Joseph turned back toward Bob.

"Wassa matter? No time for sightseeing?" Bob chuckled.

"No, there isn't, Bob. I'm trying to get things together at home. We have to take a flight back east tomorrow. Back home to Maine." Joseph was very business-like.

"Oh? Kinda sudden? What's up?" Bob glanced back and forth, from Joseph to Mrs. Howland. She was bending over to pull a rather large weed.

"My father died, Bob. I've gotta go help my mother." Joseph said quietly. Bob turned toward Joseph and looked down.

"Hey, I'm sorry, Joe. I really am. I had no idea. I wouldn't have talked about 'the suit' over there if I'd known...really." Well, thought Joseph, at least his neighbor seemed sincere. Bob turned back and watched as she returned to her house.

"Yeah, I know. I just need to find my kids."

"I saw your daughter go over to Mandy and Jonathan's house. They were talking a few minutes ago."

That turned out to be a dead end. There was no one home at Jonathan's house, so Joseph decided to try the houses of other friends on the block. At the third house Maryann's mother told Joseph that Sarah and Maryann were going to "sit around the pool". Joseph knew what that meant. Everyone knew what that meant. Maryann's mother, with the tone of her voice, knew what that meant. "The pool" belonged to Mrs. Howland. She had an open gate for all the neighborhood teens. Anne had once said that this was because Mrs. Howland was still a teenager herself. Anne had pointed out how she dressed like them, and even talked like them. Joseph thought it was sad that a thirty four year old woman needed that kind of lifestyle, and he wondered why she did. Joseph walked up to Mrs. Howland's front door. He rang the bell.

The door opened and Mrs. Howland was standing in the doorway with a towel barely wrapped around her. The bright yellow towel extended from her underarms to the middle of her thighs. Joseph cleared his throat.

"Uh, hi, um, Mrs. Anderson. Sorry to bother you, but

I'm trying to find my son and daughter. A neighbor said they might be over here." Joseph kept glancing at the yard, away from Mrs. Howland.

"Oh, please! Call me Judy! Besides, I'm not using the name 'Anderson' any more. Boy what a mistake THAT was! He took advantage of me when my second husband moved out, you know." Mrs. Howland flipped her hand and arm in a very feminine manner while holding tight to the towel around her.

Uh, sure...I just came over..." Joseph was trying to work up the courage to change the topic. Mrs. Howland wasn't giving him much of a chance, however.

"And I'm really glad you did! You're George, aren't you? The guy that teaches at the high school?" Mrs. Howland asked in a singsong voice. Joseph noticed that she had perfect, straight and very white teeth.

"Um, it's Joseph, actually..."

"Oh, Joseph. Eww. That's what my first husband's name was. We used to call him 'Joe'." She said as the corner of her lip curled up.

"Well, my friends call me Joseph, not Joe..." Joseph hated to be called "Joe".

"Well, Joseph it is! That's a good way for me to remember you! We'll be friends, then!" Mrs. Howland's magazine-perfect smile returned. Joseph chastised himself for telling her about his name.

"Um, yeah. Are my kids, my son and my daughter, over here, by any chance? The sun's almost down and we have a lot to do." Joseph looked past Mrs. Howland, trying to see into the back yard.

"Let's see. We have only a few girls in the back yard. I can go ask, if you want. Do you want to come in?" Mrs. Howland stepped back and gestured.

"Oh, no! I really have to get going. Really. I can just wait here." Joseph answered in a louder voice. He had to stop his fingers from his worst nervous habit: when he was extremely stressed he started playing with the second button on his shirt. There were too many shirts sitting in his closet recently that were missing a button. Anne had been trying to keep up with the repairs, but she had also scolded him in an effort to stop the destruction of his shirts.

"Ok, have it your way," Mrs. Howland turned, "I'll just send them out through the gate, if they're here." She walked away from the door.

"That would be great!" Joseph forced a smile. He turned and walked toward the gate on the other side of the garage, stumbling on a broken terra cotta planter near the corner of the garage.

"Good recovery, Joseph!" A man who was rolling up a hose said from the other side of the driveway. Joseph recognized the teasing voice of his old friend Conrad Hernandez. He was relieved to hear a friendly voice.

"Hey, it comes from all of my Army training!" Joseph replied. It was a standing joke between them, since Joseph had only spent a little over a year in the service just after World War II. He had fond memories of that time, but he made no claim to having saved democracy, or even to have won any medals. Conrad, on the other hand, had enjoyed a successful career in the Air Force.

"Didn't the Army teach you about fraternizing with 'the enemy'?" Conrad nodded toward Mrs. Howland's house.

"I guess I missed that day in boot camp!' Joseph smiled.

"And I suppose your Army intelligence system couldn't warn you about those land mines, either!" Conrad smiled as he pointed at the planter.

"I was absent that day, too." Joseph walked slowly toward the Hernandez house.

"Must have been! I was watching you walk down the street. You're looking a bit clumsy today, if you don't mind me saying. You're not your usual self." Conrad's forehead held a serious dip in the eyebrows.

"Nah, I don't mind. I'm having a rough day, to be honest. I'm worn out." Joseph sighed.

"Something wrong? It's not like you to hang around 'the suit'. I don't think I've ever seen you on her property. I guess THAT alone would make any man nervous." Conrad's smile returned as he motioned to his left.

"I guess you're right. It's been tough to focus. You see," Joseph took a deep breath, "my father died this morning back home in Maine."

"Oh, no. I'm sorry. That's rough. I didn't mean to make stupid jokes. I'm really sorry, Joseph." Conrad wiped his mouth with his hand and looked nervous. He put the rolled up hose down on the driveway and stepped toward Joseph.

"Oh, no, no...you've done nothing wrong. I'm just a bit lost, I guess." Joseph grabbed his friend's upper arm in a gesture of comfort. So many times Joseph had confided in Conrad; he was easy to talk to and, more importantly, he listened.

"It's so sad. All these years of you trying to find a way to reach out to him. All of these years waiting for some expression of love. I can only imagine how you feel, my friend. Pain, fear, hopes dashed, and, I might dare say, a little anger, maybe?" Conrad's voice had grown quieter.

"I think you're right on all counts, Colonel." Joseph used his friend's old military rank as he looked down at the gravel beneath his feet.

"You have the right to feel these things. He was a difficult man, from what you describe." Conrad said. He lowered his voice a notch as he waved at a neighbor from down the street who happened to be walking by.

"How're you doing, Mark!" Conrad shouted. The other man smiled and waved.

83

"Sometimes my relationship with my father felt as close as your little exchange with Mark there." Joseph answered.

"I wish I knew why it is so hard for men to build relationships with their sons. We have the same problems in my family, though they're not as severe as your situation, Joseph." Conrad said.

"I wonder. My father was so focused on work and money. That's what he taught me. I guess that's what I'm teaching Paul. I just wish I knew how to change it. I feel so helpless." Joseph shook his head.

"I think we all do, Joseph. I don't think any of us can fix it alone. Maybe a piece of the answer lies with every generation. I have to fix a little portion. My son will fix a different little part. Maybe his son will continue the healing. Hopefully someone related to me along the distant path into the future won't unravel what was accomplished with the generations that have passed on." Conrad pointed to the cement on the walkway leading into the backyard.

"Hah! Your kids left their names, I see!" Joseph smiled. He'd never noticed the little words in the walkways before. The writing seemed so child-like, and Conrad's kids were going off to college now.

"Yep. Made it so we can never move again. Not unless I dig up this slab of the concrete and take it with us!" Conrad smiled and shook his head as he mouthed the words "no way".

"Same here. I think I'd rather have a tooth removed after refusing Novocain!" Joseph replied.

"Well, I've had that happen. You'd rather move. Believe me." Conrad pointed to a bridge on the left side of his mouth. Joseph smiled.

"Dad? Can I stay here with my friends a while longer?" Sarah's voice interrupted the two men.

"Huh? Oh, Sarah! Uh, no. We have to get home. Mom and I need to talk to you two. We're definitely going to Maine for Grandpa's funeral. Where's Paul?" Joseph looked around, toward Mrs. Howland's house.

"He's not here. The last time I saw him was in the garage." Sarah turned and walked back toward Mrs. Howland's gate.

"Sarah? We have to get going..." Joseph said, with urgency in his voice.

"I know. I have to get my towel." Sarah pointed toward the gate.

"So, you're not upset?" Joseph was confused.

"No, not really. I needed an excuse to leave. I'm really not into skinny dipping." Sarah said as she opened the gate.

Joseph turned to look at Conrad, who smiled knowingly, but looked embarrassed.

"Skinny dipping? Is she pulling my leg?" He asked.

"Uh, I'd like to say I don't know, but, um, well, I do know when I have to stay out of my backyard. My wife makes me."

Conrad looked up at the clouds.

"Anne and I will have to discuss whether or not we should allow Sarah to visit Mrs. Howland's house anymore!" Joseph was upset. He turned and considered walking up to Mrs. Howland's front door and telling her what he thought of her. Conrad grabbed Joseph's forearm.

"Joseph...wait a minute. Slow down. You missed something important here. You're a success! You've done your job." He said.

"What are you talking about?" Joseph turned to look at his friend again.

"That's your problem, Army! You don't listen well! Air Force heard! What did Sarah say about the skinny dipping?" Conrad smiled as he pointed toward the side gate that Sarah had used.

"She needed an excuse to leave?" Joseph offered tentatively.

"Yes! And that she didn't feel comfortable!" Conrad winked.

"You're right. Maybe there is hope." Joseph took a step toward home.

"As long as there is another generation then there is hope, my friend." Conrad squeezed Joseph's arm. The two men looked each other in the eye for a brief moment.

"Then there is hope." Joseph nodded.

Chapter 6

The sun spent its last rays of the day as Joseph and Sarah walked back up the street toward their home. At sunset tomorrow, he thought, he'd be on the other side of the continent, back in the town that he knew as a teenager. He looked over at Sarah and realized that she was growing up in a different world from the one he knew so long ago.

Sarah's world was of television, movies, clothes stores, backyard swimming pools, and going to the market to hang out with her friends. Joseph smiled to himself. No, it was a "store" or a "market" anymore. The new generation called it a "mall". What a strange idea, he thought. Collect a few stores, put them into adjoining buildings, and then put a roof over the walkway between the stores. They call it a mall.

His world was of a corner market that he thought held every possible item a young boy could ever want. If he wanted a magazine or a comic book, the market had it. If his mother sent him out for a box of crackers, he knew that the corner market would have it. When he was a bit older, the market even installed a soda fountain, and he used to take Anne there to treat her whenever he had saved up thirty or forty cents.

He never knew he needed so many things until he moved to California after the war. Of course, back then he called it "the war", but Korea, and now Vietnam, made him say "World War Two" now. How did he ever survive without a wide orange tie, or being able to buy a book? Back then his mother took him to the library if he wanted a book. Now everyone buys a paperback at the mall.

"Dad?" A young voice interrupted Joseph's thoughts.

"Huh? What?" He replied

"I forgot what your neighborhood looks like. Was a lot like this one?" Sarah asked, while adjusting the towel wrapped around her.

"My neighborhood? Oh, no! This is so different. There are walls and fences everywhere here. Back home, there was a wall every now and then. The houses weren't as big, and most families had only one car. If you were really rich, it was a new car." Joseph smiled as he remembered the day his father had driven home in the 1936 Chevrolet. He knew he would never forget the feeling of pride as his father stepped out of that shiny black new car. All of the kids in the neighborhood were around, even that pesky little Annie. He remembered that they stood in silence as his father lectured them about staying away from the car, and to not touch it.

"Didn't your dad have some old car since you were a kid, Dad?" Sarah asked.

"Oh, no. Maybe it seemed old, but I was already out on my own when he bought that car." Joseph smiled as he pictured the old 1948 Chevrolet Woodside station wagon that his father had traded the 1936 model in for. Dad never bought anything but Chevys, Joseph remembered. He could never figure out why his father never shopped the other brands. He could still hear the echo of his father's voice from 1948, explaining that he used to buy Fords, but he didn't like the look in Henry Ford's eye when he saw his picture in the paper a few years later. Strange. Buying a car based on the look of a man in an old newspaper picture, but that was his father. He was narrow minded, opinionated, and harsh when his son cried. Joseph realized he was squeezing his right hand into a fist. He was angry.

"So you never got to drive it?" Sarah asked. Joseph noticed she was getting cold so he put his arm around her. He immediately regretted this; the water from Sarah's wet bathing suit soaked into his shirt.

"The '48 Chevy? Hah! Once, and my father never knew it." Joseph laughed.

"He never knew? What happened?" Sarah looked up and smiled.

"Well, you see, it's kinda embarrassing..." Joseph shrugged.

"Ah, come on. Tell me!" Sarah smiled.

"Well, one day I went back to visit my parents, and I wanted to go down to the creek, the one your mother and I have told you about..."

"You mean Chocolate Chip Creek? Mom told me about

it." Sarah interrupted. Joseph was surprised to learn that she had been listening. She had a terrible habit of doodling on a piece of paper whenever he or Anne would reminisce about the long-ago past.

"Hah! You remember!" Joseph shook his head.

"Of course I do! You guys talk about that place enough. Will we get to see it when we go back there tomorrow?"

"Maybe we can arrange it, honey. Maybe we can." Joseph was quieter.

"So, how did you get to drive your dad's car?" Sarah steered the conversation back to a difficult event years before.

"Well, my dad loved that old Chevy Woody. He'd wax it, polish it, and sweep it out, everything. Every week or two he'd do the same thing."

"Yeah...but that's not what I asked. So, what happened?" Sarah kept prodding. Joseph realized she was starting to remind him of Anne. She was about the right age when Anne used to pester him about dawdling and avoiding doing his homework, so many years ago. Sometimes she was so much like Anne, but you didn't want to tell her that. She was afraid she was too much like her mother. There were a lot of times he wanted to mention how much she reminded him of Anne, in a look, or the way she'd comb her hair. He had said something once or twice, but Sarah had run off crying, and mad at him. Anne had to explain to Joseph that a young girl didn't like to be thought of as being like her mother. Well, at least in her family. He went back to the story of the old car.

"Well, I got up really early one day and decided I'd wash the car for my father. I figured he'd be tired of doing it. He'd had the car about three or four years by then, and had been washing it every couple of weeks all that time. I started it up, and slowly backed it out of the little one car garage. Then I washed it. I had just finished when a young boy from up the lane walked up, put his hands on his waist and just stared at me."

"What did he want?" Sarah looked confused.

"Well, I smiled at him and figured he was confused because I wasn't my father." Joseph continued.

"That wasn't it?"

"Oh, no. It was something much more important that bothered him. I had spent about an hour and a half cleaning my father's car when the teenage boy informed me that he made his weekly spending money washing that very same Chevy! I had stolen his two dollars!" Joseph smiled.

"Two dollars is all he got paid? Is that all?" Sarah looked shocked.

"Oh, Sarah, you have to remember that two dollars back then is like ten dollars now!"

"Oh, that's right. You told me that once. So, what did you do?" Sarah nodded.

"I felt so bad that I pulled out my wallet and handed the boy two dollars. The guy seemed surprised, but took it anyway. I apologized, and he walked off." Joseph untangled himself from Sarah's hug. He was beginning to feel too wet from her bathing suit and towel.

"So, what happened next?"

"I slowly pushed the car back into the garage. It was too late in the morning, and I knew my father would hear the car being started by this time. I figured that he had his hearing aid in his ear by then, so I couldn't start it again."

"And you closed the garage door and went inside?" Sarah asked.

"That's right. There my mother was, in the kitchen, making pancakes. Mmm. She makes the best flapjacks in Maine, I think. I guess no one makes a meal as well as your own mother." Joseph nodded and wiped his mouth. He was beginning to realize how hungry he was.

"So, your father never found out?" Sarah pulled on Joseph's arm. Anne does the same thing from time to time, Joseph thought.

"Huh? Oh, no, he didn't. But my mother and I were left in a tough spot."

"Why was that?" Sarah asked.

"As soon as I had walked in, my mother asked what I had said to the boy. I told her what had happened, and she started laughing."

"What about?" Sarah wondered.

"I guess my father had paid the kid two dollars the day before and told him not to bother washing the car that week. Dad had told him that I would be doing it! Can you imagine! That kid ended up with four bucks instead of two!" Joseph had to smile. The years had taken the sting off of the embarrassment he had felt back then, he realized.

"So why was the kid upset?" Sarah asked.

"I guess he thought I'd be doing it from then on." Joseph shook his head and wondered whatever became of that curly-haired teenager.

"How did your dad know that you'd be washing the car?"

"Well, for years before that he wanted me to wash his car, and I always hated doing it..."

"Like you hate doing it now?" Sarah interrupted.

"...like I still do." Joseph gave Sarah a mock disapproving glare as he answered her.

"Oh, sorry..." Sarah acted nervous. It was a game they played over the years.

"Sure you are! Well, to continue my story, it was always a point of tension between us. I guess we were both stubborn. He wanted me to do it, and I didn't want to do it. So it was a stand-off." Joseph shrugged.

"Kinda like you and Paul?" Sarah blurted.

Joseph stopped suddenly when he heard this. He was

in front of the ash tree by their house, and he reached out and pulled off a branch. He felt a moment of pain as he remembered the recent incident at the lunch table with Paul.

"Kinda like me and Paul..." Joseph mumbled. Sarah had hit him where it hurt the most. He was more and more like his own father every year, he guessed. The idea that he was being seen in the same way he had seen his own father chafed against him terribly, but he didn't know what to do about it. Stubborn breeds stubborn, he thought.

"Sorry. I didn't want to bring that up, Dad. It just slipped out. Really." Sarah looked down. Joseph watched as the sky turned from deep blue to black. The streetlights came on about that moment.

"You'd better get inside, Sarah. You're going to catch cold."

"But I want to know something. Why did you decide to wash the car that day, Dad?"

"Well, this is it. The last question tonight. After this, you go inside." Joseph pointed toward the house.

"Ok. So, why did you do it?"

"The night before Dad had been wondering about his will. For years he wrote and re-wrote his will. He was obsessed by who would, or who would not, get his stuff. That night about twenty years ago I was sitting in the front parlor reading the newspaper. He was where he sat every Friday night, at his beat up old roll-top desk, working on papers. He had been writing probably what was the thirty-eighth version of his will, and mumbling. I was used to it. That's just how he was. At that moment, he did something strange. He looked up and blurted out that he'd give his car to whoever washed it last before he died. I looked up, confused. I couldn't figure out why he had said that." Joseph scratched at the top of his head, being careful with the thinning hair.

"I wonder who was the last person to wash it..." Sarah said as she ran toward the front of the house. She was shivering as she opened the door and went in. The light from the living room lit up the old ash tree, and Joseph's hand as it gently caressed the bark.

"So do I, Sarah. So do I." Joseph turned and looked at the bare, dark hill at the end of the street, past the block wall. He started to wonder if he really wanted to go back to Maine. He didn't really want to deal with his father's things, or the burial arrangements. He didn't know how to cope with his mother any longer. She seemed so...so old now. Joseph touched his cheek and found that it was wet. He'd been quietly crying.

"Joseph?" Anne interrupted his mental wanderings.

"Huh? Yeah?" Joseph turned. Anne was leaning on the tree trunk.

"You coming in? It's getting late. We have a lot to do, and we have to leave before dawn. The flight leaves LAX at seven, remember" She was still leaning against the trunk.

"Um, sure. I haven't found Paul yet." Joseph turned to look at the garage. The door was open and he could tell the light over his workbench was on.

"He's here. He's been in the garage working." Anne replied.

"Ok. I'll just close the garage and we'll get the bags into the station wagon."

"Are you all right?" Anne whispered as she reached out to touch him.

"Sure. What makes you think I'm not?" Joseph smiled a weak smile. It was at that moment he saw how much she had changed since he first saw here on Chocolate Chip Creek, so many years ago. She had been leaning against a tree back then, too. Her legs, her hips, looked the same way back then. Her hair had been pulled back, like it looked now.

"Oh, maybe twenty-six years of marriage tells me." Anne smiled, just like the way she did back then.

"Oh, honey. I'm not sure I can do this." Joseph was crying softly.

"We'll make it. We'll be there for each other." Anne stepped over and hugged him. He closed his eyes and tried to imagine another evening with Anne, in the forest of Maine all those years ago. He could feel her arms. They felt the same. Her head, leaning against his chest, was the same. Her hair smelled the same. He smiled as he felt the pressure of her breasts against his stomach. It was 1944 all over again.

He had felt the same way back then. He was going off to join the Army, and he didn't want to forget her hug. Joseph had memorized every feeling as he held her then. He had done the same thing under that tree so many years ago, so many miles away.

"You're right. Besides, maybe it would be good to see Chocolate Chip Creek again." Joseph looked down at the top of Anne's head and felt a pang. The gray hairs hadn't been there twenty-six years ago.

"Don't forget something. We're older, Joey, but we still love each other. That's all that matters. Until death do us part." Anne looked up at Joseph. It was at that very moment that he felt a whole lot better. Her eyes were still the beautiful shade of gray-blue that he had had the privilege of looking into for all of these years.

The couple turned toward the house, and started walking up the flagstone path. Anne stopped about three steps before the porch and pointed down.

"We really need to cement those two new stones, Joseph. I tripped on them on the way out and twisted my ankle. It's a bit sore." Anne mildly suggested.

Joseph looked down at her ankle, and realized that she had been favoring it.

"I'm really sorry, honey. What a lousy thing to happen just before going back to Maine."

"Yes, but I'll be okay. We're lucky I didn't fall. That

would have been lousy!" Anne rubbed her ankle.

"I'll get to it as soon as we get back," Joseph promised.

"Well, this time I'm holding you to it! You've just got to learn to finish projects you start!" Anne smirked, then smiled. It was one of their old jokes. He had to give his reply, as usual.

"Hey, I've got lots of projects finished!" Joseph smiled.

"Name three you've finished in the last year." Anne put her arm around her husband's waist. They stepped on to the porch.

"I got that carburetor in the Camaro!" Joseph gestured toward the garage. At that moment they heard a large crashing sound, coming from the garage. Anne and Joseph turned their heads as the jumped back.

"What was that?" Anne whispered.

"It sounded like my tool box, and glass!" Joseph pulled Anne's arm from his waist and stepped quickly off of the porch, toward the garage door.

Chapter 7

The distance from the front porch was only a few steps, which Joseph covered in a matter of a second or two. As soon as Joseph's right foot hit the driveway he immediately noticed that the garage floor was littered with tools, rags, and tiny pieces of glass. The little light shining from the workbench, to the right side of the room, was casting strangely shaped shadows across the floor. Dark lines and blobs radiated away from the light, and out to the driveway. The only things Joseph heard were an unusual slow cracking sound, and someone breathing hard.

Joseph followed the rays of the light back up toward the workbench and they led to Paul, who standing next to an overturned red and white tool stand. He was holding one of Joseph's hammers and staring at the window. Something sparkling in the dim light caught Joseph's eye, and he immediately turned to look to the right of where Paul was standing. He knew right away that there was a problem with the window that looked out from the garage to the side yard. What little light was coming in from the outside was being bent and diffused, moving at a different angle every second.

"What in the hell is going on?" Joseph tried to raise his voice, but was unable to. His chest was very tight, and the words came out of his mouth muffled. His head pounded; his blood pressure must really be up there, he thought. Anne, coming up behind him, responded. Paul, eyes wide open and mouth hanging down, just stared at the right half of the window as it slowly cracked into thousands and thousands of pieces. None of the pieces fell to the floor. Safety glass was like that.

"Slow down, Joseph. Take a breath. Breathe..." She grabbed his arm.

"I am breathing! Look at my toolbox! Look at the glass! What happened to the window? Paul! I want answers now!" Joseph was about to take a step forward, but Anne pulled on his arm.

"Joseph! Walk down the driveway first! Don't say anything you'll hate yourself for later!" Her voice was shaking. When Joseph turned to look into her face he noticed she was glaring at Paul. He looked at Paul and something tugged at his heart deep inside. Something told him that He didn't need to say much to Paul; Paul pretty much knew he had really messed up.

"I'm going to walk to the street, and then I'll be back." Joseph said in a deliberate, halting tone. Joseph had the sense about him to know that he shouldn't react at a time like this; he knew it was time to walk away for a minute, or maybe for more than just a minute. Anne had that particular look on her face, the look of patience lost. It had always been a point of contention between them. He thought she was too easy on the boy; she thought he was too hard on him. There were times, however, like this one, when he knew they were in agreement. Besides, he felt emotionally gutted. He didn't want to fight anymore. All he could feel was emptiness, the emptiness of mourning and loss. Anne squeezed his arm as he turned toward the street. She picked up a tool or two as she walked carefully into the garage. He heard her bark an order at Paul.

Slowly Joseph took one long breath after another. He looked up at the stars and remembered something his mother had told him so many years ago, after his father's father had died. "Remember, Joey, that every time someone passes away, a new star is born in heaven." He had walked out into the woods that cold Maine February night decades ago and stared for what seemed hours at the array of stars above him, looking for a new star. Joseph remembered how cold his feet were that night, and how he shivered standing in the long-melted snow of his childhood. He had wanted to see his Grandpa one more time. Now, in California, he wondered which one was his father's star. Joseph shook his head. He hated facing death, and the nastiness seemed to come more often as he grew older.

Joseph closed his eyes and tried to remember his father's face. He realized it wasn't easy; it had been too long since he had seen his father. The images of his father from years gone by came too fast; he wanted to stop them and look into the old man's eyes, but he couldn't. He remembered the day his father had fixed the chain on his bicycle, and he realized that his father seemed most happy when he was working with his hands. It was one of the few times he remembered seeing his father smile. His father had seemed almost gleeful as the chain sprocket moved around easily on his old bike.

He remembered seeing his father cry the day Anne and

he had been married. It wasn't a sobbing or break down sort of crying. He just saw tears slowly making their way down his face. Each wrinkle seemed to slow the tears down. He had studied his father's face that day. His father had taken hold of Joseph's arm just as they were to go into the church. His father had opened his mouth, but no words had come out. They stood looking at each other for a long time. Joseph remembered the strong grip his father had put on Joseph's upper arm, and how it seemed as if it would never be released. Slowly, haltingly, the strength ebbed away and the old man's hand fell dropped. The tears had seemed just as strong as before.

Joseph knew his father was suffering that day. He knew then that his father loved him, like he had never known before. When his father could not find the words he said volumes. The things he could never forget were his father's eyes. The swollen, wet lids made them seem so vibrant, and so alive.

Joseph wished he could see that face one more time. He wished that once again he could see his father's eyes as the tears rolled down that well-worn cheek. He realized that there were tears rolling down at the moment, on his own face.

He opened his eyes and shook his head. As he took another deep breath, he noticed a particularly bright and flickering light in the eastern sky, and he knew it belonged to another Paul Marino, now gone. The star was too erratic, and too distant. Yep, he thought, that's his dad. No matter what, he could never find a way to see his father's feelings, other than in his tears. He was a man who hid from emotion, like it was a shameful thing. Distant was a good word for him, Joseph thought.

Another tear left his eye as he tried to remember what the last thing he said to his father was. At that moment Joseph heard another crash from the garage, but he didn't turn to look. He knew it was just the other half of the window falling. The scattered tools and broken window didn't seem to matter much. These things were far away now. The words he and his father had exchanged only two weeks earlier were very clear. They echoed in his mind. They had talked of how Anne and he had planned on building a cabin on their land in Pine Mountain.

"I was never rich enough to own two houses at once, Joseph. Do you think this is a good idea? Costs a lot of money, you know. Like this phone call."

"It'll be simple at first, Dad. Just a place to sleep and wash your face. If we build a little every year, we should be done by the time we retire. It's a nice valley to live in."

"What's wrong with where you live now? Your mother and I have lived in this old house since two years after we married. We don't have a 'retirement house'. I just don't understand. They must do things a tad different out there in Colorado."

"California, Dad. We live in California now. We've

been here for over twenty years now." Joseph remembered how exasperated he would feel; he could never get his father to accept that he lived in California. He never understood why that was an issue.

"Whatever. You don't live in Maine, I know that."

"But we visit every other year, and the kids visit more." Joseph had replied.

"Years are lifetimes for an old man, Joseph. One day the lifetime will be gone." His father said in a quiet tone. He remembered how difficult it was for Paul and Sarah to understand their grandfather. They didn't grow up with old New England accents all around. There weren't any accents in California, they told him. They laughed at some of the words Joseph said, like 'car' and 'quarter', which sounded like 'cah' and 'quah-tah'.

"We'll see you next summer, you'll see." Joseph had responded.

"Maybe so, maybe not." Joseph's father said. Joseph felt uneasy when his father had talked like that. Besides, he knew he couldn't change the way his father thought. He was a stubborn old man. A lot like his son, Joseph thought.

"Anyway, I'm glad you're home now. Just being out of the hospital should make a man feel better!" He had answered.

"Sure 'nuff. I've gotta get off the phone. Phone call money doesn't grow on trees, now." That was his father, always worrying about money. Always.

"I understand, Dad. I just called to say that we care. I just wanted to hear your voice from home. I just...um..." Joseph was trying to postpone hanging up. Something inside was afraid that this would be the last time.

"Well, there it is. Take care of those little punkins, Paul and Sarah!" Joseph's father had said after a pause, probably trying to fill the void.

"Will do!" Joseph fought the tears.

"And, son..."

"Yeah, Dad?" Joseph had whispered.

"Love ya!"

"I...uhhh..." Joseph had been surprised. He didn't know what to say. He was able to count the number of times his father had said that to him during his whole life on one hand. He didn't even know what to say in return, as crazy as that sounds.

As he was trying to bring himself together enough to say those three words, 'I love you', he had heard the click of the phone being hung up on the other end. All he heard was the dial tone. His father's voice was gone. Little did he know that night that it was gone forever.

Joseph openly wept, there in the dark, on the driveway, as Paul and Anne cleaned up the garage behind him.

"I love you, Daddy..." He whispered, reaching for a far-away star in the eastern sky.

Joseph felt a hand against his shoulder. He looked down at the hand. It was Anne's.

"He heard you, Joey." She whispered.

"I wish I could know that..." Joseph found it hard to talk.

Chapter 8

In spite of his fear of flying, Joseph boarded the plane the next morning. He was thankful that the take-off had been smooth, and that there was very little turbulence. There was only a bump every now and then. If he had to be honest, his calm behavior at the airport hadn't been due to overcoming his anxiety; it was due to a resignation born from depression. He was still afraid to fly. His fear was overpowered by something else, something far stronger.

All he could see when he closed his eyes was the old altar of Holy Family Catholic Church, and a casket on a bier before it. It was a memory from years before, when his sister had passed away. He knew he had to deal with that scene again, and he didn't like it. He just had to endure it. This trip represented one more piece of his childhood that was no longer there.

He thought of his father as one of the pieces of china his mother kept in the cabinet in the dining room. He remembered the time, when was small, that he decided to plat with his little lead soldiers on the dining room table. The sun had come through the window just right, and reflected off of the large crystal platter on the middle shelf of that cabinet. He wanted to touch it so much, but the lock and thick cabinet glass kept him from it. Years later, when he had returned for a visit, he discovered that his mother had given the platter to his cousin who had just been married. It had belonged to their grandmother, and rightfully should have become his, but it was gone. He knew he would never see it again.

He squirmed in the airplane seat. Joseph decided he didn't want to go back to Maine again, after this trip. There seemed to be so little back there anymore for him, except his mother, and only the Lord knew how much longer she'd be there.

"How're you doing, honey?" Anne leaned over and patted his hand.

"Oh, not too bad, all things being considered." Joseph forced a smile and returned the pat on the hand. He opened his eyes and glanced out the window on the other side of his wife.

"We're somewhere over Iowa, I guess. More than halfway to Maine!" Anne commented. She had the airline map open in front of her, as she always did on a flight to Maine.

"Boston. We'll land at Boston and drive the rest of the way." Joseph corrected her.

"Boston. Well, it doesn't matter. The flight's almost half

over. We'll be in Boston before you know it." Anne smiled.

"You don't have to, Anne. I'm fine. Really." Joseph now knew what she was doing.

"I guess you're right. You don't seem too stressed this time. You're downright calm, I think." Anne folded the airline map up.

"Just tired, I guess. Too much to think about." Joseph looked up at the vent. He reached up and adjusted it, increasing the airflow.

"I can understand why." Anne nodded.

"You've surprised me a lot the last twenty-four hours, I'll have you know. Your bravery alone impressed me." Anne smiled.

"My bravery?"

"Getting on the plane this morning. You weren't even sweating." Anne looked up at Joseph's air vent.

"Oh, I'm okay." Joseph reached into the pocket in the back of the seat in front of him and pulled out the airline magazine.

"You handled the mess in the garage really well, too. You weren't even worried about using those plywood boards to cover the window. I know you were saving them for the shed in the back yard. The window will be fine while we're gone, you know." Anne watched as Joseph paged through the magazine.

"I know." Joseph returned the magazine to the seat

pocket.

"So, what're you thinking about, then? You seem so far away." Anne leaned over and whispered as the stewardess walked by. She was handing out a small menu and asking the passengers to choose their lunch.

"Just bored, I guess. I hate sitting around for a few hours with nothing to do. I guess I could decide what to have for lunch." Joseph turned to watch the stewardess as she passed.

"That's not on the menu, dear." Anne frowned as she slipped her hand over Joseph's eyes. Joseph smiled as he turned his face back toward his wife. Her hand stayed put.

"Well, at least one of us can!" Joseph smiled.

"What do you say? Should we maybe take a walk in the friendly skies of Iowa?" Anne brought her hand down.

"A walk? What about lunch?" Joseph was confused.

"A walk. Paul and Sarah said they have an upstairs on this new 747 airplane. I want to see it. Lunch will take a bit of time to get here." Anne smiled.

"An upstairs? You mean there's more than one floor? On an airplane?" Joseph looked up toward the front of the plane.

"That's what they said. Shall we explore and find it?" Anne asked.

"I'll bet that's what that big bulge of a growth on the plane behind the cockpit is for." Joseph commented on the design of the plane's body.

"Why discuss it? Let's go find it!" Anne started removing her seat belt.

"I guess so. Just as long as I don't miss lunch." Joseph followed her lead.

He was quite surprised by the size of the Boeing 747. Joseph was used to an airplane with one aisle, and one floor, like the 707. The two of them enjoyed exploring the length and breadth of the aircraft. They saved the best for last. The stairs to the second floor lounge were just ahead.

"You first, Anne!" Joseph swept his arm in front of his body, in a grand gesture.

"Thank you, my good man." Anne curtsied, with a smile. They went up the spiral staircase.

"Well, what do you know? I can't get over how much things have changed in the last few years. I can still remember taking that Constellation out of New York to go to Boston. I think that was almost fifteen years ago. Now look at this!" Joseph turned in a full circle, looking the entire room over.

"I remember how much the propellers made the plane shake, and how the sound of the engines made it hard to talk at times." Anne added as she, too, slowly turned around.

"Now it is hard to even believe that we are in the air." Joseph shook his head back and forth. Anne stepped up to her husband and put her arms around his waist.

"It's fun exploring with you." She smiled.

"Yep. Being with you made it worth it." He returned the smile.

"Shall we see if lunch has arrived yet?" Anne nodded toward the stairs.

"Oh, lunch! Now that's a reason to return to one's seat, unless airplane food hasn't changed."

"Let's go find out!" Anne stepped toward the stairs. Just at that moment the plane hit a bit of turbulence. She slipped a bit, and fell into Joseph's arms. Joseph had grabbed the edge of a counter nearby. He reached out with his left arm to steady his wife.

"Always be there in case I fall, Joseph." Anne kissed him, and they returned to their seats.

Chapter 9

There was something comforting in the drive from Boston north to Maine. The name of each small town was like a piece of chocolate candy to Joseph. He savored the old familiar sounds of his early days. Southern California was nice, with its rich Spanish names like Santa Ana, San Juan Capistrano, and Santa Barbara, but these town names tasted of childhood.

He rolled each name over in his mind as they drove through, or past, the town. Massachusetts was pure joy for

Joseph. There was the sign for the road to Swampscott. He loved the name of that town. Then came Marblehead. Sometimes he felt like he resembled that town. Next was Topsfield, and then Newburyport. As they pulled out of the gas station at Amesbury he watched for the border of New Hampshire.

One of his favorite names was the first town on the road into New Hampshire, Seabrook. The road to Exeter passed, then Greenland. He smiled as he thought about how little this little town resembled the island of that name.

"Dad?" Sarah asked from the back seat, interrupting his geography daydream.

"Huh? What? You need something, honey?" Joseph looked into the rear-view mirror.

"Can we stop in New Hampshire? My friend Maura said she used to live in New Hampshire, and I told her I'd get a post card for her here." Sarah looked out the left side window. Joseph was startled how much her young jaw looked like Anne's did, so many years ago. He smiled when he thought of her friend's name. Another great name! It was so New England! So traditional Irish!

"Sure, I guess so. What do you think, Anne?"

"That's fine with me. You know I like to shop. Just find a small little Yankee craft store and I'll be happy." Anne smiled, but Joseph noticed it had less strength in it. She was getting really tired. They all were. Joseph realized that a little

112

distraction would be good for everyone. Besides, they were almost halfway to Auburn, Maine.

"Let's go ahead and stop at Portsmouth, but we have to remember that we've lost three hours in the time zone change. It's later than we think." Joseph looked to the right, preparing to get off of the turnpike.

"Dad's right. It's five o'clock here. We feel like it's only two." Anne agreed.

"A lot of stores will be closing soon, I think." Joseph said.

"Well, let's just get a post card for Maura and get back on the road." Anne sounded tired.

"We'll see what we can find." Joseph turned toward downtown Portsmouth.

"There, Dad...there's a drug store. They usually have post cards, don't they?" Sarah asked.

"I'll bet they do. Maybe." Joseph slowed the car down.

"What about something to eat?" Paul spoke up and leaned forward. He had been quiet the entire drive from the airport.

"I was wondering when you'd ask that. How about getting a couple of hot dogs as we drive out of town?" Anne replied.

"I guess. If that's all they have around here." Paul slumped back into his seat.

"Maybe they have a hamburger place. We'll see."

Joseph added.

As Joseph stepped out of the car he felt as if forty years had been stripped off of his life. He was back in a small New England town. The moment had the same flavor, and the same smells, as the day long ago when his father had driven into Portsmouth back in the Thirties. As he shut the rental car door he looked into the window of what Sarah had called "the drug store". It wasn't a drug store, but an old general store like the one that he used to visit so many years before.

"Well, whattya know! An old fashioned general store! Just like the kind I remember! Hey, Sarah! This is what a mall looked like to my generation!" Joseph reached into the car and pulled his old Boston Red Sox hat out. He had visited this town before, when he was in his teens, and had been wearing a Red Sox hat then, too.

"What's with the hat, Dad?" Paul pointed at Joseph's head.

"Oh, nothing. Just an old tradition. I used to wear a Red Sox hat everywhere back in those days a long time ago. I just felt like doing it again." Joseph felt a little self-conscious.

"I thought you were an Angels fan? What will they think?" Paul was teasing, but Joseph was still feeling a bit sensitive about what had happened in the garage the night before, and was unable to share in the banter.

"I think Gene Autry would understand. Today, I'm twelve, and I'm a Red Sox fan." Joseph said. He gently pulled the hat off of his head. Anne noticed his look, and looked at the hat. She shook her head.

"It's okay, honey. Wear the hat." Anne said.

"Let me think about it..." Joseph gestured toward the store.

"Let's check this old place out, shall we?" She smiled and led Paul toward the front door. Sarah followed. She looked back as she entered the store and pointed at her husband's head.

The store was like a place out of time for Joseph. It seemed as if half of the boxes of goods had been there for thirty years or more. He was amazed to see old toys, and kitchen equipment. He was back in 1936 again.

"You folks aren't from around these parts, are you?" The old lady behind the counter asked in a very familiar accent.

"Well, it depends on what you mean by "from around these parts"." Joseph smiled.

"Maine, or Portsmouth." The old lady answered. He had forgotten how New Englanders were sparse in their use of words, as if extra ones cost more money.

"Originally from Auburn, Maine. Now from California." Joseph looked at the stacks of dry goods behind the counter.

"California! I always wanted to go there! Too expensive. I hear they have those freeways out there where you can drive sixty miles an hour for a hundred miles! And everybody has a job!" The lady behind the counter perked up.

"Hundreds of miles of roads, actually. We have them all over the state now. And we do have people without jobs. Times are tough there, too." A package caught Joseph's eye.

"Hey, Anne! They have those women's handkerchiefs you like here!" Joseph pointed. Just then Joseph became aware that there was something next to his leg. More accurately, there was someone by his leg. He looked down and saw a small boy, about nine years old, holding a Boston Red Sox hat.

"Excuse me, mister. Is this your hat?" The boy offered it to Joseph.

"Um, I'm not sure. I had one..." Joseph realized he had lost it somewhere.

"I saw you drop it on the floor, over there by the pop machine." Joseph knew he was in New England. No one on California called it "pop". They called it "soda" out west.

"Well, thank you! That's very nice of you to return it." Joseph took the hat that the boy was offering to him.

"It's the right thing to do." The boy replied.

"Somebody raised you right!" Joseph smiled.

"He's my grandson, and you're darn right. He's a fine boy." The old lady leaned over the counter and rubbed the young one's head.

"How about if I pay you a reward? Would you like a soda?" Joseph realized he had used the wrong word as he said it, but he hadn't caught it in time.

"What's that?" The boy turned toward his grandmother and asked gingerly, obviously afraid to offend the visitor to the store.

"A pop, Vincent. The man from California wants to buy you a pop."

"Sure! I like Grape Nehi!" Vincent smiled.

"Good choice. Here's a quarter. Go ahead and get yourself one...if it's alright with your grandmother, of course!" Joseph smiled as he withheld the money, waiting for the approval of the old lady.

"Sure. Go ahead, Vinny!" The old lady smiled.

"So, he stays with you here at the store?" Joseph watched the young boy as he inserted the quarter into the pop machine.

"Only in the summer, when school's out. His momma works now, ever since her no-good deadbeat husband left her for some loose woman from Vermont two years ago. Seems like that sort of thing's happening more and more nowadays." The old woman picked up a fly swatter and smacked the counter top. Joseph winced.

"That sort of thing?" Joseph asked. The old lady reached over and grabbed a dead fly, then threw it into the wastebasket.

"Yeah, that sort of thing. Ever since the layoffs down at the plant started, families have been breaking up left and right.

The men don't want to hang around unemployed. They'd rather take off for Boston or New York. Of course, the women have kids around, and the house, so they can't leave. For the men, it's no money, no new cars, no bowling. The women get a low paying job, and the men take off. Makes it tough putting food on the table for a youngster." The old lady shook her head and nodded toward the boy.

"I'm sorry to hear it." Joseph looked down.

"Well, what're you going to do? That's life. Besides, what kind of man runs off on his kids?" The old lady was whispering; the boy was heading back to the counter. Joseph looked up at the old lady.

"Not much of a man." Joseph replied. He turned toward his own children. Sarah was busily studying post cards, and Paul was looking over the doughnuts on the shelf toward the back of the small store. Maybe, he thought, he wasn't as bad a father as he was afraid. The little boy, Vincent, had a lost, lonely look in his eyes. Maybe, Joseph thought, having your father around, even if he was busy and not as patient as he'd like to be, and maybe pretty darn stubborn to boot, was better than not having a dad around at all.

Anne called Paul when she noticed that Sarah had made her choices from the post cards sold in the old store and had turned toward the counter to pay for them. Joseph pointed behind the counter.

"I'll take a package of those lady's handkerchiefs."
Joseph pulled his wallet out of his rear pocket. Anne and the
children arrived at the counter about that time.

"Lady's handkerchiefs?" Anne looked confused.
Joseph stared at her.

"The kind you like, Anne." He continued to stare.

"But mine are..." Anne stopped as she caught his
hidden message.

"...back home in California." Joseph finished her
sentence.

"Uh, right. Yes. In California." Anne smiled, but looked
confused.

Joseph pulled the Red Sox cap onto his head as the
old lady counted his change back to him, and winked at the
small boy lovingly drinking his Grape Nehi. Sarah picked up
her post cards, and Paul his small package of doughnuts, and
the small family walked out the door. Joseph opened the
passenger side door for his wife.

"What was that all about? The handkerchiefs? Those
aren't the style that I like, and you know it." Anne asked.
Joseph waited to answer as he rounded the car and opened
the driver's door. After he got in he inserted the key into the
ignition and started the engine.

"Just helping a little boy to grow up, that's all. His
father abandoned the family, and his grandmother in there is
watching him during the summer. His mother has a job all

day, and this is how he's going to spend his summer. I figured you could use them. I know you like the kind with flowers on them." Joseph turned around to look out the back window as he shifted the car into reverse.

"He doesn't have a father?" Sarah asked as she pulled a small doughnut out of Paul's package.

"Nope. He ran off to another state. The old lady said it was happening all over here." Joseph answered his daughter.

"Hey! Those doughnuts are mine!" Paul protested as he realized his sister had taken one from his bag.

"Come on, Paul, you can share. Besides, who said you could get those? We're stopping for a hamburger, you know." Anne scolded her son.

"Yeah, but I'm hungry now." Paul mumbled.

"Okay, have one each. Next stop: real food." Joseph replied.

Chapter 10

The sun was getting low on the horizon, and the pine trees of the rolling Maine countryside cast long shadows across the road. The winding highways in this part of New England were poorly lit, but Joseph knew the way to Auburn along State Route 4. There had been many a night when he had made this very trip on the way home from college in Boston. It wasn't a nice rental car back then, though. Joseph had kept an old 1934 Chevy through his years of college. There were a few hills in this part of Maine that he had to turn the car around and back it up. The reverse gear wasn't as worn as the others, and had a lower ratio. He wondered how many times back then he had stopped to let the radiator cool down.

The hunt for cheeseburgers had been successful back in Portsmouth, and Paul and Sarah had long since fallen asleep in the back seat. Anne looked a bit like she could use a nap. Every now and then he noticed her staring lethargically out the front window. He knew she wouldn't be awake when they pulled into the short driveway of his parents' house. As he considered the old house he realized that it belonged to his mother now. She was alone.

He eased the pressure from his foot to the gas pedal. His mouth got dry as he remembered his last phone call with his mother. She had insisted that the four of them stay at her house, but now he wasn't so sure that this was a good idea. Over the years his father had been there to intervene whenever she decided that she needed to control a situation. What would slow her down now, he wondered?

She was an enigma to Joseph. There were so many things she wouldn't do for herself. His father always did all of the driving. It was strange. She wouldn't even drive into town to get a magazine she wanted. She would wait until her husband had to go into town and then she would politely ask for a ride along. It was almost a weekly ritual. He realized that his father had died on the day he usually took his trip into town. Joseph wondered how his mother would get into town next week, or any week after that. As he considered this, Joseph noticed a tall snow stick proudly standing by the side of the road. They were placed there for the snow plows in the winter to be able to find their way along the asphalt. Joseph felt a moment of panic.

Winter! How would his mother survive out here in the winter? Joseph realized he had been mumbling when he heard Anne's voice.

"She'll be fine, honey. She'll probably get one of your aunt's to help her out." Anne whispered. She turned slowly and looked at her children, and she was satisfied that they were definitely asleep.

"They're really out. Look how Little Paul's mouth is hanging open. That only happens when he has completely checked out!" Joseph remembered how they differentiated between his father and his son. There was Little Paul and Grandpa. He felt a lump grow in his throat as he realized they didn't need the two names any longer. There was just Paul now. Paul the teenager.

"Little Paul! Huh! That seems to kick in every time we cross into Maine. I guess we won't need it any more, will we? How do you feel about that?" Anne turned toward Joseph.

"I was just thinking that. I'm not sure. Maybe this time

he'll still have to be 'Little Paul', Anne. I'm not ready to change that yet." Joseph replied, clearing his throat. Anne rubbed his knee gently. She heard a sound from Sarah's side of the backseat.

"Sarah's drooling on her sweater, her usual sign that nothing will be able to wake her!" Anne smiled.

"She'll whine about the sweater being wet," Joseph smiled as he looked into the rear view mirror.

"But the sweater will be okay, too. I can tell you're really stressed about your mom. She'll probably find a way to get along from now on. She'll have to. There are months left until winter. She'll find ways to cope. She always has."

"Probably. But I noticed something different about her. She's scared, and trying to find someone new to lean on. For sixty years she had my father to use as her crutch. I think she's never had to be on her own, Anne. What about paying the bills? Does she know how to budget her money?" Joseph gestured.

"Hands on the wheel, honey..." Anne said stiffly. Joseph returned his right hand to its proper place on the steering wheel.

"Sorry. I guess I'm wondering what we're going to find in that house." Joseph looked out to the right as he passed a small road entering the main highway.

"Are you worried about your mother, or about something else?" Anne asked. She pulled her sweater tight around her neck.

"Something else?" Joseph glanced over at his wife.

"Maybe something about your father? Are you hoping that he's made something right, after all of these years? Something you two never were able to settle?" Anne sounded really tired.

"Like what?" Joseph was unsure. There was so much that was unsettled between the two Marino men.

"Did you really ask 'like what'? I don't think we have enough time on this entire trip for me to list all of the conflicts you had with Paul Marino the Elder. Pick one, or two. Maybe pick only seventy eight!" Anne chuckled a bit, in a quiet way.

"Yeah. I just don't get it. I was never right. He was always the one who knew what he was doing. I was always the klutz, the bull in a china shop, the one who messed things up." Joseph was finding it hard to talk. He slowed down as he came to a stop sign, then the car stopped. He waited a long moment.

"Don't be so hard on yourself, honey. He had no patience with children. He expected you to do things the right way the first time," Anne comforted, "and he wasn't much of a teacher!"

"That's for sure! But he had a way of making you feel like an idiot for not thinking something all the way through. He'd make jokes about how stupid you were. When I was a small boy he made fun of me for dropping a stone on my toe.

I kept that stone in the little closet in my room for years. I couldn't leave it outside. He made a joke about me every time he saw it. One night I brought it inside. Then I remember the time I left his toolbox outside when it rained one week. The box was rusted shut when we found it the next Saturday night. Of course, the tools we needed to open the box with were inside the box itself! He'd always start saying something about how stupid a certain act was, then he'd just trail off mumbling. That time he said a long list of words like 'stupid' and 'moron'. He picked up the box and stormed off to the garage. Do you know that he welded the box to a chain, and padlocked the whole thing to his workbench?" Joseph had to smile when he thought of how boneheaded he was that time. It was a smile filled with pain, tough.

"It seems like your father could have handled that tool box incident differently. There were other ways. The rock incident was just plain mean."

"He was just trying to protect his tools. They were money, and hard to replace."

"But his son couldn't learn how to use them when they were all locked up." Anne offered.

Joseph turned to look at his wife. She was right. He had spent years begging to use the tools. He could count on one hand the number of times he had been allowed to touch them, mostly because his father was ordering him to bring him a tool while he was fixing something.

"I guess you may be right. Maybe you have to take a chance and let someone try again. Maybe one mistake shouldn't be the end of the world..." Joseph looked left and right, and then accelerated into the intersection.

"Kind of like how Little Paul dropped your tool box on the garage floor, and hit the window with the hammer because he was trying to save it from getting dinged up because it would hit the hard concrete?" Anne reminded her husband of the incident just the night before.

"Kinda. I guess I was too harsh last night about using tools in the future?" Joseph felt a bit sheepish. He had forbidden Paul from using them again without Joseph being there.

"You think?" Anne smiled.

"Okay, I was too hard on him." Joseph shook his head. She was right, but he hated that sometime.

"Can you see it from his point of view, now? He was trying to help you. Your tools were all over the workbench. So what if he was lacking one critical skill. He didn't understand that he had pushed the box halfway off the tool bench while straightening it out, and it was unbalanced."

"I know. And you're right. There were no tools seriously damaged, and the window is easy to fix."

"Easier to fix than a boy's view of himself." Anne replied as she pointed to the left side of the car, about one hundred yards ahead.

"Huh? What is it? A sign?" Joseph glanced toward where she was pointing, and returned to watching the road in front of the car.

"There it is! Norway!" Anne smiled as she thought of her hometown.

"Oh, yes! Norway! The land I always wanted to visit!" Joseph reached back into the far recesses of his mind and dusted off the old line he used to say to Anne.

"Sweden. It was Sweden, Joseph. You always wanted to go to Sweden."

"Didn't I used to say that Sweden was near Norway, though? Something about the water?" Joseph realized that his memory had grown foggy over the years.

"Well, you're close. I can't believe you forgot! You used to say you would come up to see me at my grandparent's place in Norway on your way to Sweden. You said you always wanted to go to Sweden. I'd reply by telling you that Norway was in between Maine and Sweden, so stop by anytime, and that I'd hitch a ride with you. Of course, it took you a long time to get out to Norway." Anne smiled and sat up. Joseph slowed the car down, almost to a stop, as they came close to the sign.

"I remember! I read a book about Stockholm, Sweden, and the canals they had there! Somebody called it the 'Venice of the North'!" He smiled as the memory became clearer.

"Joseph," Anne smiled and slid over toward her

husband, "remember how we used to ride close to each other?"

"I remember." Joseph whispered. He stopped the car, and put the transmission into 'park'. He stared at the large word 'Norway' on the sign.

"You still want to go to Sweden, don't you?" Anne put her head on Joseph's shoulder.

"Or Norway. Either one would be fine."

"We'll get there. In time. You'll see." Anne smiled. She closed her eyes and squeezed her husband's arm. Joseph's arm stiffened suddenly.

"The time! Oh, wow! We'd better get going! I told my mother we'd be there an hour ago, and we still have twenty more minutes to go!" Joseph sat up and shifted the transmission back into 'drive'. He stared straight ahead, into the dark woods.

"Oh, well. So much for going back in time a bit. It won't matter, honey. The kids will be out all night, and you know your mother stays up half the night anyway. Her insomnia is probably a lot worse now." Anne tried to reassure Joseph.

"Yeah, but she may be worried about us." Joseph licked his lips. He hadn't taken his foot off of the brake pedal yet. He was staring, but not driving.

"What's going on, honey?" Anne rubbed Joseph's arm.

"We're back, Annie. I always felt that way every time I saw that sign pointing to the road to Norway. I'm not sure I can do this. He's dead. I can't go there. I just can't handle it all, Annie." Joseph trembled. He grabbed on to the steering wheel with an iron grip.

"You're handling it already. We're almost there. It's the same old town you used to know. Well, maybe they have a new gas station or something. Your mother still lives in the same old house."

"Which holds his clothes. His books are there. His old, rusty collection of barbed wire is still there." Joseph whispered. Anne moved away from her husband.

"And the rusty old tool box is still there, too?" Anne lovingly said. It wasn't really a question. She was just trying to shine a light on what was really making her husband tremble.

"And the rusty tool box." Joseph repeated slowly.

"Maybe you'll find something there you haven't expected, honey. Maybe not everything is unpleasant. Besides, we're together, and we can handle it. We always have. We made it through when you had to move away for the summer for that job."

"I remember. We did make it, didn't we?" Joseph relaxed his grip on the steering wheel. He was still staring straight ahead.

"Yep. We made it all the other times, too. When Sarah was sick, we made it. That's why I have that string of pearls. Every pearl stands for a time when we made it, even if it didn't feel like it at the time." Anne continued to rub her husband's arm. He turned to look at her. Joseph was crying gently.

"I don't know how I would have made this trip without you, Anne." He smiled.

"And I don't know how I would have made it without you," Anne replied.

"Well, let's pass by Norway this time. Let's go to Auburn."

"How about a kiss first, like we used to do?" Anne giggled.

"Hah! A Yarmouth kiss!" Joseph smiled broadly, remembering something from a long time ago.

"Oh my gosh! I remember! Our first kiss after we were engaged! When we went to the beach near Yarmouth!" Anne's eyes sparkled in the dim car light. Joseph thought she looked twenty-five years younger.

"Do you remember what I said? Joseph asked, with the smile still on his face.

"How in the world could I forget, oh great King of Puns! You stood right next to the town hall." Anne leaned over toward Joseph.

"Yep! 'I want to give you a kiss on Yar-mouth!' Joseph laughed as he leaned over to kiss his wife.

"Well, here's one for YOUR mouth!" Anne replied with a laugh Joseph knew he hadn't heard in too many years. An old sign with the word 'Norway' on it had transported them back in time over a quarter of a century.

"Oh, geesh, Dad!" Paul mumbled from the back seat.

"Yeah, gross! Mushy stuff from your parents! Too much showing here, Mom!" Sarah waved her hand in front of her face. Joseph could tell Sarah was trying to settle in and go back to sleep. It was the same way she'd done it on every other long car trip. Come to think of it, Paul was doing the same.

Joseph and Anne didn't look back. The looked into each other's eyes and kissed, the old Yarmouth way.

"Let's go see what we will find at that old house in the woods." Joseph shifted the car into drive, and the car moved forward.

"I agree. Maybe we'll like something we'll find there." Anne messed up her husband's hair playfully. Joseph smiled as the car passed another milepost.

"Maybe I'll find that old rusty tool box. Or that stone. Maybe it would be good to put these things behind me. Or get rid of them in the dump!" Joseph found a bit of determination.

"Now you're on the right track, Joey!" Anne smiled.

"Unbelievable! Here we are, in Auburn, Maine! We're Yarmouth kissing, and you're calling me Joey again! What year is it?" Joseph laughed.

"Who cares?" Anne smiled. Joseph heard grumbling from the back seat.

"How much longer until we're there? I can't handle this

anymore! No teenager should have to deal with this after a long day like this one." Paul rolled over to face the door next to him.

"Just around the next bend of the road!" Joseph smiled as he answered.

Chapter 11

It seemed as if time had stood still when Joseph turned the car onto his the street of his childhood. As he slowly drove down the street he remembered the families of the days before television, before jet aircraft, and before the fifty star United States flag.

On the right side of the lane, at the corner, were the Jacobsens. Peter Jacobsen was two years older than Joseph. When Peter went off and joined the Navy in 1942, as Joseph was finishing college, his parents had put a rectangular flag with a blue star sewn on to it in their front window. A year and a half later Joseph was standing on their lawn, talking with Mr. Jacobsen, when a Navy officer pulled up in an official government car. Joseph was impressed by how neat and proper the man in the white uniform looked. Joseph didn't know that he had come to deliver a telegram that would change that household forever. Joseph would never forget the polite, but forced, smile on the man's face. He was concerned when he saw Mr. Jacobsen's hands shaking. He dropped the shovel he had been using to till his small Victory garden, and his right hand reached up to cover his mouth.

The Jacobsen house was still there, but he never knew what happened to Peter's parents. The last time he saw them was at Peter's funeral at the Lutheran Church in town. Joseph went to the funeral against his priest's counsel; Peter had taught him how to hit a baseball when he was a child. He had to be there. Joseph wished that the Church had dropped its rule against visiting non-Catholic churches decades before they actually did. The Jacobsens packed up and moved the following autumn, while he was away at Army basic training.

Next door to the Jacobsens was the Rath family. They had a boy who was a few years younger than Joseph was, and they called him Jimmy. His real name was Peter, but there was already a Peter in the neighborhood, so he ended up being Jimmy. Joseph smiled as he remembered suggesting the name because no one knew a Jimmy around the area. Years later Peter Rath had grown up and moved to Chicago. He hadn't heard from him in over twenty years. Peter's parents died, and the house was sold. The new owners died only two years ago.

Across the street, on the left side, lived pretty Mary Ann. Joseph couldn't remember her last name, and that bothered him. Mary Ann was a name Joseph didn't mention to Anne. Mary Anne was the same age as Joseph was, and Anne had been certain that Joseph and Mary Anne were a "thing". Joseph had to smile. He didn't think Mary Ann had ever noticed him.

"Wasn't that Mary Ann's house?" Anne said in a gruff tone. Joseph had to smile. She was right on cue.

"Mary Ann who?" Joseph asked, feigning ignorance.

"Oh, come on. Mary Ann Hobart, that's who!" Anne folded her arms.

Joseph was stunned when he heard Mary Ann's last name. It brought back a flood of memories. Anne had a nickname for her...the 'Tasmanian Devil'. It was the only time he'd ever seen Anne so jealous.

"I remember you had a nickname for her!" Joseph decided a little teasing was in order.

"Oh, yes, I did. I remember the day she earned it, too."

"She earned it?" Joseph turned to look at his wife.

"Yep. She had her sister Helen slip a note into my geography book at school. I think it was Helen that put it there, though. Helen Hobart always hated me. I remember every word of it still! She wrote: 'Joey likes my new dress. Have a good day, Helen.'" Anne looked away. Joseph smiled when he thought of how long ago that had been, and how innocent it seemed in 1971.

"So, why the 'Tasmanian Devil'?" Joseph prodded.

"The capital of Tasmania is Hobart. And you knew that, mister geography teacher." Anne was genuinely angry, Joseph realized.

"Anne, I'm only teasing. It's a long time ago, and who knows what's happened to that family anyway. It's okay now to let it go..."

"We'll see. We'll see." Anne turned to face the front of the car. Joseph applied the brake, and the car slowed down. They were in front of his old house.

"Well, here we are. Finally!" Joseph said as he leaned back in the seat.

"I see the front porch light is on. I'll bet your mother is sitting inside, waiting." Anne squinted, trying to see inside the front window.

"Nah. Knowing Mom, she's in the back room, with her hearing aid out, sewing some curtain or blouse. I think this used to be her sewing night." Joseph turned to look at the children, sleeping in the back seat.

"Well, should we wake them up?" He asked.

"I guess so...hey, Paul! Sarah! We're here! We're at Grandpa's and Grandma's..." Anne stopped in mid-sentence. She realized too late that she had mentioned both of them. She turned to look at Joseph.

"It's okay, honey. Old habits are hard to break." Joseph looked at his old house. It was hard to believe his father was no longer there. He felt his throat tighten, and tears well up. There was the sign his father had made many years ago. It looked old and weather-beaten now. The 'O' at the end of the name seemed a bit worn, and the sign seemed to say 'MARIN'. The old stone planter Joseph's father had built for his mother was still there in front of the mailbox. Joseph felt a wave of sadness as he noticed the weeds growing around that old monument to a man's stubborn attitude. His father had promised it would be done in 1937, but had put it off all year. During a cold New Year's Eve he went out and finished it. He never forgot to mention how it had been done in 1937. Barely.

Joseph could see, even in the darkness, that the house needed paint. He wondered how much else needed to be done.

"We're here?" Paul was the first to wake up. He struggled to straighten up and started to open the right rear car door.

"Whoa! Hold on! Let me pull into the driveway!" Joseph pulled his foot off of the brake and they eased on to the Marino property.

"What? Where are we?" Sarah was waking up.

"We're in Auburn! Grandma's house!" Anne replied as she looked at Joseph and rubbed his arm.

"Let's go see if I'm right. My mother never locked the kitchen door, so let's go in that way." Joseph smiled a bit.

"Don't you think we should just knock on the front door?" Anne was obviously worried.

"Nah! I used to always use the kitchen door. Besides, maybe she has some chocolate chip cookies out on the counter!" Joseph licked his lips.

"Oh, the famous cookies again! I guess it's worth a try!" Anne smiled as they all got out of the car. The air was a bit cool, even for Maine.

"Smell that air! Pine!" Joseph took a deep breath.

They went around to the side of the house, and Joseph strained to see the words he had scratched in the cement by the steps. He had come home from college one June and his father had poured a new walk in front of the steps. Joseph took a stick and wrote in the wet cement. Of course his father had never known. He pushed aside some weeds, and there were the old words.

"What are you doing, Dad?" Sarah was rubbing her eyes.

"Looking for something I wrote when I was twenty-one. I wrote it on the cement here. My Dad never saw it. I made sure. Hey, Anne! That happened exactly thirty years ago this month! Whattya know!" Joseph smiled.

"What does it say?" Paul asked, as he leaned over to see it.

"Joey loves Annie 1941. Here it is! Hey...wait a minute! What the...when did he write that?" Joseph, astonished, pointed behind the words, next to the boards of the steps.

"I saw you do it, son. I was looking out the window! Dad. 1970" Anne chuckled as she read the words out loud.

"Hah! He must've done that when he had to fix the walkway last year, Dad!" Paul laughed.

"I guess he got the last word in on that one, huh?" Anne had to laugh. Joseph's smile faded. His old man had done it to him again.

"Let's go see Ma..." He mumbled as he reached for the side door. It was locked.

"Darn...I can't believe it. The door's locked!" Joseph tried again.

"I guess she's changed her ways, honey. Let's go to the front door." Anne suggested. Paul and Sarah were already walking to the front of the house.

"But she's left this door open for as long as I can remember. What in the world is wrong...?" Joseph trailed off.

"Your father isn't here anymore, remember?" Anne slipped her arm into her husband's as they walked up front.

"Yeah. I guess." Joseph whispered. Paul and Sarah were waiting on the front porch for their parents, who were only two or three steps behind them.

"Should we knock?" Sarah asked.

"On my own front door? No. My mother always said that this was still my house." Joseph reached for the doorknob. It turned easily. The door was a like a portal into his high school days. There on the shelf was his senior portrait, still in the old pine frame as it had always been. His sixth grade geography bee trophy was still there, too. The old grandfather clock still made the click-clack sound. It was 1938 again, he thought.

"Ma? It's me...Joey!" Joseph called out in an ordinary voice. There was no answer.

"Maybe she has her hearing aid out, like you said, honey." Anne held her husband's arm.

"There's no sound from the sewing machine." Joseph stood still and looked down the hall. It was dark.

"It's really quiet. Could she have gone out?" Anne whispered.

"I can't believe it." Joseph slowly walked toward the hall. Anne looked into the kitchen.

"Ma! It's me, Joey!" Are you here? He called again.

"No one in the kitchen. No cookies, either." Anne said.

"This is definitely not the way she does things. I don't like it, Anne." Joseph said, worried.

"Come on, slow down. I'm sure she's in bed. Let's try the bedrooms." Anne suggested.

"Yeah, let's do that." Joseph turned on the light in the hallway.

"You two stay in the living room." Anne motioned for Paul and Sarah to sit down.

"Can we turn on the television?" Sarah asked as she sat down on the couch.

"Go ahead, but keep the volume low. We'll be right out.

"Ma? It's Joseph, and Anne, and the kids. We're here,

from California!" Joseph called out as he looked into the bedroom that his mother used as a sewing room. There were pieces of dark cloth all over the floor, scattered here and there.

"Wow! She wasn't happy with the way something was turning out!" Anne whispered.

"No, she wasn't. I think that one piece looks torn, like it was ripped apart." Joseph pointed at the corner of the room.

"I think it was!" Anne was whispering more quietly.

"Let's check my parents' room. I mean, my mother's room." Joseph turned down the hall. As he passed his own room he noticed there was no light on in it. There was a faint light from behind the partially closed door to his mother's room.

"There's a light on. Maybe she fell asleep reading." Anne suggested.

"Just what I was thinking." Joseph replied, also in a whisper. They stepped quietly to the door and opened it slowly. Joseph opened his mouth, but couldn't speak.

"Ma?" Anne called out.

"She's not in here, either. What's going on? Ma? Are you in the bathroom?" Joseph, more agitated now, called out louder.

"Where else can she be? She's not here. She knew we were coming tonight. We're only about a half-hour late, and we called." Anne's voice was laced with fear.

"Shhh. Slow down, Anne. She's here. Maybe in the garage?" Joseph turned to go back down the hall.

"Wait! Listen!" Anne put her hand up in front of her husband's mouth, as if to silence him.

"Listen to what?" He asked.

"Shhh! I hear a voice!" Anne looked toward Joseph's old bedroom.

"In my room?" Joseph was confused. The light was off, and there was no one in the bed. The desk chair was empty, too.

"Yes, there it is!" Anne stepped into the room and turned on the light.

"Ma?" She called out.

"Annie? Is that you, Annie?" A quiet voice answered from the other side of the bed.

"And me, too, Ma - Joey." Joseph gingerly stepped around the bed. His mother was lying on her side, next to the bed, on the floor. She was holding an old stuffed teddy bear that Joseph had received from his grandfather many years before. Joseph immediately felt a wave of strong emotion. There were many, many nights that he had fallen asleep with that bear when he had been frightened as a child.

"It's okay now, Ma. Everything's going to be okay." Anne whispered as she sat on the edge of the bed. Joseph heard the children walking down the hall.

"Go back out to the living room, guys. Everything's

okay." Joseph was on the verge of tears. Strangely, the only thing Paul did was look into the room, and then he went back down the hallway. Joseph knew by the sound of Paul's feet on the old hardwood floors.

"Ma? Do you need anything?" Anne asked. She reached down and stroked her mother-in-law's arm.

"Oh, no. I'm doing just fine right now."

"Okay. I was just worried it was kind of cold down there on the floor." Anne said, gently.

"I suppose. I think I hurt my knee. It's hard to get up." Joseph's mother answered.

"Here, maybe I can help. Maybe we can get you on to the bed. The kids want to see you, Ma." Joseph stood next to his mother. He started to tremble. Never had he realized how small and frail she had become. She was so gray, and her skin was so white. Where was the young, strong mother who had taught him how to ride a bike?

"That would be nice." She answered.

Joseph leaned over and scooped her into his arms. He gently placed her on the bed as Anne pulled the covers over her legs. She reached over to take the teddy bear.

"Oh, please, not the bear. Please let me have the bear..." Joseph's mother had a pleading look in her face.

"Oh, sorry. Of course." Anne touched her mother-in-law's cheek instead.

"Oh, no. The bear is there for you, Ma. We wouldn't

dream of taking it!" Joseph smiled weakly.

Chapter 12

Joseph looked down at his mother; he didn't quite know what to say or do. He'd never been in this situation before. He turned and looked at Anne. She shrugged.

"Did you have a rough night, Ma? Do you need to talk?" Joseph whispered. He pulled his old desk chair toward the bed and sat on it, then sharply shifted his eyes toward the door as he looked at Anne. Anne got the signal, then turned and slowly walked out of the room, toward the other small bedroom.

"Oh, I wasn't having much luck with the sewing machine. I didn't have enough black material." Joseph's mother sighed as she looked at her son. It appeared to Joseph that she was studying his every detail. Even his shirt pocket seemed to interest her.

"Enough material for what?" Joseph asked.

"For the...um...church...um..." Joseph's mother turned toward the window. She was unable to finish her thought. He realized his mother was having a hard time facing the idea of going to the little local church for her husband's funeral. It was the same church in which Paul Marino had married Julie White just before World War I. She had been but twenty-one that day. Back then she was proud of her dark, chestnut-brown hair. Over the years it had turned more and more gray. Now the strands seemed more white than gray.

It was the same church where Julie White's parents had been married a couple of decades before that event. Grandpa William Marino had married his bride Virginia there also. It was home.

Joseph had been baptized a few years after the wedding of his parents in the little font next to the altar where Paul and Julie had recited their vows. He had been born just a year and a half after his father had returned from the trenches of northern France, where he had beaten the Kaiser single-handedly (or at least that was what Joseph's father had told him).

It was the church where lives and marriages were started, and where they finished. Holy water marked the beginnings, and consecrated earth sealed the endings. Joseph's mother's grandfather had helped seal the stained glass windows. Her grandmother had carried the stones for the steps in her skirt when she was a teenager. There were many Marinos and Whites buried in the town cemetery nearby. Now there would be one more. Joseph understood why this trip to the church was the hardest for his mother.

"You know, we could take you into town and get you something nice, Ma. You should have something nice to the church on a special day." Joseph reached out and rubbed his mother's arm.

"I wore a white dress there one day a long, long time ago." Julie stared out the window, into the Maine darkness.

"And it was beautiful, Ma. You should have another nice dress."

"It's strange, Joey. You wear a white dress the day your marriage starts and a black one when it ends." Julie started crying softly. She closed her eyes.

Joseph opened his mouth, but couldn't think of anything to say. He shook his head, as if he were chastising himself, and just continued rubbing her arm. He found it hard to speak. He stared at his old desk. There were his teen mementoes, still there. His high school and graduation announcements were still in the frames on the wall. He studied the words 'Boston College' slowly. It seemed like a long time ago. 1944 was an eternity ago, he thought. Joseph cleared his throat.

"Let's get you a new one, Ma." Joseph said. He was surprised to see a panicked look in his mother's face.

"Oh, I can't afford that, Joey. I've been running all over the house to find enough money to pay the light bill. I'm still short two dollars. Will they turn off the electricity, Joey?" Julie looked at her son and pleaded.

"What...?" Joseph started.

"The electricity. I have to pay it. They called. It wasn't paid on the first. Oh, Joey, I just don't know where to get the money for next month's bills. I have to go to the bank and see how much is left. I think after paying for the burial there's only a few hundred left. Our monthly check won't cover all of the bills." Julie explained. She started listing each utility bill that she was expecting.

"Ma, shh, don't worry. I'll drive down there in the morning and take care of it. Maybe Anne can help with the dress. She's pretty good about those kinds of things." Joseph looked out into the hall. Anne was standing just inside the doorway. She was shaking her head in a very distinctly negative gesture.

"Anne can help?" Julie turned to look toward the door. Anne suddenly stopped her head motion.

"I think you need something new, Ma. What do you say, Joseph? Our treat?" Anne was trying to send a message to her husband with her eyes.

"Uh, sure. I think you're right." Joseph was confused.

"I couldn't do that to you. You have the kids, and bills of your own. Maybe I could just wear my Sunday church dress." Julie tried to sit up, but stopped with a pained expression on her face.

"Nonsense, Ma. Does something hurt?" Joseph reached out to help his mother.

"I think I've just been lying down too long. I need to get up and move around." Julie struggled to sit up.

"Maybe the kids would like to see you?" Anne smiled and reached out to help her mother-in-law stand up.

"Oh, yes! The kids! I have some cake for them! They must be hungry! Where are my little kittens?" Julie smiled as she moved toward the door.

"In the living room, watching TV." Anne stood back as Julie left the room.

"Paulie? Baby Sarah? Grandma has something for you!" Julie called out as she walked down the hall. Anne looked at her husband, and stopped him with her hand as he followed his mother out of the room.

"Joseph, wait." Anne whispered.

"Huh?" Joseph was confused.

"I looked over the material in the other room. It's a collection of old black pieces of cloth that have been stitched and re-stitched together. It's a mess. There's no way I could make a dress out of that in a month!" Anne frowned.

"Is that why it's all over the room?" Joseph whispered.

"Annie? Joey?" Come and get some cake! Paulie and Sarah have already eaten almost half of it!" Julie called from the living room. Joseph looked down and had to smile. He knew it was actually Paul alone who had eaten almost half of the cake, no matter what flavor it was. Joseph had to smile when he thought of the times that Paul had eaten something and couldn't tell Joseph what the flavor of the item had been. Paul often inhaled his food so fast that no one knew exactly what the boy had eaten.

"Be right there, Ma!" Joseph loudly replied, then

returned to his whispering as they left the bedroom.

"Do you think you can get her something in town tomorrow?" Joseph asked.

"I think we'll have more luck in town than in that other bedroom!" Anne answered.

"You can do that while I take care of her electric bill. Then we can go to the funeral home." Joseph frowned. He realized he would have to confront two of his least favorite chores in one day: visiting a funeral home and paying a bill.

As Joseph and Anne entered the living room, Paul and Sarah were busy telling their grandmother about trying to come in the back door earlier. Julie was sitting in an easy chair, intensely studying her grandchildren.

"...and Dad was confused about the back door being locked, so we told him to try the front door." Paul rattled off, his mouth full of cake.

"Yeah, and it was unlocked so we just came in." Sarah finished Paul's thought, then took a bite of cake. At least she finished her sentence before she took a bite, Joseph thought.

"You know, children, your grandfather and I fought over that back door being unlocked for years. He used to sneak out the back for a drink of his corn liquor sometimes. I used to hate that. Then he jimmied the lock so that I couldn't hear the door open at night. Except I could, really." Julie smiled, and looked down.

"Is that why that door always opened smoothly, but the

front door scraped the wood on the floor?" Joseph looked at the front door. He realized it hadn't scraped tonight, as they had entered.

"Oh, he finally saved up enough money to buy that planer-blade-thingy to scrape the door. Finished it just last month. Had to pester him for years, though. Whenever someone brought his or her car to his shop to be fixed, he'd finish it right nice and quick. Home chores took months. Sometimes years!" Julie smiled again, and looked at the door. She shook her head.

Anne looked over at Joseph with an accusing stare as she sat down on the couch.

"What?" Joseph gestured at his wife with his arms up as he moved toward the other end of the couch.

"Sound familiar?" Anne tilted her head and looked toward the door.

"Our door works fine!" Joseph answered with a frown.

"What about your faucet in our bathroom?" Anne smiled and raised her eyebrows as she reached for a piece of cake. Joseph cleared his throat nervously.

"So, Ma, what are the sleeping arrangements?" Joseph asked sheepishly as he reached for a piece of cake. He definitely wanted to avoid the subject of the bathroom faucet, and any comparisons with his father.

Chapter 13

Joseph's first night's sleep in Maine in many years was not a comfortable experience. Joseph and Anne had been given the master bedroom, while Joseph's mother stayed in his childhood room. Paul and Sarah had fallen asleep on the couches in the living room. Their grandmother had tucked them in with some blankets and pillows.

Falling asleep after a very long day traveling across the United States was not hard at all. Staying asleep was the struggle, Joseph discovered. The most difficult issues were the physical factors that contributed to the situation. Joseph's father bought something new only if he was forced to, and he kept repairing household items well beyond the useful life of the item. There was no exception to this rule of Paul Marino the Elder when it came to his own mattress. Three or four times during the middle of the night Joseph had awakened because something was stabbing him in the side, or in the leg. As he adjusted himself, and felt around the mattress under him, he discovered a myriad of lumpy items under the sheets. Twice Joseph pulled the sheet from the corner of the mattress, trying to adjust an offending lump, much to Anne's discomfort.

It was a night of incredulous discovery for Joseph. The first time he pulled the sheet back, after his calf had been wounded by the lower half of the bed, he discovered that his father had used the better part of a roll of duct tape to fasten a large piece of canvas to the lower third of the mattress. In places the duct tape had wadded up, obviously from years of someone tossing and turning all over it, into a very unpleasant looking mass. He could tell that his father had used a curved upholstery needle to roughly finish the edges and permanently attach the canvas to the bed. What Joseph couldn't figure out was why his father had left the duct tape all over the canvas. As he pulled at one piece of the tape he discovered the reason. The duct tape must have pre-dated the repair to the bed, for it had been used to cover up a number of nasty moth holes in the old canvas. A bit of faded lettering on one edge of the canvas in the dim light caught his eye. When he moved close to investigate he discovered the letters "BSA". At that very moment Joseph realized that he had slept with this very piece of canvas in the past, about thirty-five years before. It was his old Boy Scout tent, or at least a part of it!

An hour or two later, after finding a couple of more items in the bed (including a 1945 edition of National Geographic Magazine), as he had shifted to lie on his right side, something felt like it jumped out and nipped him in the arm pit. Joseph jumped up out of the bed, turned the bedside light on and massaged his offended body part.

"Joseph?" Anne whispered.

"Huh? Yeah? Sorry if I woke you up," Joseph mumbled. He had his arm up high as he was rubbing the underside of it.

"Why are you putting on deodorant in the middle of the

night?" Anne asked as she used her right hand to shield her eyes from the light.

"Come on, Anne. I'm not. Something reached out from inside of the bed and nipped at my arm pit." Joseph grumbled. He wondered if the local motel had a vacancy.

"What? Something inside the bed? What are you talking about?" Anne put her head back on the pillow.

"Something nipped me. Here, look. There's a red mark. I swear something bit me! I'm not joking!" Joseph was irritated.

"I don't think your mother has bedbugs in her house, Joseph. Go back to sleep." Anne turned away from her husband.

"Anne, I didn't mean a bug. A bug wouldn't leave a welt like this!" Joseph snapped as he pointed inside his armpit.

"What was it then?" Anne was getting harder to understand. She was mumbling.

"A piranha. I swear he must have kept piranha in here. Maybe one or two are still alive in there." Joseph answered. He couldn't imagine what had bitten him.

"Ok, then. Let's go back to sleep." Anne was now almost impossible to understand.

"You know the stories about people keeping millions of dollars under the mattress? Well, I'll bet he kept twelve dollars under there and invested something like eight hundred on protecting those twelve one dollar bills. I figure he kept piranha in here. Maybe sharks." Joseph was enjoying himself. He realized he had years of frustration with his father's tightwad attitude pent up inside. Anne rolled back toward her husband.

"What in the world are you talking about? Are you having a bad dream or something?" Anne covered her eyes again.

"No. I'm having a bad horizontal experience. I'm fine as long as I'm vertical. Maybe I could sleep standing up." Joseph nodded and congratulated himself on the brilliant solution to the problem at hand, or, actually, leg and underarm. He wondered why he sounded as good as Johnny Carson on the Tonight Show when it was three-thirty in the morning, but not in the afternoon.

"Do you want to switch sides? My side of the bed seems fine. I don't mind. If it means we can turn the light out and get some sleep, I'll do it. We don't need your wee-hours-of-the-morning humor." Anne barked. Joseph scanned the room and spotted a throw blanket on the chair in the corner of the room.

"Nah, you just go back to sleep. I'll just lay this blanket under me. Maybe that'll keep the piranhas at bay. They hate wool, you know." Joseph pulled the sheets back and was about to throw the blanket over the mattress, as a sort of pad, when he saw something unusual. A short zipper, in the side of the mattress, near the pillow, had obviously been sewn there by either his father or his mother. Joseph leaned over

153

and studied the sewing work. It was too rough to have been his mother's handiwork, he thought. His mother always tied off the ends of the thread neatly. This was really sloppy work. He knew his father had done it.

"Whatever you say, Joseph. Let's just get some sleep." Anne's breathing became more shallow and rhythmic.

"Anne. Wake up." Joseph was trembling.

"Huh? What now?" Anne didn't turn over.

"Really. I mean it. You have to see this." Joseph knelt by the bed. He scraped his left hand across his day-old beard growth and shook his head.

Slowly, and quietly, Joseph pulled the zipper open. He spread the mattress apart and peered inside. It was too dark to tell what was in the pocket, or whatever one would call this, in the mattress. He licked his lips and rubbed his mouth with his palm as he tried to decide if he should stick his hand in to investigate. He decided, as a right-hander, to risk his left hand. Slowly he pushed his hand deeper and deeper into the mattress. When his arm was in halfway to his elbow he felt something metallic and hard. Slowly he pulled whatever it was out. As the metal object came out from inside the mattress, Joseph saw that it was a very recognizable piece of metal. It was a common, rusted, pry-hubcaps-from-the-wheel tire iron. Joseph shook his head. He gently lowered the tire iron to the floor and sat on the edge of the bed. He didn't know whether to laugh or to cry. What a ridiculous situation, he thought. A tire iron in the mattress! Ludicrous!

"What is it?" Anne asked, still facing away from Joseph.

"A stupid tire iron. Who in their right mind would keep a tire iron in their mattress?" Joseph shook his head.

"I think you just answered your own question. Consider the 'right mind' idea carefully. Now, let's go to sleep?" Anne was pleading.

"Oh, yeah, I guess you're right. And my father thought I was strange. I guess this piece of 'iron-clad' evidence oughta convince the jury which Marino had a few screws loose. Or hub caps." Joseph had to smile at his own pun.

"Okay. I've had enough. Can we go to sleep now?" Anne was still facing the other way, and she was pulling the blanket up over her shoulder.

At that moment, probably due to the pressure of his body on the mattress, two one hundred dollar bills dropped out of the zippered opening onto the floor. Joseph felt his mouth drop.

"Anne. Look." Joseph whispered.

"No more, please." Anne mumbled.

He decided that he needed to go back into the mattress. He returned to his previous kneeling position on the floor next to the bed. Slowly, once again, he pushed his hand inside. As he got close to having his arm in up to his elbow he felt something, something distinctly paper-like. He slowly pulled a large handful of whatever it was toward the opening. Joseph realized there were other handfuls deeper inside. As he removed his hand from the bed he found that he was holding fifty or sixty one hundred-dollar bills.

"Holy mackerel! Anne You have to see this!" Joseph was stunned. He grabbed on to the money with both hands.

"No! Definitely not! Can't it wait until the morning? It's really way too late. Should I go sleep in the living room?" Anne snapped as she hit her pillow.

"Please, Anne. You have to look. I mean it. Just once. I promise you won't be disappointed." Joseph held the money up high enough that Anne would be able to see it if she just rolled over.

"This had better be good. I'm losing my patience. If you can't..." Anne stopped in mid-sentence as her mouth fell open and he eyes widened, "...oh my gosh! Are those things what I think they are?"

"If you think they're hundred dollar bills, then you're right." Joseph was counting them. Anne rolled completely over and sat up, on Joseph's side of the bed. A few more bills fell out.

"Joseph! There must be thousands of dollars in there! Your mother doesn't know?" Anne's mouth was still hanging open.

"I don't think she does! Not according to what she said last night before bed. I don't think she was lying to us. Mom doesn't lie." Joseph looked up at his wife.

"I don't believe it..." Anne whispered.

"Anne...close your mouth." Joseph smiled.

"But she was crying because she didn't have the money to buy enough material to make a black dress for her husband's funeral!" Anne covered her mouth.

"Maybe she needs to just buy one. What do you think?" Joseph waved the wad of bills back and forth. Anne followed the bills, almost mesmerized.

"Or maybe twelve?" Anne shook her head.

Chapter 14

"Joseph? I've made waffles! Come and eat!" Joseph's mother had opened the bedroom door a bit, and was gesturing with her left hand.

"Huh?" Joseph sat up and looked at his mother.

"Waffles! Breakfast is ready!" Julie Marino smiled.

"Anne? Breakfast..." Joseph sat up and turned toward his wife. The bed was empty next to him.

"Oh, for heaven's sake, Joseph, she's been up for an hour now! You're the last one up! I saved you two waffles, but you'd better hurry. Your children can sure put the food away!" His mother slowly shut the door.

"As if she had to tell me! I'm the one who's had to watch his paycheck consumed by two non-stop eating machines!" Joseph smiled and scratched the back of his head. Slowly he moved one leg, then the other, out of the bed and onto the floor. Joseph looked around the room. It was as if nothing had changed. Ever. When he was three years old he used to slowly open the slightly ajar door to the room and climb into the bed next to his mother. A picture of his mother's parents had been on the nightstand back then. It was still there. The old quilt that Julie Marino put on the end of her bed every Christmas was still on the quilt stand in the corner, but now it had a plastic cover on it.

Joseph was about to stand when he remembered the money inside the mattress. He jumped up and looked between the bed and nightstand, where he had carefully hidden it in the middle of the night. It was gone. Joseph climbed over the bed, banging his knee in the process on some other piece of metal in the mattress, and looked between the nightstand and bed on the other side. Nothing. He dropped to his knees and looked under the bed. Still nothing, except the usual Christmas boxes that his mother always kept there. He sat up and wiped his mouth as he scanned the remainder of the room. At that moment Anne walked in, carrying a plate.

"I wondered how long you'd be, so I thought I'd serve you breakfast in bed. Actually, it was your mother's idea..." Anne closed the door, "but I thought it was a good one, so...Joseph? Is something wrong?" She asked. Anne looked confused as she studied Joseph's position on the floor.

"Um, I'm not sure. I think I lost something. Something important. Really valuable." Joseph raised his eyebrows. He rubbed his face with both hands. Maybe, he thought, he had found the money in the mattress only in his dream.

"Where did you last see it?" Anne asked, as any mother would when her child came to her because of a lost toy.

"It was between the bed and the nightstand. I thought it was on my side, but it wasn't there, so I decided to check this side of the bed." Joseph shook his head. Sometimes, he thought, dreams were too cruel.

"Was it in a paper bag?" Anne put the dish of waffles and bacon down on the bed.

"Yes! Where is it?" Joseph asked, afraid of the answer. He sat up.

"I hid it in the bathroom, under the sink. I didn't want anyone finding it." Anne whispered as she walked over toward the bathroom door. She nodded in that direction and Joseph followed.

"Thank God! I thought I was dreaming!" Joseph replied.

"Now THAT was too real to have been a dream. Besides, I got up a couple of hours ago and counted it." Anne's voice was unsteady.

"So...?" Joseph leaned forward, waved his hand and

asked

"I don't believe it, Joseph. I counted three hundred and nineteen one hundred dollar bills. Thirty one thousand, nine hundred dollars!"

"Holy mackerel! How in the world did he get that kind of money? No, wait. Don't answer that," Joseph put his hand up, "the mattress the money was found in is the answer. There are all the things they went without all of those years, right there in that bag." Joseph pointed and shook his head.

"I think they should have spent a little of it on a mattress. That was one of the worst night sleeps I've ever had." Anne rubbed her back.

"I thought it wasn't that bad for you? You were just lying there all night!" Joseph frowned.

"That's because if I moved one way or the other I got jabbed by something." They both turned to look at the bed.

"Just when I thought I was better than my father in one thing, like where I put my tools, I get one-upped by a bag of cash." Joseph shook his head.

"Honey, this is probably his entire retirement account. Your mother said they only had a couple of hundred dollars left in the bank after paying for the burial expenses." Anne rubbed her husband's upper arm.

"That feels good. That's where I wrenched my arm. Get it? Wrench? Wrenched?" Joseph smiled weakly. Anne smiled back.

"Joseph, I think you're wrong." Anne looked into the bag.

"About the bad pun? Yeah. Sorry." Joseph shook his head and looked down.

"No. About the money. About your father showing you up. As much money as this seems, I wonder how much this would have been if your father had put it in the bank?" Anne shrugged. Joseph looked up, and then down at the bag.

"Holy cow, you're right. If he's been hoarding this for thirty years..."

"Or more..." Anne interrupted.

"...or more..." Joseph nodded, "it could have easily been a hundred thousand!" He looked up at his wife and smiled.

"I think so." Anne returned the smile.

"Thanks, honey." Joseph hugged his wife.

"So, what are we going to do with it? I mean, should we just leave it next to the bed and let your mother find it?" Anne asked.

"I don't know. She'd probably think it belonged to someone else. She'd probably give it all to the church! Every single extra dime we ever had went to the church. If Ma ever found money, it went to the church." Joseph scratched the back of his head.

"Why do you keep scratching your head?" Anne reached up and pulled his head down. She turned her husband around.

"I dunno. My scalp feels a little irritated in one place." Joseph replied.

"Well, I'll be. There's a circular mark on your head. Nothing serious. Did your father collect something round, about the size of, maybe, a quarter?" Anne made a circle approximating the mark on her husband's head as Joseph turned and faced her.

"Something in my pillow? I never thought of that. I just thought my dandruff had come back. But my mother put fresh cases on the pillows." Joseph shook his head.

"Let's take a look." Anne walked back into the bedroom. Joseph followed.

The two of them pulled the pillowcase from the pillow, and then unzipped the cloth cover. There was another zipper, a smaller one, obviously hand sewn into the pillow, on the edge of the pillow.

"Why is it I'm not surprised this time?" Joseph asked. Anne gestures, wondering if Joseph wanted to "do the honors" and be the one to put his hand in and investigate. He shook his head and made an "I leave this one to you" gesture with his right hand while rubbing the back of his head with his left. Anne unzipped the pillow. Slowly she slipped her hand in.

"I found something. It feels like shiny metal. Smooth." She pulled her hand out. Joseph easily recognized a socket bit.

"Huh! A socket! In the pillow!" Joseph was startled by a noise from the door.

"What are you two doing? We've been waiting out in the kitchen for you." It was Joseph's mother.

"Uh, hi, Ma. We were just, um, just..." Joseph looked at Anne, and hoped she'd see the pleading in his eye.

"We were just making the bed up, Ma. We know you have a lot to do today. We thought we'd help." Anne smoothed the pillow and placed it at the head of the bed.

"Oh!" Julie whispered. She was staring at the pillow. She wasn't moving.

"Is something wrong, Ma?" Joseph asked.

"Um, well, if you must know, that is your father's piggy bank." Julie whispered. She looked out into the hall, to see if anyone was standing there.

"Piggy bank?" Joseph was amused.

"He kept his valuables in there. And some money. He figured no one could steal it right out from under his head." Julie picked up the extra sheet on the end of the bed and started smoothing it.

"Oh, so you know. We weren't sure." Anne smiled.

"Oh, yes, I do know. I was going to look in there next to find some money to pay the electric company. Have you looked inside?" Julie tightened her lips.

"Well, only a bit." Anne smiled and flashed the socket, hoping Joseph would catch the pun.

"Ma, keeping your money in your bed can't work. You need to put it in a bank." Joseph rolled his eyes when he saw Anne grinning at him, holding a socket. He'd tell her later it was a socket, not a 'bit'.

"Well, first of all, it was in the pillow, not in the bed. He said only a fool would put his money in a mattress. He kept his in his pillow. Secondly, we lost everything back in nineteen hundred and twenty nine to those bankers. It seems like anything left in that pillow was more than those crooked bankers left us back then. You must have remembered. You were nine, and wanted a bicycle for your birthday. All we could get you was a new pair of pants, and you were none too excited!" Julie shook her head and smiled a tense, small smile.

"I do remember..." Joseph was surprised.

"Well, let's see how much he had in there, then." Julie stepped up to pick up the pillow. She unzipped it and started rummaging through. At that moment, Anne looked behind her at Joseph and shrugged She pointed at the paper bag in her hand, and then she mouthed the words "s-a-y w-e f-o-u-n-d t-h-i-s i-n t-h-e p-i-l-l-o-w".

"Ma, we found..." Just as Joseph was about to say his line, he was interrupted.

"See, I told you! Look here! We have almost one hundred dollars in here! I can pay the electric bill now!" Julie smiled as she turned to face her son.

"Ma, like I was saying, we found a lot more, um, in there." He gestured toward the pillow. He hated lying to his mother, but knew he had no choice. There was no other way she'd believe him. She didn't believe her husband had hidden any money in the old mattress, so this was the only chance Joseph had to have her believe the money was hers.

"More? Where?" Julie looked around. Anne raised the bag.

"A bag full? I don't believe it. You're just giving out charity." Julie frowned.

"Ma, take my word for it. There's no way we could give away that kind of money. We could afford to pay off our mortgage with that!" Joseph smiled. Julie opened the bag and then dropped it. She covered her mouth with both of her hands.

"Ma?" Joseph stepped next to his mother.

"Oh my God, Joseph Marino. There must be five thousand dollars in there!" Julie whispered.

"Thirty one thousand nine hundred, to be exact." Anne replied as she picked up the bag.

"That can't be our money! No! Maybe it belongs to the church!" Julie continued to stare at the bag as Anne shook her head and ran her fingers through her own hair.

"Ma, we found it in this room, last night. It's yours. Dad probably saved money over the years to make sure you'd be okay." Joseph said.

"He used to put his mark on every bill bigger than a five all his life. If this is his money, the bills will tell." Julie picked up the bag. She pulled a handful of bills out, and inspected them one by one. She walked over to the desk, opened the drawer and pulled a magnifying glass out.

"Is there a mark, Ma?" Anne leaned over and squinted at the bill Julie was checking.

"There it is. It's his money, to be sure!" Julie shook her head.

"Where, Ma?" Joseph leaned over and stared.

"Right here, do you see the tiny capital letters 'PM' between the words 'UNITED' and 'STATES'?" Julie handed Joseph the magnifying glass.

"Oh, Lord! Ma's right! I don't believe it! How did he do that?" Joseph shook his head. Anne stepped over next to Joseph and looked into the glass. She smiled.

"With this very same magnifying glass!" Julie smiled.

"That must have taken him a lot of time over the years."

"Well, I guess he did it while working with his stamp collection." Julie pointed at the bottom drawer of the desk.

"Stamps?" Anne asked.

"Yep. Since about 1900, he's been doing it." Julie pulled some more bills out of the bags and inspected them. Anne looked at Joseph and raised her eyebrows.

"Ma! Have you had someone look at those stamps? They may be worth a lot of money!" Joseph suggested.

"Never thought of it. Who'd want some old stamps? It was just an old man's way to pass the time. Now, how in the world did that old coot get this amount of money into that pillow?" Julie shook her head in a gesture of disbelief.

"Um, Ma, I know what he said about putting your money into a mattress, but did you see the zipper on the side?" Joseph pointed to the mattress.

"Oh, sure. That's where he kept his tools! He always said, 'sleep on your tools and no one steals them'!"

"He had more in there besides tools!" Joseph shook his head.

"And to think I never knew...huh!" Julie sat on the edge of the bed and continued counting.

Chapter 15

Joseph, Anne and Julie left Paul and Sarah at home, watching television, and drove into Auburn. After a long discussion on the way, Joseph managed to convince his mother that the bank was the best place to keep her newfound money. He felt guilty about how he had done this, however. He had used fear. Simply, he had mentioned how worried he was. He explained that he thought his father had protected the money all of these years, and it wouldn't be safe anymore without him around. Julie had quietly agreed after Anne had said that she felt Joseph was right.

Their first stop was at the bank, where they deposited almost the entire sum into the family bank account. Julie held some back to help pay for the expenses of the day. It had been quite a surprise for the old banker, who had to summon a guard to watch over transaction. The guard to the vault transported the bills swiftly, with Julie walking beside him. She seemed downright nervous about leaving that amount of money in the bank. Joseph pointed out that the bank was federally insured, and that Julie had a receipt, the bank book showing the deposit. They started walking along the sidewalk, window-shopping. Three doors down was a small women's clothes store.

"Hey, Ma! Here's a place for getting a dress! You should! You deserve one!" Joseph pointed.

"I agree. I'm sure we can find something really nice in here, Ma." Anne touched her mother-in-law's elbow.

"Well, as long as it isn't too expensive!" Julie looked very nervous.

"I'll tell you what, Ma. You and Anne get a nice dress, and I'll take a walk, um, down the street..." Joseph was staring at a corner building two blocks away. Julie was studying a dress in the display window, as Anne was, until she noticed Joseph's faraway look. She turned to trace Joseph's stare.

"Why don't you go in and look around, Ma." Anne said to Julie.

"Why, sure. You know, they have some pretty nice

satin looking bolts of cloth here!" Julie entered the store. Anne smiled a half-smile at her mother-in-law and then turned back to her husband.

"What's going on, Joseph?" She touched his arm.

"I think I need to take a walk to the funeral home, Anne. I need to, um, I don't know, see him." Joseph whispered as he looked quickly into the dress shop.

"I understand. Do you think it's a good idea to go in all alone?" Anne whispered as well, smiling whenever her mother-in-law looked out the window, which seemed often.

"I don't know, but I have to try, Anne. If I'm not back in an hour, come and get me. Maybe you'll have to lead me out, but I have to try." Joseph smiled at his wife and looked down the street again.

"Okay, but walk out if you can't handle it, honey. There's no shame in doing that. It's not an easy thing to do." Anne took a short step toward the dress shop, but hesitated.

"Go on in, Anne. I'll make it. I may not be fine, but I'll make it." Joseph leaned over and squeezed his wife's arm. He started walking down the street.

Chapter 16

The latch on the door seemed to be made of lead. Joseph had to squeeze with more strength than he thought he had. He finally heard the familiar click as the lock gave way.

The sign right in front of his face said 'Clay Brothers Mortuary'. He leaned into the heavy wooden door, which made the sign appear larger, and the huge portal gave way, exposing a dimly lit, cavernous room, with a dozen or two candles at the front. Joseph hesitated and licked his lips. Maybe, he thought, this wasn't such a good idea. He took one step inside, and waited until his vision adjusted to the lower lighting.

Slowly he walked inside, further with each step. There was a strange echo inside this room, as if there was nothing soft; everything was a hard surface. Joseph's foot scraped along the wooden floor, and it seemed to be heard everywhere. He stopped. He took another step. Then a third.

"Can I help you, sir?" A quiet, kind voice said as Joseph jumped back, quickly.

"Huh? I'm sorry! I didn't know you were there." Joseph was breathing hard. His mouth was dry. There was a man standing in front of him who looked like he had not been outside in months. He had a dark, maybe black, suit on, and a white shirt, with a black tie. Joseph licked his lips again, and started fumbling with his shirt button.

"Oh, no problem, sir. I'm used to that. What can I do for you?" The man asked.

"Oh, me? Nothing, I guess. I'm still alive, and, um, I'm just fine. I don't need anything. Really." Joseph pulled harder at his shirt button.

"Oh, no, sir, that's not what I meant," the man smiled

and leaned back a bit, "I meant, is there something here you would like to see?"

"Um, no. Not really." Joseph really didn't want to be in the room at all.

"So, why have you come into the mortuary?" The man asked.

"Um, well, you see..." Joseph was fumbling for words, and on his button."

"Sir, if you don't mind me saying so, you're going to lose that button..." The man in the dark suit pointed to Joseph's shirt. At that moment a loud 'SNAP' echoed through the room, followed by the tinkling sound of a plastic button bouncing on a wooden floor.

"Oh, I'm sorry. Here, let me clean that up!" Joseph reached in the direction the button flew.

"Sir, it's quite alright. We can find it," the other man said.

"Oh, yes. Right. Joseph stopped and turned toward the doorway. He felt an overwhelming need to see the light of day.

"Let's start over. Hello, I'm Jim Clay, and I run this place. And you are?" The man extended his hand. Joseph meekly shook it, and then criticized himself for offering a "dishrag handshake". His high school physical education teacher had told the boys never to shake like that, but he had done it.

"Um, Marino. Joseph Marino." Joseph felt better just being able to see the light outside, and the cars driving by.

"Joey Marino? Boy Scout Troop thirty six?" The man's tone of voice changed.

"Huh? Uh, yeah. That was me. Do I know you?" Joseph looked into the man's face. He seemed somewhat familiar, especially around the eyes.

"Jimmy Clay, Joey! It's me, Jimmy! Do you remember the campouts on Chocolate Chip Creek?" The man smiled broadly and extended his arm again.

"Oh, my gosh! Yes, Jimmy Clay! I didn't recognize you! I thought your father ran this place!" Joseph was feeling a bit better. He got a second chance to shake hands, and he made sure it was not a dishrag this time.

"Hah! He did, until he died five years ago. Now my son and I run it." Jimmy gestured for Joseph to go inside the office to the right of the door.

"Your son?" Joseph asked.

"Yep. He's nineteen now, believe it or not. Works here with me. Fourth generation, I'll have you know!"

"I'll be!" Joseph smiled as he looked at the photographs on the wall. Jimmy moved around to sit on the opposite side of the desk, and then he gestured for Joseph to sit across from him.

"So, I can figure out why you're back in town. I'm really sorry, Joseph." Jimmy seemed downright sincere. That was hard to believe, since the two of them hadn't exactly been close friends. To this day Joseph still believed that Jimmy stole his Scout flashlight, the one he had saved for a year to buy.

"Yeah. It's been a rough week." Joseph looked at the opposite wall, which was covered with old newspaper clippings.

"So, you live in Colorado now, I hear." Jimmy sat back and loosened his tie.

"Uh, no. California. I moved to Colorado for a couple of years, but decided to go further west." Joseph replied. Joseph wondered how many more years he'd have to explain that he lived in California, not Colorado.

"I see. Have you told your mother? She told me Colorado." Jimmy smiled and lifted his eyebrows. When Joseph saw that expression he remembered how much he despised that kid years ago. Now he really hated being in the funeral home. Jimmy Clay had always managed to be around to take advantage of situations.

It was Jimmy who had threatened to tell Joseph's mother about sneaking out of the house in the middle of the night to catch frogs one summer, between their seventh and eighth grade years. Jimmy wanted Joseph's new pen, or he'd tell. Joseph kept the pen, but he spent the rest of that summer cutting weeds around the cornrows at old man Schrier's farm because of that. Joseph had left his father's fishing box at the creek, and had gone back looking for it. Of course he couldn't find it. Joseph was just going to play dumb about where the fishing tackle box had gone. Jimmy Clay ruined all that by telling his parents what had happened. Joseph paid for that tackle box. The next summer he spotted Jimmy with his father's old box at the creek. Joseph squeezed his hand into a fist, and looked out the window.

"She's confused, that's all. My dad's death really hit her hard." Joseph started to rise. He decided he'd had enough. Too much, actually.

"Where're you going? Sit a while, we have a lot of catching up to do!" Jimmy rose with his guest.

"There's not much to catch up on, Jimmy. We weren't that close back then, and I'll only be here for a day or two more, anyway. Besides, I'm really tired." Tired of being around you, Joseph thought

"So, why'd you drop by?" Jimmy asked.

"I wanted to see...I mean..." Joseph felt like his mouth was suddenly made out of cotton.

"Your dad?" Jimmy whispered.

"Yeah. My dad. I just wanted to see him one last time, I mean, alone. You know what I mean..." Joseph was getting more nervous.

"I understand, Joey. Here, let me show you the way. Jimmy gestured toward the office door, back into the dark room.

"Thanks." As Joseph walked away he spotted a photograph of Jimmy, obviously from years before, in a fishing boat, holding a large catch. A thought struck Joseph. Maybe he could solve a decades old mystery.

"I see you're quite the fisherman, Jimmy." Joseph pointed at the faded image.

"Huh? Oh, that! Sure! I used to spend a lot of time on the water, but I don't get out much anymore, though." Jimmy squinted at the picture.

"Too bad! It looks like you enjoy it! I'm glad to see that the old fishing gear I gave you back in school started a lifelong hobby for you." Joseph squinted, trying to make details out in the photo. Joseph looked over toward his old schoolmate.

"Oh, yeah. I had a lot of fun with that old kit. I don't remember what happened to it..." Jimmy said as he walked out the door. Joseph followed the mortuary director, and he was feeling much better.

"This way, Joey. Your father is in the side viewing room." Jimmy slowly pushed a door into a side room.

Joseph felt a moment of weakness. For some reason he couldn't work his own legs. His mouth got dry again. After a moment of working up the courage, he gently stepped up to the doorway. Jimmy's arm was stretched in front of Joseph, blocking the path.

"Joey...wait..." Jimmy whispered.

"Yeah? What?" Joseph whispered in return, not

because he would wake anyone, but he couldn't find the strength to speak much louder. He had to admit, even to himself, that he was frightened.

"I wanted to ask something before you go in." Jimmy had a kind tone in his voice.

"Sure, what is it?" Joseph looked at Jimmy.

"Could you put in a word to your mother for me? I've offered her five hundred dollars for your dad's old forty-eight Chevy Woody." Jimmy smiled. Joseph couldn't believe it. His mouth dropped, and he couldn't decide what to say.

"Don't worry, Jimmy, I'll talk to her. Believe me, I will." Joseph smiled a tiny, polite smile. He decided that he'd make sure Jimmy never touched that old thing.

"Thanks. You are a friend, Joey." Jimmy smiled. It was then that Joseph, in the close quarters of that small entryway to the side chamber, noticed that Jimmy's front two teeth had a slightly different hue to them, and he remembered why. He remembered how his fist hurt that day in tenth grade. Joseph suddenly felt better.

"I guess so. A friend does what he knows is best." Joseph smiled broadly.

Chapter 17

Joseph felt a deep sense of relief as he watched Jimmy leave the small side chamber of the funeral home. He really wanted to be alone with his father, one last time. Slowly, one arm after another, he removed his sweater. He held it firmly in his left hand as he wiped his mouth with the right hand.

Slowly, carefully, Joseph looked around the room. He studied each of the bright, colorful stained glass windows that lined each side of the room. He recognized many of the Bible stories they portrayed. The first one was the story of the wedding, when Jesus turned the water into wine. The third one from the front portrayed the woman washing Jesus' feet, and the middle one on the other side showed a man who looked like what Joseph thought would be Jesus, carrying a lamb from a thorn bush. It was then that it struck him. It was the story of the Prodigal Son. The lost, forsaken son returns to the fold. Joseph moved slowly to the pew nearest that image, and held on. For the longest time he stared at it. It wasn't long before his throat felt more and more swollen, and tears began to fall from his eyes.

He knew what he was doing. He was avoiding the object in the middle of the room at the front. He clenched his teeth, and slowly stepped closer to the casket that held his father's body. He licked his lips, and unconsciously reached for the second button of his shirt. He was startled to discover it was missing, and then he remembered why.

The casket was deep, deep reddish brown. That was strange, he thought. The color was called "auburn". It seemed appropriate for someone in this town to be buried in an "auburn" casket. Joseph smiled, knowing his father, the King of Puns, would enjoy this final pun. Joseph toyed with how the pun would come together. 'He was buried in auburn.' Or maybe it would be better to write it as 'He was buried in Auburn, capital and lower case.'

Just then Joseph caught the sight of his father's face. He had crept to the edge, and now he looked upon the face of the man who had carried him into the doctor's office when he had broken his leg when he was twelve. There were the eyebrows of the man who frowned through the glass of the front of the neighborhood market one day. Joseph had snuck into the store to buy a candy bar even though his father had told him not to. As he turned to leave, there were those eyebrows. The pun flew from Joseph's mind. Joseph's mouth fell open.

"Daddy..." Joseph whispered. He knew that even if he wanted to, he could not yell. Whispering was too hard. There was a terrible trembling in his throat. Twice he tried to reach out, but he was afraid to touch his father. He shook his head. His father wouldn't be hurt if he touched him. Slowly, carefully, Joseph reached out and approached his father's cheek with his right hand. He stopped only a finger's width away.

"Daddy? Please?" Joseph's voice was almost gone. He stopped, wondering why he had said the word 'please', then lowered and shook his head. Everything seemed so cloudy and confusing. He looked up again, after collecting himself a bit, took his right index finger, the one his father had taught him was called "Mister Pointer", and gently touched the old man's cheek. It was cold, and Joseph began to cry. Full sobbing erupted when he looked down and saw a poorly disguised scar on his father's throat, from his last surgery.

"Daddy? No?" Joseph's sweater fell quietly to the floor, and he clumsily kneeled next to the casket, which shook gently, and he was unable to restrain his tears. There were moments when his sobbing made it difficult for him to stay upright, and not fall over. It was then that he grabbed on to the auburn casket, and allowed his forehead to rest on the side. His chest heaved over and over again as the tears flowed without restraint.

After a period of time (he had no idea how long it was), Joseph slowed himself down inside. He looked up, trying to clear his throat, and took a deep breath. There, on the upper portions of the wall, was a crucifix, with a warm, glowing, golden light crossing it.

"I am the resurrection and the life..." Joseph mouthed the words he knew so well from Sunday school years ago. He repeated it, over and over again. There was no way he could speak anymore. He cleared his throat and tried to say something. He sat back on his heels.

"I don't know what to say, God. I don't know what to do. I can't believe in anything anymore, God. I guess this is what faith is. I just hold on to what you said in the book...I have nothing else to hold on to." Joseph sobbed again. He slowly opened his eyes and decided to try to look on his father's body again. He took another deep breath and returned to his knees.

You can do this, he reminded himself. There he was, Joseph thought. Paul Marino, the elder. He did look good in that old blue suit, Joseph acknowledged. His hair was neatly arranged, and he looked as if he would wake up at any time. Joseph felt tears well up again as he remembered climbing into his father's bed, so many decades ago, thinking he had been asleep. As Joseph crept closer, his father opened his eyes and shouted, "BOO". Joseph smiled as he recalled how he had jumped across the bed. He remembered how his father told him, years later, that he could have won a broad jump award for nine year olds!

"Please say boo, Daddy. Please say boo." Joseph cried again and looked down at the floor. Once again he mustered the courage to look on his father. He raised his head again, and took a deep breath. He decided to say what he had come to say.

"Dad...I wanted to say I'm sorry. I'm sorry I let you down all those times. I'm sorry I never could fix a machine right. I'm sorry I didn't know the names of all of those tools. I'm sorry I read too many books." A sob overcame Joseph as he remembered how he would read into the late hours of the night in his room, sometimes with an old flashlight under his blanket. The image of his father, drunk and angry, yelling at him to go to sleep, was seared into his mind.

"Oh, Dad. Please tell me that you love me. Please..." Joseph put his head on the edge of the casket, as if he was waiting to hear the words he longed to hear. Tears fell from his cheek and arched gracefully to the boards on the floor. Small droplets scattered in every direction after the impact.

"I'm sorry." Joseph straightened, feeling vulnerable and weak. He always felt guilty for crying. Joseph stood up, slowly, then leaned back over to pick up his sweater. As he did so, he noticed the corner of a small piece of paper in his father's coat pocket. It looked like it was a small, yellowed piece of paper, the kind his father had kept in his desk drawer for years. Joseph reached for the paper, and then stopped. He looked around, toward the doorway, and saw that no one was in the room. Slowly he pulled the paper out, opened it and read. It was in his father's scrawling handwriting.

Julie-

I've thought about it, and you're right. Now I'm scared to death. I don't know what to do. I haven't told him that I love him in more years than I can remember. Now I can never say it to him again. Please tell me what to do!

Paul

Joseph cried for what seemed like days to him, and when he was able to stop he found himself on his right side, lying on the floor, holding his chest. After a few minutes he became aware that someone was rubbing his arm.

"Huh? Ma?" Joseph whispered.

"Shh. It's me, honey. Anne. I'm here. You're going to be alright." She whispered.

"Anne?" Joseph sat up and ran his hand through his hair.

"Yes, it's me." She was sitting next to him on the floor, with her legs to one side. Her purse was between them. She started to stand up, but struggled because of her dress.

"I'm sorry. I guess I was quite a spectacle. I hope I wasn't on the floor for long." He rose first, and reached down to help her.

"Oh, no. I can understand. It was only a few minutes. This is a tough place, honey. No one wants to see their father like...like this." Joseph could tell that Anne had been crying, and not just a little bit. She was having a hard time speaking.

"Oh, gosh, Anne, are you okay?" Joseph pulled his wife toward him.

"I guess." Anne whispered. Joseph looked at Anne. Her eyes had a far-away, listless look in them. Her mouth turned down so strongly, and her skin seemed pale. He did the only thing he knew how to do. He surrounded her in his arms and hugged her.

"Where' Ma?" Joseph whispered.

"Um..." Anne was unable to talk.

"Shhh. It's okay." Joseph decided to just wait. His timing was always bad, he thought.

"She's at the show store." Anne took a deep breath.

"Just take it as you can, honey." Joseph said.

"Getting new shoes. Black ones. I came to tell you." Anne sighed.

"Thanks. Maybe we should go. We'll be back for the Rosary. And then there's tomorrow." Joseph's voice fell in volume.

"Tomorrow..." Anne repeated. They slowly walked toward the door, still in each other's arms. Joseph took one last look as they went through the doorway. He put his arm out to push the door and noticed the little piece of paper. Anne noticed it as well.

"What's that?"

"A gift from my father...the Christmas present I've always wanted!" Joseph smiled weakly.

Chapter 18

Joseph rose in the middle of the night. He had been sleeping much better with the money and tools removed from the mattress, but it was the time, and he had to see if he could live something from long ago. Slowly and quietly he slipped his pants on, then his shoes. He reached into his duffel bag, near the door to the hallway, and pulled out a small, white box. Anne stirred a bit as he slipped his sweatshirt over his head. He stood, arms over his head, with the sweater halfway down his body. He decided to stand motionless for a number of seconds as she settled back down. He looked at his wristwatch. It was almost one twenty. Only three minutes left! Joseph pulled his old Boston Red Sox hat down on top of his head. He moved as quickly as possible, and yet made little sound.

The sweater fell effortlessly down onto his shoulders, and then he straightened his belt. As he was running his hand through his hair he leaned over and looked out of his mother's window at his intended destination: the garage. It had been a long time since he had played "Oyster". "Oyster" had started when he was dating Anne, so many years ago. He took a breath and shook his head as he realized someone was missing.

He stepped gently down the hall, and through the living room. He thought it was strange that he didn't need a light; every piece of furniture that was in the house was in the same location as they had been when he was a teen. He shook his head as he thought of his mother replacing each item two years ago when they re-carpeted the house. Joseph wondered if his mother had measured the distance that each item was from the nearest wall.

As he approached the back door he grasped the doorknob and turned it. Well, at least he tried to turn it. His hand slipped along the old, polished brass doorknob with no effect on the door.

"Darn! Locked!" Joseph whispered to himself. For a moment Joseph looked down at the floor and considered his options. His mother had installed a deadbolt lock on the back door that would not open without the key. He realized that he couldn't search the house for the key, so he decided to go out through the front door. He looked at his watch: one twenty-two. Not much time left.

He placed each foot slowly and carefully, choosing where each step would land with great care as he went through the living room. He knew where the squeaky boards were, and he wanted to avoid them.

The front door opened easily, and Joseph was able to shut it behind him with no trouble whatsoever. As he looked around he realized how much he had missed the beautiful pines of Maine. The moon, almost full, cast a grayish glow over the front yard, and made the pines appear empty with blackness. Only the outer branches and the ground under the trees were bright. He looked around, half hoping someone would be there. The night was still, except for an occasional gust of wind running between the trees. A strong along the top of the trees earned his attention. The moon was now hiding, rather poorly, behind the top of the tallest tree in the yard.

"I'm back, Moon Friend! It's been a while. I see you've taken care of my childhood for me!" Joseph whispered, as if he had a relationship with the light in the sky. He felt his lips pull back, in a smile. Sometimes he wished he could tear away the years and be in high school again. He closed his eyes and listened for the light wind that played in the branches of the trees in the early Maine summer. They produced a symphony of sound for him.

"I hear you, Wind of Long Ago!" Joseph smiled as he remembered the many summer nights he and his friend Petey Barnes had snuck out to meet in front of the old garage. He opened his eyes. A thought crashed in on his dreams. Why hadn't he kept in touch with Petey all these years? He looked down the street, toward Petey Barnes' house.

"Where are you, Petey? You're supposed to be here tonight. I was there for you when your dog died. Don't you remember? We double-shook on it! No matter when, no matter who, we'd be at the old garage at one twenty-three the night before a funeral. But you're not here." Joseph walked slowly toward the garage. He studied each stone in the pathway, seeing his past, but hoping for a sign of his future, somehow. He could still feel every one of those stones. A ridge on a large stone caught his attention. Joseph knew the stone was a deep red color, but it had been robbed of its hue by the harsh light of the moon.

"I remember you, old friend. You're the one who fought with me for so long. You didn't want to line up with the other ones. I almost threw you away, but you seemed so right for this place in the walk." Joseph squatted and caressed the old rock. He let his fingers trace the craggy outline, and then placed his palm down flat in the middle of the stone.

"We may never see one another again, old rock. I don't know. But you'll always be with me, no matter where I go." The wind brushed against Joseph's back. He looked up and decided he'd dawdled enough. With strength in his legs he walked briskly to the side door of the garage.

Turning on the light switch only produced a dim glow in the garage. Slowly Joseph scanned the realm of his father. Paul Marino's tools were where they should be, on the bench to Joseph's right. His father's tools were always where they should be, he thought.

As Joseph turned to the left the sight of a very large, maroon and wood-covered Chevrolet greeted him. It was his father's 1948 Chevy Woody. Joseph's mouth dropped as it dawned on him that the car looked as it did twenty years before, when he had last been in the garage. He could see that the dust on the paint was recent, and that the chrome still shined, even in the dim light.

"Well, you sure did care for this car, Dad." Joseph said in a quiet voice, but not in a whisper. He stepped over to the left front fender and gently touched the paint. Step by step he walked slowly down the side of the garage, next to the car, tracing its many curves and angles with his left hand. As he was finishing his finger-trip he turned to face the driver's side door.

"I guess I don't have to ask you any more, Dad. I'll just get in!" He put his hand into the handle of the door and pulled. The door opened with only a small amount of effort. Joseph was startled that the interior light still came on! He turned and slid into the driver's seat.

Joseph slowly panned across the fabulous dashboard of the old car. The chrome in the gauges, and in the old handed clock, still looked like new. The seat looked a bit worse for wear, but everything else made Joseph feel like it was 1948 again. He marveled at the large steering wheel with the chrome horn rim inside of it, and he checked to see how much gas was in the car. Joseph looked at the workbench next to him.

"It's mine now, Dad. All those years of fighting over so many things, they're all gone now. I can't believe what we used to fight over. I remember Ma telling me to "pick your fights". She wondered how important they were.

Joseph turned toward the passenger-side door. He opened his eyes wide when he noticed the scratch in the inside panel of the right-side door.

"Oh, there's a great example," Joseph pointed, then dropped his hand when he realized that he was the only one there. The bulge in his pants pocket reminded him of why he was in the old garage in the wee hours of the night. For a full minute, though, Joseph stared at the scratch. The imagery was too powerful.

"I had to take the new shovel blade out of the car. I swung it away from your hand, thinking I was being helpful. Instead, I have to look at that the rest of my days." A tear ran down Joseph's cheek.

"What was the point?" He whispered. Slowly he dug into his front pocket and removed the little white box.

"Where should I put it?" He asked as he scanned the inside of the old car. He considered the dash area in front of the driver, the area right above the clock (appropriate for his mission), but decided to leave the box on the passenger seat. That would do it, he thought.

His eyelids were feeling heavier by the minute, and Joseph knew that he couldn't last much longer. He had to get back to the house. Step by step, Joseph backed himself out of the car and the garage. As he was shutting the side door he was surprised by a gruff male voice.

"What're you doing in Scoutmaster Marino's garage?" Joseph heard. He felt the sweat beading up in his hands.

"I'm Paul Marino's son. Joseph. I was just checking the garage." He answered. Joseph was too afraid to turn around.

"I know it's you, Joey. And you're late!" The voice

warmed a great deal. Joseph felt the voice sounded familiar.

"Late?" Joseph smiled as he turned.

"Late!" A man with salt and pepper gray in his hair smiled back.

"Do I know you? You look familiar." Joseph gestured with the palms of his hands turned up.

"You don't have a clue?" The older man smiled back.

"Sorry, no." Joseph raised his eyebrows. Now he was really uncomfortable.

"What time do you have?" The man pointed at Joseph's left wrist.

"One thirty three..." It was that moment that it dawned on him.

"Petey?" Joseph pushed down on his eyebrows and smiled.

"Who else do you think would be stupid enough to come out here at one-thirty in the morning? I haven't forgotten!" Petey Barnes smiled and extended a hand to shake.

"Shake hands? Nah. Here!" Joseph smiled as he reached out and hugged his boyhood friend.

"Anne said you might be out here." Petey returned the smile.

"Anne?" Joseph was surprised.

"I recognized her near the store yesterday. We talked and she reminded me of our old tradition."

"My gosh...!" Joseph shook his head.

"I'm sorry about your father, Joey. I know how hard this must be for you. He was a hard man to get close to. For anyone." Petey looked down. Joseph remembered when Petey's father had died while they were in college. Two years later Petey had come to Joseph's father to ask how to ask a girl to marry him. Joseph's father had been gruff.

"Yeah, I remember what he said to you in that garage one night about this time of year, when we were in college." Joseph pointed over his shoulder.

"Yep. He just continued tightening a bolt and said 'marry me'. He didn't even bother to look up. He didn't know how nervous I was back then." Petey turned and looked at the moon.

"I'm sorry." Joseph apologized for his father. He always wondered why he apologized so much, even for the behavior of others. Petey looked into Joseph's eyes.

"Don't worry about it, Joey." Petey shrugged and looked away. He squinted as he looked into the face of the moon. Joseph felt the discomfort growing. It was quiet for a long time. What do you talk about with your old best high school friend after so many years? An idea struck him.

"So, nobody told me you live in Auburn, Petey! I thought you'd moved away years ago. I remember how you said you wanted to get as far away from this town as you could someday." Joseph looked into the moon with his friend.

He studied the rabbit's face in the moon. He remembered holding a piece of paper up between his eyes and the moon, and trying to trace the image. He could never get it quite right. He saw that he didn't quite know how to relate to Petey now.

"Nah. I just happen to need to check up on the old place. I rent it out, you know." Petey glanced at his friend, who was still studying the moon.

"So, where do you live now?" Joseph

"I did get out of this state, Joey, but not far. I live in Portsmouth, New Hampshire." Petey turned his eyes away from Joseph.

"Well, I'll be! I stopped in a little store in that town on the drive up here from Boston!" Joseph smiled.

"On the main road?" Petey looked right at his friend.

"Yes! It was on the right. Why?" Joseph asked.

"Hah! Were you wearing that hat?" Petey pointed to Joseph's head.

"Uh, well, carrying it." Joseph was confused.

"And did you buy a small kid a pop?" Petey smiled.

"Yeah...?" Joseph tilted his head to the right.

"I heard all about it. That was my sister-in-law's grandson. He was over at our house for dinner that night and told me all about a tall stranger who bought him a soda. The way he described how you had dropped the Boston hat reminded me of you, that night we went to the drug store for a shake, and that girl tried to kiss you. But I thought, nah, couldn't be. But it was you!"

"Yep. I thought he deserved a soda. He could have just hidden the hat and I never would have figured out where it went."

"Nope, not him. He's an honest kid." The uncomfortable silence returned.

"Wait a minute! If you're renting out your old place, then your mother is...is..." Joseph didn't want to finish the sentence.

"She died about four years ago, Joey." Petey finished the sentence as he lowered his head and pushed a stick on the lawn with his right foot.

"Oh, no. And I wasn't there for you the night before her funeral." Joseph frowned.

"It's okay, Joey. You made a memory for a little boy in my sister-in-law's store." Petey looked up again in to the sky.

"I guess..." Joseph whispered.

"Look, I've gotta get going. I'm staying with my cousin Nancy and her husband, and I can't stay out as late as I used to." Petey offered his right hand. Joseph sensed Petey's discomfort and slowly reached out and grabbed the worn-out looking hands.

"I understand." Joseph wanted to say something, but couldn't quite find the words. Petey started walking away, looking up into the sky.

"Petey?" Joseph whispered loudly.

"Yeah?" Petey stopped and turned halfway around.

"Thanks." Joseph smiled. Petey smiled back and gently waved. Joseph felt nervous. He feared that this might be the last time they'd meet.

"But...Petey?" Joseph called out again. Once again, Petey stopped, but this time he continued looking at the moon.

"Yeah?" He replied.

"Did you ever think it would turn out like this? I mean, life?" Joseph felt a tear drop from his eye. Petey pulled his sweater closed.

"Have you ever noticed how the man in the moon looked more like a rabbit as you got older?" Petey asked. Joseph looked up.

"I guess." Joseph shrugged.

"Which one is it? A man or a rabbit?" Petey asked.

"I don't know. Neither, I guess. The picture's just a bunch of mountains and valleys, anyway." Joseph squinted at the moon.

"I think you have your answer." Petey turned and looked into Joseph's eyes as he smiled a weak, half-smile. The lines of pain around his old friend's eyes struck Joseph.

"I care, Petey. We're still the same boys who threw the baseball around this yard." Joseph fumbled, trying to find a way to comfort the boy who shared so many of growing up with Joseph. It was as if they were brothers. Joseph just looked at his old friend, wondering what had made him so full of hurt.

"I don't know. I think it's gone, Joseph." Petey barely smiled, turned and walked around the pine tree on the far side of the garage. The gray light of the moon seemed to swallow him up.

"Gone..." Joseph repeated. He kept his eyes on Petey's outline in the moonlight as long as he could.

Chapter 19

"Joseph? Wake up! We have to get going. There's a lot to do!" Anne said in a quiet voice.

"Huh? Wake up?" Joseph could not open his eyes. He felt like his head was buried in the pillow. His current existence consisted of darkness and the voice of his wife, and only those things.

"Yes. Wake up! We have to get ready to go to the church." Anne said in a hurried tone. Joseph opened his eyes quickly. He opened his eyes quickly, and looked at the closet door. At that moment he remembered that it was the day of his father's funeral.

"Oh, no!" He exclaimed as he sat up. He felt dizzy. Joseph grabbed wildly at the bedpost. He was thinking of using it as a crutch while standing up.

"Hey, whoa! No need to panic!" Anne calmly quieted her husband.

"Huh?" Joseph rubbed his eyes and looked at the window. The rays of the morning sun were dancing on the carpet, in rhythm with the slightly swaying pine branches outside.

"We'd better get ready. The kids left a few minutes ago with your mother. She wanted to take a walk with them." Anne said as she removed her slip from her suitcase.

"I think I see." Joseph squinted as he watched Paul and Sarah walk toward the garage. It felt strange for Joseph to see his mother in black. She was wearing a black dress, black stockings, and black shoes. The new outfit looked like it fit her well, Joseph thought, but he wasn't surprised. Anne knew how to pick clothing out. It was very strange, however, to see her in black. Her favorite style involved a lot of bright flowers. It was rare that he had seen his mother in something dressed in even one color.

"I hung your black suit just inside the door. Are you going to shower?" Anne continued pulling the clothing she had brought along for the funeral out of her suitcase.

"Yeah, I guess I'd better." Joseph stepped out of bed and rubbed his hair as he walked into the bathroom. He felt a chill as he turned the water on. He hated waiting for the water to warm up. Joseph slowly shut the door to the bathroom.

"Joseph?" Anne asked.

"Yeah?" Her husband turned as he removed his undershirt. He looked out of the slight opening in the doorway with his left eye.

"Can we take a walk before we leave? Just a short one? I think I need a few minutes walking in the woods." Anne's voice was trembling. Joseph could see that she was fidgeting with her nylons.

"I guess so. What's going on? Are you having a hard time?" Joseph stayed in the bathroom; he didn't want to leave just as the warm water was starting to fill the shower area with steam. He rarely saw Anne like this.

"It's hard seeing your mother in that dress. I don't think I've ever seen her in anything but a floral print. Her eyes were so, well, so empty looking. She just sat in the living room, staring out the window." Anne's frown grew more pronounced.

"I know how you feel. Joseph said as he turned to check the shower. It was ready.

"The shower must be ready. There's steam pouring out into the bedroom!" Anne pointed with her right hand, which was holding her nylons.

"Yep. And you know how short a time that water lasts, with their twenty gallon water heater!" Joseph raised his eyebrows and gestured toward the shower. Anne smiled, but not for long.

"Get in there!" She said as she turned. Joseph shut the door and entered the shower.

Showering gave way to drying. Joseph pulled clean

underwear and socks out of his suitcase and placed them on the bed. As he was dressing he remembered that he had to say a few words at the funeral mass. He shook his head as he tried to bring together all of the jumbled thoughts and emotions. From the pocket of his suitcase he pulled out a slightly wrinkled piece of paper, something he didn't want to forget. On the airplane to Maine Joseph had written down some kind of eulogy speech. He didn't know if he could have done better, or worse, but he knew he had to write something down.

Almost reverently, Joseph folded the paper into thirds, walked to the closet door, and tucked it into his suit coat inner pocket. As he turned away from the closet he decided he should look it over one time, while the emotions were still under control. He dreaded how he'd feel in two hours.

He unfolded the paper and started to read it, to himself, in a whisper:

On the plane flight here from California I decided to write some memories of my father down. I wanted all of us to remember Paul Marino.

He was my dad. He was my mother's husband. He was the grandfather to my two children, and my son is named after him. But don't you think he was more than just that?

Many here today know that he worked on the cars that you owned over the years. Many people didn't know that he fought in World War I, the war he called 'The Great War". But he was more! Just seeing him as those things would rob him of the very nature of who he was. We need more insights into his world.

Well, he was thrifty with his money. He liked to have his tools neatly organized. He always wore plaid shirts. He ate shredded wheat for breakfast, and sometimes oatmeal. But have we done him justice now? No. There is still something missing. How can I share with you about who he was inside?

I could tell you about how he got angry with me when I unwrapped one of the Christmas presents set aside for my mother, in front of her. I must have been three.

I could also tell you about how he brought me comfort when my little dog Braun died. My father's big, wrinkled hands rubbed my hair and neck. He said he understood because he was about the age I was back then when his dog had died. I can still close my eyes and see the one tear coming down his cheek, and the far-away stare that he had.

I can remember how he cried as we stood in the vestibule of this very church, waiting for the signal to move over to the altar on my wedding day. His big, wrinkled left hand grabbed my upper arm with an iron grip that day. It was a struggle for him, but he said three words. I love you. He didn't say that phrase much in his life, but when he did, he meant it.

He took care of all of us in the family, from me to the cat he adopted and kept in the garage for years. He told my mother that it was a stray, but it wasn't. Sorry to break this to you, but he wanted that cat, Ma.

I guess this helps us to see who he really was. All of these memories were of him as an adult, though. We shouldn't forget that he was a child, once. Not too many here today can see him as one. I can't. My mother can. He's home with his Ma and Dad today, and one of his sisters. I hope they're picking flowers in the woods behind their house right now, like they used to. I remember him crying as he talked of his mother once.

He had a childhood, and a family few of us really knew. There was one incident that really let me see Paul Marino the little boy. I need to share it with you, because I'm the only one who ever saw it. It was at breakfast about four years ago. During the last time I visited with him I was surprised to find him late one morning eating a bowl of cereal in the living room. I had gone out to that room to use the one telephone in the house. I was startled. He was smiling, and occasionally laughing, at a cartoon character on the television set. He almost didn't notice me as I picked up the phone. I shook my head and chuckled as I dialed home. During that talk with my wife that long ago morning I could   hear my children laughing in the background. When I asked her what was going on, she reminded me that it was Saturday morning and the kids were eating breakfast by the television, watching cartoons. I turned and watched him for a long minute. It was as if he was in the same room as my Paul and Sarah. He was able to surprise me even in the last few years of his life.

Could this be what I wanted to tell you? Maybe so. I'm afraid to step down from this podium, in fear that I missed something important that you needed to know about him. I hope you'll allow me to continue this eulogy over the years to come, as I live the rest of my life as a testimony to his wisdom, his strength, his hopes, his dreams, and his weaknesses.

You see, I guess much of what I am today, good and bad, is his handiwork.

I miss you, Dad. I'll always be your little buddy Joey!

Joseph pulled a pen out of his coat pocket and added a phrase to the speech:

I got the note, Dad. I love you, too.

"Going over the eulogy speech I saw you writing on the plane?" Anne rubbed Joseph's arm.

"Uh, yeah." Joseph replied, unable to say more.

"Wanna take a walk, Joey?" Anne smiled.

"I think I need to now." Joseph whispered.

As Joseph and Anne walked out the back door, Joseph stopped his wife and pointed down.

"Is this the sort of walkway you want in your garden?" He asked. Anne looked down and smiled.

"Someday, maybe. Maybe from the garden to the side

gate." She replied.

Just as they turned toward the garage, Paul the Younger walked up and pushed something into his mother's hand. Anne looked at her son with a look that visually shouted confusion.

"What's this, Paul?" Anne's eyebrows were pulled down in the middle, over her nose. Joseph leaned over to see what she was holding. He couldn't quite see what it was. It appeared to be a small, white jewelry box, the kind Joseph received whenever he bought a small item of jewelry for Anne.

"I found it in the garage. It looks like one of your weird gray stones." Paul shook his head. Anne opened the box and pulled back the paper.

"It looks like what?" Joseph felt his eyebrows push up in the middle. He started to panic. At that moment Anne pulled a small, gray object out of the box.

"A pearl! Where did you get it in the garage?" Anne smiled.

"It was in that old woody car. Grandma said I could sit in it." Paul turned and smiled at his grandmother.

"Can't you leave something alone when something doesn't belong to you?" Joseph growled. He had planned exactly what to say to Anne when he gave her the latest addition to her pearl necklace. Now it was ruined. His own son had given the pearl to his wife!

"Hey, Dad, back off! I thought it would be better to

bring it into the house. You can't leave jewelry sitting inside an old car in a garage " Paul frowned.

"Joseph! Paul! Please don't fight!" Joseph's mother scolded. Joseph was still staring at his son.

"Sometimes, Paul, the best way to deal with a situation is to NOT deal with the situation! You've got to leave things alone!" Joseph shouted. Sarah stepped away and started walking toward the front of the house. Joseph's mother stepped back as she grabbed Paul's arm.

"Joseph! Shh! Please! It's not worth it! Remember what day this is! It's fine. I have it, and I like it just fine!" Anne showed him the pearl.

"You're doing it again. Shielding him from taking responsibility for what he's done." Joseph grumbled.

"Joseph, I am not. I just don't want a fight. Not today." Anne shook her head. Her eyes were pleading.

"So, you stand up for him because you don't want a fight." Joseph turned away.

"No!" Anne whispered.

"So, you and I fight instead of me fighting with him. I suppose that's much better! He gets off, we punish each other!" Joseph pointed at Paul. Anne looked at her son and shook her head.

"No." Anne said.

"I don't think you get it. He doesn't think things through. My window back home is ruined because he couldn't think his actions through first. Now this. Every week it's one thing or another." Joseph briskly walked off toward the garage. He had saved this particular pearl for a special moment, to remember something that was a milestone in their lives. Ever since he had given her the original pearl, a discolored specimen, early in their marriage he had found another one that was just right for each memorable occasion. Each pearl was just a bit flawed, each one discolored a little differently. There was a pearl for the births of their children. Another one came along to mark the deaths of her parents. Buying their first home meant getting a new pearl.

But each presentation had been in a unique situation. Each time it went flawlessly, like it had been well planned. Now, after more than a dozen pearls, something went wrong, and on one of the toughest emotional days of his life. It was Paul's fault.

"Joseph...please!" Anne was trying to catch up to him.

"Please what?" Joseph said gruffly, refusing to look around.

"Don't leave me alone. Not on a day like today. Don't do this. We can't get through this alone. Don't let this stand between us." Joseph stopped just in front of the entrance to the garage. He could tell that Anne was crying by the ebbs and flows of her voice.

"Anne, I wanted you to connect that pearl with my father's old Chevy. I had it placed just right inside the car. I knew where you'd look if you sat in the car. But now it's just a box thrown around in the back yard. I needed to do this right, Anne." Joseph's voice tempered a bit.

"But I need something else. I need you to be close. I'm hurting here, Joey." Anne sobbed. It was always tough for Joseph to hear his wife crying. He took a deep breath and looked up at the old wooden shingles on the garage, partially covered with moss. Joseph knew in his heart he had to put aside the stewing anger brewing inside. He had to find a way. What was driving this rage?

"Maybe we're all really stressed, honey." Joseph's voice softened.

"We are." Anne whispered as she came up behind him. She put her arms around him, from the back, and put her head down on his back. She was still sobbing.

"Tell me." Joseph whispered in return.

"Tell you what?" Anne replied.

"I know you. Some thought went through your mind and sent you into a panic this morning. I can only guess this time that it had something to do with death." Joseph wrapped his arms around hers. She didn't respond with the spoken word, but he felt her head nod up and down on his back. He'd found the problem.

"Is it about us?" Joseph knew that she worried about their relationship a lot. Heck, she worried about every relationship in the family! He did sense that she was touching and hugging more than usual. Maybe that was his clue, he thought.

"Yes..." Anne's sobbing increased.

"Something you can't get out of your mind, but you're having a hard time saying it?" Joseph asked.

"Yes." Anne nodded against his back again.

"So, go ahead. Just say it. Don't worry. You know I'll listen." Joseph was trying to be strong. He felt a strong urge to play with the button near the top of his shirt. Anne's arms kept him from doing so.

"I know you'll listen, but there's no answer. There can't be, until it's too late." Anne's sobbing slowed down.

"So, what's the question that can't have an answer until it's too late?" Joseph smirked.

"Well, it's really two questions."

"Okay, so what are they?" Joseph was trying to be patient.

"Which one of us will die first? What will the one left do?" Anne sobbed again. Joseph took a deep breath and held it. He hadn't expected that sort of question.

"I don't know, and I don't know how to find out..." Joseph whispered.

"Only when it is too late..." Anne said.

Joseph turned his head as he heard an ambulance siren in the distance. He took a deep breath as he realized it wasn't heading in their direction.

"Only when it's too late..." Joseph repeated.

Chapter 20

Joseph studied the trees in the little park across the street from the church as he waited on the sidewalk for the hearse to pull into the proper position for the unloading of the casket. So many memories flooded into his mind.

The tree just across the street was the pine that he and Petey had tried to climb one Sunday while waiting for his parents after church services. An old man had scolded them about how small the tree was and had lectured them on the foolishness of asking too much of a little tree. That's how the trunks were warped, he had said. The tree was a solid, dominating, shadow-casting pine now. As Joseph followed the trunk from the ground up, he noticed a bit of a "kink" in it. About one-third of the way up. He shook his head, telling himself that he hadn't done that. Joseph looked again. Even if he had bent the tree all those years ago, and the current "kink" was the result, the tree was firmly rooted now, and looked as if it would last forever. Joseph knew better, though.

Beyond the tree, next to a walkway, was the old water fountain Joseph used to wash his hands in before crossing the street back to the church. So many games of tag ended there. So many splashes of water from that fountain had hit little Joey in his face back then. Joseph was surprised that water still gushed forth, though unevenly. The stone sides of the fountain seemed more worn now, and less colorful. Joseph wondered if this was the price for anything or anyone who hung around this Earth too long.

A sudden slam of a door returned Joseph to the task at hand. He turned his head and saw the gleaming brass handle that was firmly attached to the head of his father's casket. A strange, eerie feeling overpowered Joseph. It was as if everything was blurring into a fog. Nothing was clear anymore, except the shiny, golden brass handle. He couldn't seem to recognize faces, voices or any of the other items around him.

"Joseph, as his son, you should have the place of honor, in front." A Voice that should have been familiar, somehow, whispered.

"Uh-huh." Joseph nodded as he stepped forward. He stared at the handle.

"Joseph? Go ahead and grab the handle with your right hand. Good." The voice continued. Joseph slowly reached out for the handle. It seemed as if it was far, far out of his reach.

"You've got it, just squeeze your fingers and you'll be fine." The Voice sounded relieved.

The metal of the handle was cold. Too cold, Joseph thought. His arm seemed suspended in time and space. He wasn't sure he could lift the casket. Just then the Voice continued.

"Now, first, we'll all just lift as high as our belts first. Don't worry, it won't be too heavy." The Voice said, but Joseph was unsure. He pulled, and the box seemed to float upward. The Voice spoke again.

"Good. Now, step back four paces. Yes, good." Joseph just did as he was told. He looked up and into the Mouth that spoke the Voice. Whatever the Voice told him to do, he would just do.

"Now, we have to turn to the right. The men in the back will just turn slowly. Men in front, step to the right until I tell you to stop." Joseph was mesmerized by how softly and gently the Voice was speaking. He looked down and realized that the casket wasn't as heavy as he thought it would be.

"You're doing just fine. Now we have to walk forward three paces, then stop." The Voice continued. Joseph counted out three steps. He looked forward and saw the steps to the church in front of him.

"Very good. Now we have to go up the five steps to the church. Let's keep the casket level as we go up. Men in front, lower your arms a bit as you step up. Men in the rear, you'll have to pull up to your belt level, and a bit higher." Joseph noticed that the Voice took a deep breath. He lowered his right arm a little bit more as he went up each step.

"Excellent. We're almost there. Very good, men." The Voice sounded more and more tired.

"We'll just go in through the double doors, and walk down the aisle of the church. Just one foot in front of the other. Nothing to it. You've got the idea. Keep walking. Slowly, now." The Voice seemed to add a new phrase of encouragement with every other step.

As they approached the front of the church, Joseph looked up and noticed the old, simple crucifix he remembered from his childhood. It was there when he had made his First Communion. His Confirmation was here as well. He stood on this place with Anne one bright day in October years ago.

Joseph tried to remember his anniversary. Was it the twelfth? No. That was another holiday...what was that? Joseph felt his mouth drying out. He couldn't remember the important dates of his life anymore! He was always so good at remembering dates. What was happening?

"We're there. Now, we have to slowly lower the casket on to the platform beneath it. On a count of three we will lower..." The Voice said.

"One..." Joseph heard the number, and tried to remember if his anniversary was the first. It had a '1' in the number, he thought.

"Two..." The Voice was quieter. No, there was no number two in the date he had married Anne. He was pretty sure of that.

"Three." The Voice said the number with finality. Joseph let go of the handle to the casket. The answer came to him.

"Eleven." Joseph mumbled. He had been married on the eleventh of October. He looked up at the crucifix.

"It's alright, Joseph." The Voice whispered. Joseph looked at his arm, where someone was holding it. It was gently pulling him to the left.

"Come sit with me, honey." Another voice said. It was a very familiar female voice. Joseph looked to his left as he sat down.

"Anne?" He asked.

"It's fine, Joey. You did just fine." Anne said as she squeezed his arm.

Joseph turned toward the front and watched the priest enter from the side of the altar area. He instinctively moved his right arm to his forehead as he heard the priest say the words that were so familiar to him.

"In the name of the Father..." Joseph felt his right arm drop toward the middle of his jacket, as if it knew what to do. Joseph repeated the word 'father' to himself.

"...and in the name of the Son..." It was strange. Joseph's right arm pulled upward toward the point of his shoulder. He whispered the word 'son'.

"...and in the name of the Holy Spirit."

Images and phrases floated in and out of Joseph's mind as the funeral mass progressed. Panic welled up from time to time. He wasn't sure where he was, and why he was there. Every so often he caught sight of his father's casket, and then he knew why he was there, and that felt even worse. He felt someone pull at his left arm.

"It's your turn, Joey. Your turn to talk..." Anne whispered. He looked from her face out to the aisle, stood and made his way to the front of the church. He stood, silently, on the lower step of the altar, not sure where to go. A young boy, dressed in a long, white robe, led him to a podium to one side of the altar.

Joseph remembered a piece of paper that he had put into his pocket, and reached in for it. There was nothing there. Joseph licked his lips slowly as he looked out on the crowd gathered before him. Slowly he moved his hand to the other side of his jacket, and felt relief when he touched the paper within. He lifted the paper form the inner pocket of his jacket, unfolded it and laid it on the wooden podium in front of him. He adjusted his glasses, pushing them back on his nose. Someone coughed in the middle of the assembly. Joseph cleared his throat. It seemed so dry.

"Please forgive me. I wrote out a few words to say today, but I seem to be having trouble reading my own writing, not even with my glasses." Joseph smiled weakly. There was a light and respectful chuckle from the audience. Joseph realized the notes in front of him wouldn't help much. Panic welled up, and he looked to his wife, and he often did when he was frightened.

Joseph looked down at Anne. She was nodding and smiling; he knew what she would be saying to him. Of course, she'd be encouraging. He looked to Anne's side and saw his mother. She seemed to be staring to Joseph's left. He followed the line of her sight, and there was the casket.

"I wanted to say some things about my father. Well, actually, to tell the truth, there are some things I wanted to say to my father, but I can't anymore. I hope you don't mind, but I need to talk to my father today. It's my last chance. For so many years I saw him as an old man who worked and fixed things. He wasn't much of a man who hugged, or kissed you on the head, but he was my dad."

Joseph closed his eyes, took a deep breath and then turned to looked at the casket. As he opened his eyes there was the sleeping, silent face of his father, beneath the door of the open casket. He stared, hoping, somehow, that his father would wake up.

"Dad, I got your note yesterday. I can't tell you how much that piece of paper meant to me. I have it here, in my wallet." Tears started to flow down Joseph's face.

"I felt a little cheated, though, Dad. I couldn't say 'I love you' back. I'm afraid that you never really knew how much you meant to me. You were my hero. You were there to pull me out of the creek when I was a kid who only thought he could swim, but who was really too stubborn to listen to anyone else, especially you." Joseph took another breath.

"I was stubborn, but I love you. I've been sick all week about how my stubbornness cost us so many years of tension. I wish I had one of those years back." Joseph wiped his cheek.

"I was robbed, Dad, when you passed away. I wanted to let you to know that I forgave you for the nights you drank too much. Please know that you're forgiven, Dad." Joseph looked toward Anne, to see if he was doing all right. She was nodding.

"I've got to be honest, Dad. I wasn't robbed. I robbed myself of all of those years. We robbed each other. No one robbed us." Joseph sobbed lightly. He looked at Anne, who was looking down.

Sitting behind Anne were Paul and Sarah. Paul was staring at the casket. Sarah was, like her mother, looking down. Joseph remembered a scene from a few years before.

"Dad, I never could understand how my children could say 'I love you' to you, and hug you, yet we were so far apart. Please forgive me for being jealous of my own children and how they could find a way to touch you when I couldn't, Dad. But I'm happy that they could love you, and be loved by you. Maybe through them you knew that I loved you." Sarah looked up at her father. Joseph smiled at her.

"I know we fought over so many stupid things. I know you had your faults, like I have my own. How I wish I could go back and stop those stupid fights before they started. Now they seem so really foolish. I remember Ma telling me that I should choose my fights. I thought that meant 'go find a fight'. Now I see that I should have asked myself if the fight of that moment was worth it." Joseph looked at his mother and smiled. She wiped the corner of her eye. Joseph turned back to the casket.

"But, Dad, I wanted to tell you about a day when I saw you in a different way. Maybe you don't remember a few years ago, but I had come back to visit. It was that time when you and I went fishing. The next morning, I walked out into the living room and you were watching Saturday morning cartoons and eating a bowl of cereal. You were laughing, just like my kids laughed. You were eating sugared cereal, just like my kids ate. I even noticed that you sat up in your chair just like my kids did. Dad, it changed everything for me. You weren't a mechanic anymore. You were a kid again. I remember how you loved the Red Sox. Boy, did you curse them for trading 'the Babe'. But you still wore their hat to the local high school field to watch a game." Joseph folded his paper and lifted it toward his pocket.

"Dad, you taught me that when someone forgets to play, they grow old. I was ashamed to think that I never sit down and watched cartoons anymore. You were younger than I was." Joseph looked at Paul, who was nodding. Joseph felt the rise of a bit of anger, and then remembered his own words.

"I pray, Dad, that God will help me to understand what's going on in my relationships. I think you really opened my eyes that one Saturday morning. I hope you got to watch hours and hours of cartoons. I'm sad I never knew which one was your favorite."

"Well, Dad, I have to go now. I talk too much, you used to say, and you were right. I think I've learned that I keep talking sometimes when I'm scared. I guess maybe by doing this I can avoid something. Today, I can't avoid what we have to do here." Joseph pulled the front of his coat together, and then buttoned the upper button. Slowly he raised his hand toward the second button of his shirt, under his tie.

"You know, Dad, you used to tell me not to play with my shirt button when I was nervous. Just this one time I won't. It's okay if you win this one." Joseph lowered his hand and looked at his father's face. Slowly, out of his pants pocket, Joseph pulled out a small, crisp, clean light blue envelope.

"I wrote you a little note, Dad. I wanted to give it to you now. I found the envelope in your desk." Joseph stepped away from the podium and toward the casket. He opened the envelope and pulled out the piece of paper that was inside.

Dear Dad,

Thanks for what you wrote. I understand that you couldn't talk toward the end. Your words meant everything to me. Never forget that I LOVE YOU, TOO!

Love, your son,

Joseph

Joseph gently returned the paper to the envelope, and then sealed it. He opened the outer pocket of his father's coat, and stopped. He decided that this wasn't the place to put it. Even though it was hard to do, Joseph lifted his father's hand and slid the envelope underneath. Tears flowed. Joseph reached up and caressed his father's left cheek.

"Good-bye, Dad. I love you."

Chapter 21

"Come on, Dad. Why can't we just stay here?" Paul whined from the back seat as Joseph started the car. Joseph smiled as he waved at his mother, who was standing in her front window watching them. Joseph carefully and cautiously backed the car out of the driveway, into the street. He had remembered another scene similar to this one, when he was a teenager, and a new driver.

Joseph had only been driving a month or two when he had backed his father's old car out into the street, at the same time a local delivery truck was passing by. Joseph had missed the front bumper of that truck by only a few inches. His mother had been standing in the same place she was in now. He can never forget the look on her face as she saw the truck coming down the street. He had been watching her, as she frantically pantomimed and pointed in the window, instead of looking behind him. Joseph had always thought it was a bizarre situation. If she hadn't been making faces he might have turned and scanned the street. Of course, he now realized if he had just stopped the car and tried to figure out her signal everything would have been okay.

"Paul, I'm not going to explain it again. Your grandmother asked to be alone for a little while. That's all you need to know. Sometimes we have to think of the needs of others first. This is one of those times." Joseph turned to look at Anne. He gestured with his eyes toward the back seat. He was trying to signal that he was at the limit with Paul. The funeral and burial of his father had been enough for Joseph; he was out of emotional energy.

"Let's find something to do. It's been a hard day. How about taking a drive out toward Norway?" Anne smiled as she pointed west.

"Don't you mean Sweden?" Joseph smiled. He shifted the car into drive and moved forward, away from his mother's house. He watched through the rear view mirror as she turned from the window and disappeared into the dimly lit house. Joseph hesitated for a moment. He wanted to be there for her, but she had been very insistent. He sensed a longing in her eyes when she was standing in the window, but he couldn't quite understand it. If she had wanted them to stay, why was she asking them to leave?

"Nope. I mean Norway. The country where they fly one of your other favorites, the red and white flag with the blue cross." Anne smiled. Joseph stopped the car.

"Oh, no!" He exclaimed as he pushed on the brake pedal.

"What?" Anne turned to look behind the car, as if Joseph had seen something while looking in the mirror.

"I think I left that flag up on my backyard pole at home!" Joseph put his hand in front of his mouth.

"There's not much we can do now, honey. I don't think the Kingdom of Norway will declare war on the United States because of it or anything." Anne replied. Joseph had to smile at that image.

"I guess not. I'll stop and call Conrad. Maybe he can go into the back yard and bring it down." Joseph offered.

"Is it something you really need to worry about right now?" Anne asked.

"Well, maybe not, but...well, it's important to me." Joseph replied.

"I guess you'll worry if you don't. Might as well stop at the first phone booth and call. Just get it over with." Anne pulled the windshield shade down as the car turned to the west.

* * * * *

"Hi, Conrad! It's Joseph, back in Maine!" Joseph cupped his left hand around his left ear while standing in the phone booth. In his right hand he held the phone receiver. He hated how these old phone booths sounded like echo chambers.

"Conrad! How are things going back there?" The distant voice of his friend said.

"As well as can be expected, all things considered. The funeral and burial went smoothly. "

"I know how rough those are. Your Dad was a veteran, wasn't he? Was there a flag on the casket?" Conrad asked.

"Yeah. My mother got the flag. I don't know where they found a big old 48 star flag, though. I'm not surprised, really. Dad never flew the 50 star." Joseph adjusted his left hand.

"They still have them. Probably the local VFW or somebody found one for him. They still make them, for all of us old-timers who grew under the 48." Joseph thought this was strange. He thought the 50 star pattern was fine. After all, he thought, there are 50 states. Sure, he was born under the 48, but he liked the 50 star pattern better.

"I think the funeral director arranged it." Joseph offered.

"Yeah, probably. So, you didn't call just to tell me about a 48 star flag, I'm sure!" Conrad sounded nervous.

"Well, Anne and I are on our way to Norway with the kids and." Joseph was interrupted.

"Norway? What in the heck are you doing going from

Maine to Norway?" Conrad sounded surprised.

"Oh, no! I mean Norway, Maine. Not Norway the country. We have a town back here near my town of Auburn. It's called Norway. I think some old-country Norwegians settled there a long time ago." Joseph explained.

"Oh, I get it. So you called me to tell me you're going to Norway, Maine?" Conrad asked.

"Well, no. The town reminded me of my Norwegian flag." Joseph was interrupted again.

"But I'm not Norwegian. My family was from Central America." Conrad said.

"No, wait. Listen. I think I left my Norwegian flag on the pole in my back yard. I put it up in honor of us coming back here and visiting Norway before we left. I feel sick that it may have been up day and night since then. I wanted to ask if you'd go over and take it down. I wouldn't want to start an international incident!" Joseph was embarrassed.

"It's done. I took care of it yesterday. The flag's here in my living room." Conrad answered.

"Oh, good. What a relief!" Joseph physically felt better.

"I don't think there's much to worry about, though. I was stationed in Norway once. They're not the type to start a war over that kind of thing. They're pretty decent people, you know." Conrad chuckled.

"Right you are, Colonel! I knew I could count on you. I'm sorry, Conrad. I've been really stressed. It is kind of silly to worry about that." Joseph replied, with relief. He threw his old friend's rank into the conversation as a way of saying thanks.

"I'd say you're right, Lieutenant. Carry on." Conrad verbally put on his eagle wings.

"Carry on?" Joseph was not catching on.

"Yes. But not too much!" Conrad chuckled again. Joseph smiled when he realized he'd heard that phrase from Conrad just about every week since he met him. It was always the same. Using his best military demeanor Conrad would bark the order 'carry on', then soften to let the joke of "but not too much" slip out. Joseph could see Conrad's wink and smile in his mind.

A phone call without a pun from his friend wouldn't be right. It seemed like it had been twenty-five years since the two of them started 'playing military', but it had only really been five or six. Sometimes it was embarrassing, but Joseph knew he'd never trade one sentence of their silly banter for anything.

"Yes, sir! We'll be crossing Chocolate Chip Creek at fourteen hundred hours, sir!" Joseph played along.

"Secure the beachhead, Army! Just call anytime if you need air support, even for a flag!" He thought he could actually hear Conrad's smile.

"Thanks, Conrad. It was good to hear your voice today." Joseph said. He smiled. He wanted to tell his friend how much he had been cheered up, but decided not to. They said their good-byes and then Joseph hung the phone up.

* * * * *

"So, you worried about nothing, huh?" Anne asked as Joseph turned the ignition key.

"Yep. Conrad took care of it, like I should have known he would." Joseph replied.

"Chocolate Chip Creek is only a couple of miles from here. How about we stop?" Anne smiled.

"That was my idea, too!" Joseph smiled briefly. He liked the idea of visiting their childhood meeting spot, but the emotion had been tempered by the funeral and burial. Joseph steered the car back onto the highway to Norway and accelerated.

"We're going to a creek?" Sarah asked from the back seat.

"Well, a special creek. Your father and I met there, a long time ago." Anne turned to explain to her daughter. She saw Paul, on the other end of the back seat, throwing something out the window.

"Paul! Don't throw trash out the window." Anne's voice had an alarmed tone to it.

"Come on, Mom. It's just a gun wrapper. Don't get worked up over it." Paul grumbled as he slumped back into his seat and stared out the window.

"Paul Marino! DO not talk to your mother like that. She's right!" Joseph pulled his head back to be able to see his son in the rear-view mirror.

"Joseph, please. Just keep your eyes on the road. I can handle this." Anne pointed toward the windshield. Joseph kept talking.

"Paul, it's been a really hard day for every one of us. Can you help all of us out by just not back-talking?" Joseph felt his blood pressure rise.

"Yeah, sure. Whatever." Paul answered. Joseph didn't feel better about the situation.

"What's eating you, son?" Anne asked. It seemed like she had decided to take a different direction.

"Eating me? Nothing's eating me. It's just that nobody listens to me." Paul sat up a bit.

"Paul, right now we have to listen to Grandma. What she needs, she gets today. I'm sure you can understand why. We do want to listen to you. You probably hurt like the rest of us do." Anne explained.

"You mean about Grandpa? Sure. But I don't understand why Sarah and I couldn't have stayed at her house. She said I could sit in Grandpa's old car, and maybe start it." Paul looked out the side window. A boy was riding his bicycle on the other side of the road. He turned and watched as he rode away from them.

"I know, Paul, but she probably realized that being alone would be better for herself right now." Anne offered.

"That's not what she said." Paul kept watching the boy

on the bike.

"What do you mean?" Anne asked. Joseph looked at his son in the rear view mirror.

"She told me she just didn't want to see Dad and I fight over the car." Paul turned back around and faced the front. Joseph slowed down as they approached a stop sign. The car stopped.

"What do you mean 'fight over the car'?" Joseph asked. He knew he was tense. His grip on the steering wheel made his fingernails white. He wasn't sure he wanted to hear the answer to his own question.

"Like we fight over other things." Paul said in a monotone.

"Paul, why would you and your father fight over the car?" Anne asked, and then looked at her husband. Joseph waited for Paul's answer before moving forward.

"Listen, I don't want to talk about it. Let's just go." Paul sat up and looked out the side window again.

"Paul. I saw you talking to your grandmother out by the garage. What do you think she said? I want to know." Joseph was getting angry.

"Listen, she was telling me about that funeral guy, and how he came up to her after the funeral and asked about the old car, that's all." Paul gestured with open hands.

"The old car? My father's Woody?" Joseph was angry. He'd forgotten about how his old childhood enemy had wanted the old car.

"Yes. The Woody." Paul shook his head. Joseph turned to look at Anne.

"Anne, we have to go back. That snake Jimmy at the funeral home's probably already backing the Woody out!" Joseph was shaking.

"He can't, Dad." Paul answered. Anne and Joseph turned to face their son.

"Why not?" Joseph asked. Paul reached into his pocket.

"Because I have the keys here." Paul answered. Joseph felt relieved. He put the car into drive again and pulled forward, through the intersection. For once he was glad his son had taken the initiative and grabbed the keys.

"So, why do you have the keys, son?" Anne asked. Joseph turned to look at his wife. He was confused about why she asked that question. Anne had her eyebrows pushed down over her eyes, as if she was worried.

"What does it matter, Anne? Jimmy the Snake can't get the car now, so it's not an issue." Joseph replied.

"I think it may become an issue, Joseph. Remember, Paul is fifteen years old. Do you need to tell us anything, Paul?" Anne continued to look at her son. Joseph was looking into the rear-view mirror more often now.

"No, why?" Paul looked out the window.

"I was just outside the window when you were talking to

your grandmother, Paul. It makes sense now." Anne frowned. Paul sat up and looked at his mother. Joseph noticed that his son had a startled look on his face.

"You were eavesdropping? You were listening to my private conversation?" Paul was upset.

"Listen, mister. The window was open and I was throwing out the garbage. Besides, let's talk about that sales job you were doing on your grandmother." Anne barked. Joseph was concerned, but still confused.

"Wait a minute. What sales pitch? What are you talking about?" Joseph asked.

"Pull the car over, Joseph. I think I see what's going on here." Anne pointed to a parking lot on the side of the road.

"Mom! There's nothing 'going on'!" Paul protested. Joseph pulled into the used car lot, stopped and put the transmission in park. He turned to face his son, completely baffled by what was going on.

"So, why didn't Grandma want us around?" Anne asked.

"I don't know!" Paul protested.

"I think you know darn right well what I'm getting at. I think I can remember to the exact word the last thing she said to us before we left. Do want me to repeat it, or do you want to explain?" Anne growled.

"Anne? What is this all about?" Joseph asked.

"I know, Mom. I can tell you what they were talking

about." Sarah frowned at her brother.

"You said you'd shut up!" Paul shouted at his sister.

"Yeah, but what do I get out of it? Nothing!" Sarah replied.

"Enough! Will someone explain what in the hell is going on here?" Joseph barked. Suddenly the car was quiet. They were startled by a knock on the driver's side window. Joseph turned and saw a smiling man in a suit with a tie that definitely didn't match. He rolled down the window.

"Yes?" Joseph asked.

"Are you folks here because of our advertised special? I see you have a teen driver in the back! Maybe he'd be interested in a nineteen sixty-five Chevy! I can let it go for under two-thousand!" The man clasped his hands together and nodded to his left.

"No, sorry. We're just stopping to discuss something, that's all. We're not in the market for a car." Joseph started rolling up the window. The man shoved his sleeve and arm into it.

"I can see you're someone who drives a hard bargain. You really should test drive it!"

"Get your arm out of my window, and leave us alone. Like I said, we're discussing something personal here!" Joseph growled. The man pulled his arm back. One of the buttons at the end of his sleeve popped off as it pulled against the window edge. The man brushed the sleeve off and walked away. He searched the ground for the button and mumbled at the Marinos as he left.

"He looks mad!" Sarah exclaimed.

"Did it to himself!" Joseph answered.

"Well, Paul? I haven't forgotten why we're parked here. Shall I tell your father what I think is going on, or do you want to tell him yourself?" Anne had not stopped staring at her son.

"Okay! Geesh! Listen, it wasn't my fault. She told me about the burial guy..." Paul started.

"Funeral director." Joseph corrected.

"Joseph, stop. It doesn't matter what his title was. I want to hear what this is all about." Anne said.

"Okay, so I said it was too bad somebody in the family couldn't have it..." Paul put his hands up, palms up.

"So you asked her for the car?" Joseph jumped in, with anger.

"No! That's when she told me it had already been decided and was in the will!" Paul barked back at his father.

"You lower your tone of voice, young man. You're wrong, and you know it." Joseph said while angrily pointing. He was staring at Paul.

"Dad, I did nothing wrong. You and Mom are the ones looking at this all wrong." Paul slumped back in his seat with a defeated look on his face.

"So, what happened to the car?" Anne asked.

"It' mine. Grandpa and Grandma gave it to me." Paul

said in almost a whisper. Joseph's mouth dropped. Anne gasped.

"What?" Joseph asked.

"Dad, they gave it to me. Here are the keys." Paul waved the keys above the level of the front seat.

"Keys are one thing. Title is another, son." Joseph was finding it hard to control his anger.

"Well, she gave me this piece of paper." Paul pulled it from his back pocket and handed it toward his mother. Joseph intercepted it and then unfolded it.

"Damn! They both signed it over to Paul! Both signatures! I don't believe it! They did this long before he died!" Joseph handed it to Anne, then turned and faced forward.

"Joseph, it isn't Paul's fault. Your mother was trying to do it in a way that would avoid a fight. What I heard makes sense now. She was giving him the car." Anne studied the vehicle title.

"Thanks, Mom. Yes. That's exactly what happened." Paul exclaimed.

"Joseph, I'm sure there is a good reason behind this..." Anne touched her husband's arm.

"Behind what? Dad has a car. Now I do, too!" Paul explained.

"It's not that simple, Paul." Anne turned to answer.

"I think it is." Paul said. Joseph sat up and turned

around.

"Damn it, Paul. I've wanted that car for over twenty years now. My father knew that. This was a slap in my face." Joseph noticed that his hands were shaking.

"Joseph, please. The language." Anne urged her husband.

"Let's just get to Chocolate Chip Creek." Joseph grumbled as he started the car. He quickly threw it into gear when he noticed that the salesman was returning.

"Huh. I wonder what he wants?" Anne asked as they pulled onto the highway.

"I don't know and I don't care!" Joseph exclaimed.

"Probably this coat thingy here on my dress..." Sarah said as she picked up the button.

Chapter 22

"It's right through here, guys!" Joseph called out as he pulled a pine bough back, exposing a trail.

"Joseph, it doesn't look right." Anne said as she stepped over a stone in the path. Joseph scanned ahead, and nodded.

"You're right, but this is the only trail that goes downhill. I know it was downhill from that big rock. Of course, the little shopping center wasn't there back then..." Joseph shook his head.

"Why don't Sarah and I go wait back at the store? We could get a soda." Paul wiped his forehead. Joseph turned and stared at his son. He wasn't sure he wanted him along after the little news about the old Woody. Joseph seethed with anger, and wondered if this is exactly what his father had wanted.

"Oh, come on. It's only a hundred yards more. It's not like it's an all-day hike. We left the car ten minutes ago!" Joseph said with disgust. Not only did Paul have the title to the Woody, but he was also whining about a hike that was no longer than three hundred yards. He took a deep breath as he realized that this is probably what passed the pain from one generation to the next. He looked back at Paul and tried to remember that it had been the decision of Joseph's father and mother to give him the car, not his own. Yes, sure, Paul was happy to get it. Any teenager would love a 1948 Chevy! Maybe it would be good to let the anger wash away here, on Chocolate Chip Creek, he thought.

"Look! Joseph! The big boulder!" Anne pointed as her husband turned. In the distance, through the trees, Joseph saw an old familiar friend. He used to call it 'Grandfather Stone'. He had to smile as he remembered all the 'conversations' he had had with the old rock. He used to find answers here. Somehow, from inside, the answers always showed themselves to him when he was alone here in the woods. He knew there wasn't really any magic in it. He just talked to the rock and somehow the peace in his heart showed him the way to knowing what was right. How he missed that rock, he thought.

"Oh, yes. That's Grandpa, alright!" Joseph smiled. Joseph wiped his mouth, then pulled a handkerchief out to wipe his forehead.

"Grandpa?" Sarah asked as the followed the overgrown trail.

"Your father used to call that one 'Grandfather Stone". It's the biggest rock on Chocolate Chip Creek!" Anne pushed some tree limbs aside.

"So, is that little dribble of water your cookie creek?" Paul pointed downhill.

"Not 'cookie creek'. Chocolate Chip Creek. But I never knew what the real name of this stream is." Joseph broke through the trees and walked briskly toward Grandfather Stone.

"So why do you guys call it 'Chocolate Chip'?" Sarah asked.

"That's where your father promised to marry me." Anne said as she reached the stream bank, littered with leaves and twigs.

"So what's that got to do with chocolate chips?" Sarah asked.

"Well, I didn't believe your father. So I said 'prove it'. Remember, he was a big eighteen year old. I was just twelve.

My mother had told \me not to trust older boys! She told me to always get proof." Anne smiled at her husband. Joseph was able to smile when he remembered that moment, in spite of the fading anger about the car. He felt a softening in his heart. He was upstream, closer to Grandfather Stone. Maybe that was why.

"That's exactly what she did. So I asked her how I could prove it." Joseph returned the smile.

"And I told him to throw something valuable into the creek. Then I would believe him." Anne looked into the water. Stones lined the bottom.

"And you guys know how much I love chocolate chip cookies!" Joseph pretended to search the creek.

"What do you see, Dad?" Sarah looked concerned.

"Not much. Every time I come back here I look for those cookies! Some lucky fish had a good day back then." Joseph smiled.

"Well, some of us came prepared!" Anne reached into her large purse and pulled out a plastic bag. Paul and Sarah noticed immediately.

"Oh, cookies?" Paul stepped toward his mother. Sarah followed.

"I think your father should go first. After all, he lost three cookies here once."

"Five." Joseph said in a matter-of-fact tone. He walked over to where Anne was.

"Five?" Anne asked.

"Five. I remember that I had packed six, and I took one and ate it just before I threw the rest in. Only," Joseph looked into the plastic bag and selected a large, homemade chocolate-chip cookie, "I wrapped my cookies in my mother's old kerchief back then. No plastic bags back then." Joseph bit into the cookie and smiled. There was something soothing about a homemade chocolate chip cookie.

"Yep. Your father just up and threw the cookies right into this very creek." Anne smiled as she bit into a smaller cookie. Paul and Sarah grabbed one each and wolfed them down. Immediately they asked for another one. Anne looked at her husband, and Joseph nodded. The kids pulled two additional cookies each out of the bag and walked over to a rocky ledge, where they sat down and leisurely nibbled the cookies. Anne stepped closer to her husband.

"Who would have guessed that our kids would be here, eating those cookies, right where we started our relationship?" Joseph smiled and shook his head.

"I never would have seen it. So, was it the right choice all those years ago?" Anne asked tentatively as she looked at Joseph.

"We've had our rough times. But today, this morning, in the church, when I looked at you, and when I saw your smile, I knew there was no question." Joseph reached out and pulled Anne toward him.

"You did fine, by the way. You looked so confused when you pulled out that piece of paper. What happened to your notes?" Anne asked.

"I don't really know. It was hard for me to read. My eyes were so watery, and it was so hazy." Joseph looked down.

"I think you were in a bit of shock, honey. You looked so, I don't know, lost, or something." Anne whispered.

"I was lost." Joseph raised his eyebrows.

"No. I don't think that's the right word for what I saw in your face. Maybe you were just scared." Anne comforted.

"I must have mumbled and drifted like a lost drunk up on that podium." Joseph shook his head.

"No. You didn't. Everything you said was true, and loving. That's all that mattered." Anne looked at her husband's mouth.

"It probably made no sense." Joseph pulled at a stick hanging from a tree branch.

"What you said was from the heart, and that's all that mattered." Anne consoled her husband. She put her right index finger in front of his lips.

"Thanks." Joseph whispered. Anne moved Joseph's chin toward the large rock overlooking the whole scene.

"I remember one time I actually caught you talking to Grandfather Stone. Remember?" Anne smiled. Joseph felt his cheek blush.

"Oh, I keep trying to forget, but someone keeps reminding me!" Joseph smiled.

"Do you remember what you were saying?" Anne asked with a smile.

"Not really, but you haven't forgotten!" Joseph smiled.

"How about a hint?"

"Okay..." Joseph nodded.

"Our wedding. The day after. Driving down that road." Anne pointed back toward where their car was.

"Yeah..." Joseph was still not sure.

"You had to tell Grandfather something?" Anne flashed her wedding ring at her husband.

"Oh, yeah! 'We're married, Grandpa!'" Joseph blushed.

"Yep!" Anne said as she turned and looked up.

"Well, it's your turn, then!" Joseph pointed upward.

"Well, we're back, Grandfather Stone!" Anne said in a loud voice

"Is that it?" Joseph pretended to be disappointed.

"Okay, then...AND WE BROUGHT KIDS! How's that?" Anne had a large smile on her face.

"Better...!" Joseph chuckled.

"What? What did you say?" Paul called out to his mother.

"She was just talking to the rock, Paul! That's how your mother is!" Joseph winked and gestured with his head.

"So, what would we tell Grandpa about all the things

and people and dreams in our lives now?" Anne pointed at the old rock.

"Let's see." Joseph looked at the massive piece of glacial debris. There was so much to talk about.

"Well, we could tell him that we're trying to build a little cabin in the mountains." Joseph shrugged.

"That's good. How about our house, and the garden?" Anne added.

"Yep. That works. Joseph agreed. Just then Anne stood up a bit straighter; she was staring at the upper ledge of the rock.

"Hey, remember when you scratched our initials on Grandpa's shoulder?" Anne spoke up and pointed.

"Oh, yes I do! I still have the stick back home in the garage!" Joseph laughed.

"I remember! You couldn't quite reach where you wanted to scratch our initials, and you tied the little rock onto a stick with one of your shoelaces!" Anne smiled.

"Let's go see if they're still there!" Joseph slapped his thigh and walked toward the large stone.

"Yes!" Anne followed.

"Can we just stay here this time?" Sarah called out.

"Sure. Only real Maine kids are allowed on Grandfather Stone!" Joseph smiled broadly. The two climbed the left side of the rock, stopping every now and then to study the rock's face.

"Hey, you kept the stick, but whatever happened to the little stone that you actually used to scratch into the big rock? Anne asked.

"You don't remember? Just as I finished scratching our initials in the stone broke through the shoelaces and fell deep into the large crack on the side of Grandfather Stone." Joseph reached up for a handhold. He looked to his right.

"Wait a minute. I think it's right there, Anne!" Joseph pointed into a crack in the face.

"Where?" Anne held on to her husband.

"Just under that crack. I remember that I did it there, where it would be protected by the little overhang." Joseph squinted to see if he could read anything.

"Well, can you read anything?" Anne asked.

"I think so. Right next to ours is a clear set of initials. See them? They say E plus C." Joseph pointed.

"Okay. I see those. They're clear." Anne replied.

"Now look to the left."

"I see it! J plus A! It's still there!" Anne giggled.

"Hey, when I scratch 'em in, they stay scratched in!" Joseph let out a little laugh of his own.

"We're still here on Chocolate Chip Creek, Joey!" Anne put her head on her husband's shoulder.

"We'll always be here, no matter what." Joseph reached up and caressed Anne's chin.

"Let's make a new promise here, Joey." Anne looked

up at Joseph.

"What kind of promise?"

"If anything should ever separate us, we'll meet here."
Anne said quietly. There was a tear on her face.

"You mean, what we talked about yesterday? About
one of us being left?" Joseph whispered. Anne nodded.

"That's what I mean." She said.

"We'll meet here, then. We'll stay here." Joseph
whispered again. He leaned over and kissed Anne on the
forehead. She looked into his eyes, and he felt strong tears
well up. Her blue eyes always got brighter whenever she
cried. Looking into her eyes was like looking into the blue of
the sky itself today, he thought.

"Here." Anne mouthed, with no sound.

"Forever. Here on Chocolate Chip Creek." Joseph
mouthed in return, tears in his eyes.

Chapter 23

Joseph took a deep breath as he turned the key in the
car to shut off the engine. He wasn't as angry as he had been
a couple of hours earlier, but he needed to talk to his mother
about why she had given the car to Paul. He shook his head
when he thought of the logistics of getting the old car back to
California. There were no two ways about it to Paul. Paul had
to have the car back home. Joseph had been prepared to

leave the car in the garage in his mother's house for another year, and then have it shipped to California. He figured it would take a year to scrape together the money to ship it. Now this. And it had to be settled tonight. They were scheduled to leave the day after tomorrow.

Joseph remained in the car as Anne, Paul and Sarah stepped out. He just sat, with his arms draped over the steering wheel, facing the front of the house. He considered how difficult this conversation would be. No wonder, he thought, she wanted to be alone after the funeral. She must have figured that time would mellow him. Joseph smiled as he realized his mother must have planned it this way. She knew Joseph would be caught in the middle. She knew it was harder to disagree with a gift like this one if the boy was directly involved. Joseph pulled his arms down, opened the door and stepped out. As he turned, his mother stepped out of the front door. She was still wearing the black dress that she had bought in town.

"So, did you make it to your 'Chocolate Chip Creek'?" She asked. Joseph smiled a small, curt smile.

"Oh, yeah, Ma. We got there. It was nice." Joseph pushed the car keys into his pocket.

"It hasn't changed a bit! Our initials are still on the old Grandfather Stone, and the creek still looks the same. Everything's the same!" Anne exclaimed, almost in joy.

"Except for the little store by the road, and the

overgrown trees, I guess." Joseph looked at Anne and raised his eyebrows.

"Well, except for those little things." Anne smiled.

"Well, it was nice to return to our favorite spot." Joseph smiled again.

"So, you had a nice time, then? I'm glad. It was such a hard morning." Julie Marino said in a monotone as she glanced at Joseph.

"There was a little stress, Ma, and we have to talk about it." Joseph looked directly into his mother's eyes.

"Not tonight. I'm tired. I've made some pasta for dinner, and I've kept it warm for you. I made it the way you like it, Joseph. Meat sauce with rigatoni! Are you hungry, Sarah?" Julie looked at her granddaughter, then walked over and hugged her.

"Ma...come on..." Joseph gestured with a shrug of his shoulders.

"Joseph, let's have dinner, shall we?" Anne turned her face away from Joseph's mother and frowned.

"What? Oh, come on, Anne! We don't have much time!" Joseph whispered.

"We have enough time to have a nice dinner at home with your mother." Anne strained her eyes at her husband. Her facial muscles spoke volumes. Anne put her left arm into Joseph's right arm. It was a look Joseph had seen before, like when he had said no to Sarah going out on her first date two months ago. He had given in after he had seen that look.

"Okay. Fine. Dinner." Joseph tightened his upper lip, and the two of them stepped toward the front door. Sarah and Julie, arm in arm, followed.

"Sarah, after dinner I want to give you something!" Joseph heard his mother say. Joseph tilted his head toward Anne.

"Probably the keys to this house, I'd guess". He whispered.

"Joseph, stop!" Anne whispered back.

* * * * *

"Ma, that was too much. You really served it up tonight!" Joseph smiled, and then pushed himself back from the table as he took a sip of ice-cold water.

"Yeah, Grandma, it was great!" Paul said as he chewed on a piece of garlic bread.

"Hey, Paul! Either talk or eat, but not both at the same time!" Anne scolded.

"Oh, it's alright, Anne. I see him so little. I don't mind." Julie stood up and gathered a few used and empty plates in front of her.

"Did you make the bread yourself, Grandma?" Sarah asked, and then looked at her mother, who was frowning. She stopped as she was about to take a bite.

"Oh, dear, no! I just bought a loaf of French bread and doctored it up a bit." Julie smiled as she turned toward the kitchen carrying an armful of plates.

"Here, Ma, let me help..." Joseph stood up and reached for some of the plates. Julie turned away.

"You don't have to, really. I can handle it. It's nice to be able to cook for a family again." Julie replied. Joseph didn't quite know what to do, so he looked at Anne. Anne was shifting her eyes back and forth, from Joseph to his chair. It was an obvious signal, so Joseph sat down. His mother walked into the kitchen.

"Anne, we have to bring it up. Tomorrow is our last full day here. We have to tell her that we can't take the car." Joseph whispered to his wife. Paul stopped chewing.

"What do you mean 'we can't take the car'?" He said.

"This is for your mother and I to work out, Paul. You have no place in this discussion." Joseph said, not looking at his son. Paul pounded on the table.

"I don't? It's my car, so I DO have a place in this!" He growled. Joseph turned his head and glared at Paul. He lifted his hand and pointed at the boy.

"You have a place in this discussion when I say you have a place in it. You have no idea what problems this brings up!" Joseph said in anger, but he kept control of the volume.

"Yes I do know what problems this brings up. We have to drive the car four thousand miles across the country. That's a lot of work!" Paul stood his ground. Joseph felt his ears getting more and more flushed. Anne looked down at the floor, to her right side.

"First of all, it's more like three thousand miles, and there is no 'we' in this. Either your mother or I would have to drive." Joseph paused to catch his breath. Anne leaned forward.

"Joseph! Please!" She pleaded as she looked toward the kitchen. Joseph leaned forward toward Paul. Paul didn't move. Joseph continued to stare at his son.

"Anne. I can handle it. Listen to the facts, Paul. One, you don't have a license. Two, you couldn't possibly drive a three speed column shift. Three, the steering wheel is a lot larger than what anything you've driven with, considering also how little you've driven."

"Then we'll find another way to get it home!" Paul said, through his teeth.

"Yes, we will. Next year, if you can save enough money." Joseph leaned back.

"That's not possible, Joseph." Julie was standing in the kitchen door.

"Ma? What?" Joseph sat up.

"It has to go now. It's in the will. Your father wrote it up two months ago. If you don't take the car, I have to sell the car, and I have one bid already. Jimmy, the nice boy at the mortuary, has offered three hundred dollars for it." Julie pulled a paper from her apron pocket, as if she had prepared for this confrontation.

"He's not a boy, Ma. He's my age. You're joking, right? He didn't put that in the will, did he?" Joseph stared at his mother.

"He did. I have your copy of it right here." She pulled another paper from her apron.

"Do you have a contract with a trucking company to drive it west in there, too?" Joseph said sarcastically.

"Joseph! Your mother! Don't talk to her like that!" Anne scolded.

"Anne, I feel set up," Joseph decided to speak what he felt, "and I'm trapped no matter which way this goes. Listen, I either have to find a way to get that thing home, or let Jimmy the Snake take the car. If I let Jimmy take it, Paul will stew over it for years. If I drive it home, I have to face a week of driving!"

"A week? Joseph, it's only about sixteen hundred miles to Colorado." Julie interrupted her son.

"Ma! We live in California! We've lived there for years! It's three thousand long, dry, empty miles!" Joseph felt the need to walk away. He stood up and stormed out the front door. Anne followed.

"Joseph!" Anne slowly shut the door. Joseph was standing two or three steps off the porch.

"What?" Joseph barked.

"Slow down. We can work this out. I know we can.

There has to be another way." Anne whispered.

"Yeah. An accident could happen in the garage tonight." Joseph growled.

"Oh, no! Don't say that!" Anne scolded her husband. She folded her arms.

"Anne, I'm stuck. I'm trapped. No matter which way I turn, I have a mess here to deal with, and she manipulated me into it." Joseph pointed back over his shoulder.

"We'll find a way that will work. I know it." Anne said.

"Don't you mean that I'll just give in? Come on. This is the way she knew it would go. I'd be willing to bet that she even approached the Snake to see if he'd buy it, just because she knew darn right well that he and I can't stand each other! Of all the people in this town, why do you think it was Jimmy the Snake who put in the bid? Think about it! They gave it to Paul just to stick it to me, right between the rear shoulder blades!" Joseph shook his head.

"Then let Jimmy have it. Paul will get over it. Maybe we can tell him that we'll find a way to get him a part time job and help him buy a used car next year. That'll work." Anne offered.

"No way. That's how my parents promised it to me, but they could never deliver. I only got a car because I went off to college and found a piece of junk to buy. This was their way of..." Joseph paused as he saw something he hadn't seen before.

"Joseph? What is it?" Anne stepped closer.

"Oh, Lord! I know what he did!" Joseph whispered.

"What did who do?" Anne asked.

"My father! I remember how he looked one night when I yelled at him, right on this very porch!" Joseph turned and looked at the old steps.

"Yelled at him about what?" Anne frowned.

"I see it! Anne! It's not what I thought! Back when I was a senior in high school, I yelled at Dad right here, and I said he couldn't possibly understand how it felt to have no car!"

"So?" Anne raised her eyebrows.

"I remember what he said in return!" Joseph exclaimed.

"What was it?"

"I should have seen it! He said 'I hope you'll be able to give your son a car someday. You can't know how much I hurt because I can't give one to you.'"

"He said that? Your father?" Anne asked.

"Yes! Then he just walked away, into the trees in the back yard!" Joseph looked to his left and squinted, as if he was looking for someone. He heard the door gently being shut behind him.

"You made your father very happy tonight, Joseph." Julie said.

"Ma? What?" Joseph turned toward his mother. Anne

did the same.

"He never knew if you ever listened to him. He wondered. Seriously, he did!" Julie said. Joseph noticed a tear stain on his mother's cheek.

"If I ever heard him?" Joseph asked.

"Yes. It broke my heart how you two never listened to each other. You two just avoided each other and there was nothing I could do!" Julie cried.

"It's okay, Ma..." Anne walked over to her mother-in-law and touched her arm.

"You don't know how that hurt your father. He was a mechanic. His own son should have a car. He felt like he failed." Julie continued.

"But, Ma. Why didn't he just talk to me about this? We could have worked things out! There didn't have to be a 'gun at my head'." Joseph made the shape of a pistol with his thumb and index finger, and then pointed it at his head.

"Are you sure, Joseph? It sounds so reasonable now, when he is...he is...gone." Julie sobbed. Joseph realized his mother was right. The little note he had found in his father's suit in the funeral home seemed like a summary of their whole relationship. They couldn't talk to each other. Joseph slowly nodded.

"I suppose you're right, Ma." Joseph whispered as he looked down and scratched the back of his head.

"Joseph Marino, your father kept that car in that garage

to be able to give it to your son. He didn't want you to feel as low as he felt that day on this porch. Don't you think he wanted to buy a new pickup several times? No, he kept driving his old one so he could keep the old Woody." Julie pushed her hair back on her head.

Joseph nodded. He saw it all now, from his father's perspective. The money in the mattress was to keep his mother well after he was gone. That took care of her. The car would take care of the pain with Joseph. It made sense. It was warped, and poorly thought out, but it made sense. It was his father's penance for all the years of alcoholism. It wasn't much, but he could see that his father had to do it this way. It was the only way he knew how to do it.

"We'll find a way, Ma." Joseph smiled weakly, and then looked at Anne, who smiled back.

"So, how about some homemade chocolate chip cookies for dessert? Julie smiled back. From behind them they heard two teenagers answer.

"I'll take a couple!"

"Me, too!"

"I guess it's cookies, then!" Joseph walked toward the door.

"But you don't have to throw them into the cold creek water this time, Joey!" Anne smiled.

"Only into cold milk this time, Anne. Just cold milk." Joseph answered as he smiled faintly.

PART TWO

The Journey

Chapter 24

Joseph pulled on the handle, and the old wooden door stuck on the right, just as it always did. He smiled as he recalled leaning to his left as he raised the door. As if thirty years had not passed Joseph leaned to the left and the door gave way. The light of early morning streamed into the dusty clapboard shelter in the woods as if it were excited to be returning to its source.

There it was: the 1948 Chevrolet Woodside station wagon. Joseph just stood for a while and remembered how his father had called him to tell him that he had finally bought a new car for himself. He remembered how his father's voice sounded so much younger that day. He shook his head as he realized how many years had passed. Everything looked the same, but the back door was covered in a layer of dust. Joseph could barely read the old Maine license plate. He gently ran his index finger over the letters and numbers on the plate and wiped some of the dirt off.

The Maine colors back in 1948 were black, with orange letters and numbers. The colors were still strong. There wasn't much rust or corrosion on the plate. Back home, in 1971, California plates were black with yellow letters. Too similar, Joseph thought. He chuckled at the word

'VACATIONLAND' on the bottom of the license plate. Some vacation, he thought. Even the long drive to California wouldn't be much of a relaxing drive. Joseph looked up suddenly.

He shuddered as he considered the challenge of driving a twenty-three year old car across the country. How well had his father kept the car up? Would it be able to make the journey? A mechanic needed to take a quick look at the critical parts of the car and let him know, Joseph thought. He smiled when he considered the irony of having a stranger trained in car repair assess the fitness of an old mechanic's own car.

"Are you ready, Paul?" Joseph turned and called out toward the house. He heard the sound of tennis shoes gently scraping on the stone walkway outside.

"I'm ready!" Paul replied as he ran into the garage.

"We really need to have someone look under the hood, and at the brakes. If we're going to do this drive then we need to know that the car's going to make it." Joseph said.

"Yeah. I wouldn't want to get stuck somewhere." Paul nodded.

"Or worse." Joseph put out his open hand. Paul reached into his pocket and pulled out the keys.

"Worse?" Paul's forehead wrinkled as his eyebrows went up.

"Well, we don't need to discuss it. Let's just make sure

we've got as safe a vehicle as we can get." Joseph turned sideways as he worked his way to the driver's door.

"Should I get in? The other side of the garage is pretty crammed with stuff!" Paul looked to the right of the car.

"No. Let me pull out first, if this thing starts." Joseph opened the door and slid behind the wheel. He was amazed at how much cars had changed. There was so much more chrome on the dashboard back in 1948. The steering wheel was a lot larger back then. He smiled as he noticed the silvery metal ring inside of the steering wheel; it was the horn ring.

"Well, Woody, old man, time to see if you can still move it down the road." Joseph found the ignition switch. He inserted the key and turned it. Nothing happened.

"Well? Dad? Are you going to start it?" Paul called out.

"Hold on! I'm working on it!" Joseph tried to remember what he was doing wrong. He knew there was something else he had to do. He looked around the dashboard; there was no clue there. He leaned over and looked on the floorboard, near the gas pedal. There it was, a sort of a button. A starter button! Now he remembered!

"Is there a problem?" Paul asked.

"Well, there was, but I think I figured it out. I forgot that these things had a floor button starter. Let's try it now!" Joseph turned the key and stepped on the starter. The engine groaned, sputtered, and stopped.

"That didn't sound so good..." Paul sounded worried, Joseph thought.

"Well, it's normal for a car that's been sitting for a long time. Let me try again." Joseph repeated the procedure. After an initial groan, the engine roared to life.

"Hey! The old Woody still has it! What do you know?" Paul smiled as he exclaimed. Joseph watched his son through the rear view mirror. He had to admit it made him happy to see Paul enjoying this important moment.

"Yep, he's still got it!" Joseph shouted.

"He?" Paul answered.

"He. My father named him 'Kit Carson'. Hey, move out of the way! I'm going to back him out!" Joseph smiled as he studied the gauges on the dash. After looking into the rear view mirror Joseph grabbed onto the shift lever on the steering column and moved it into reverse. The car lurched back. Slowly it moved into the sunlight.

"We're moving, Paul! Hop in!" Joseph felt downright giddy. The passenger door opened and Paul eagerly plopped down on the seat.

"So, why'd he call this thing 'Kit Carson'?" Paul asked.

"Well, my dad thought this thing looked like a modern covered wagon, with the wood on the side. So, he named it after a pioneer of the old west." Joseph looked out the front window and remembered something else. "Of course, my father liked puns, you know, Paul."

"Yeah? Like what?"

"A kit meant someone's equipment. So he called it his 'Kit'. His equipment." Joseph explained as he turned around so he could finish backing down the long side driveway. Anne, Julie and Sarah were watching from the front porch. Joseph and Paul waved. Each of them was wearing a big smile.

"What about 'Carson'?" Paul asked.

"Carson? I guess it was just a last name, and a famous guy!" Joseph answered.

"Huh. I thought it meant 'car for son'." Paul shrugged. Joseph stopped the car and looked across to the other side. Paul was studying the inner door paneling.

"Huh! I never saw it that way! 'Equipment for my son!' I guess it could work!" Joseph truly felt surprised.

* * * * *

Joseph found the car difficult to drive, compared to his 1968 Chevrolet Camaro. While his car was easy to steer, and full of power, he discovered the old Woody was tough to turn and much louder inside. He sighed as he considered driving the old crate across the country. His arms would definitely feel like rubber after this trip! He worked the wheel to the right as he pulled into the little mechanic's garage that used to be owned by his father. The old sign was still hanging over the doorway: Marino's Reliable Automobile Repair Service. Joseph could tell that his father had never replaced that sign.

He remembered painting it as a teenager, in their back yard. There were probably seven or eight layers of paint on top of his original letters now.

An older, white-haired man wearing gray overalls and carrying a blue shop rag walked toward the car from inside the open garage doorway. Joseph rolled the window on the driver's side down.

"Hey! Isn't that Old Man Marino's Woody?" The man asked.

"Well, it was. Now it belongs to Young Man Marino." Joseph pointed with his thumb toward his son. The older man squinted as he looked into the car.

"You guys related to Paul Marino?" The white haired man rubbed the back of his neck with his left hand.

"Well, I'm his son, and this," Joseph again pointed toward Paul, "is his grandson, Paul. Same name."

"Well. I'll be. Now I recognize you two. I was at your father's funeral. I felt real bad about his passing. He really meant a lot to me." The white haired man extended his hand, as if to shake, then looked carefully at it and decided differently.

"How about we take a rain check on that?" Joseph asked politely, with a curt smile.

"Yeah, one of the problems with being the boss and the head mechanic. When I have to shake hands with customers, or go over to the bank to fill out papers, I run into this hassle."

The man smiled. Joseph felt as if he could relate to this man, but he didn't know why. There was kindliness in his eyes.

"You must be Tom? Are you the guy my father sold his place to?" Joseph asked.

The white haired man pointed down to the area above his own breast pocket, and then frowned. He looked down at a large oily blob on that area of his overalls. He wiped at the sear with no affect.

"Well, my name used to be sewn onto my overalls right here. Well, actually, it still is here, just that it's covered with grease from a leaky can I had to hold over my head for twenty minutes this morning! Yep. I'm Tom."

"I'm Joseph, and this is 'Young' Paul Marino. I grew up here, but now we're from California." Joseph opened the door and stepped out.

"California? Paul told me y'all's from Colorado." Tom looked confused.

Joseph smiled a small, pained smile, and shook his head.

"It's a long story. I lived there after I left Maine many years ago, but only for a couple of years. We moved to the L.A. area a long time ago. My father never liked the idea of me living in California, I guess." Joseph explained.

"Oh, I see! I think I understand what he meant. I heard that California's got some real strange folks out there. Fruits and nuts, they say." Tom raised his eyes, and continued wiping his greasy, oily hands with the blue rag.

"Well, about as many as any other state has, I guess." Joseph felt uncomfortable with the topic at hand. He was surprised how that expression had crossed the country.

"I suppose..." Tom looked at Joseph for a long time. Joseph licked his lips. Maybe he hadn't said the right thing.

"Well, uh, Tom, I detect a bit of a twang in your voice. You didn't grow up in Maine." Joseph pointed out. He thought this would change the subject.

"Nah, North Carolina's my home. Last year - no, maybe it's been almost two years now - my wife, well, she passed on sudden like. My daughter had moved up here with her husband and kids, so I was stuck alone. Her husband got some job with the county here. He's some sort of land use planner or something. My daughter called me and told me to come visit, so I did. Well, I drove through town, stopped for some gas here at your dad's old place, and we started chatting. He showed me his collection of license plates on the wall, and I noticed he didn't have a North Carolina plate. I told him I'd be able to get one for him, seeing that I run a garage down there. So, you see, he -" Tom was interrupted by Joseph, who was fidgeting with his keys and looking around. Joseph was sorry he had asked the question about Tom's childhood.

"Excuse me, Tom. I'm really sorry, but we're running a bit behind here. I'm wondering if I could ask a favor..." Tom interrupted Joseph.

"A favor? Why, heck yes! Just go ahead and interrupt. You see, I know I talk too much. A favor? You know, Old Paul Marino sold this place right cheap to me, and he stayed around for some time showing me the ropes, so I figure I owe him. 'Cept he's passed away. I guess I could help his family." Tom frowned and looked down.

"Well, that's nice of you to help. What we need to know is if this Woody's fit to make the drive out to California. I want to know if things are in good enough shape, like the engine, transmission and brakes." Joseph pointed at the front of the car, and then looked at Paul, who was watching two girls as they went into the small store next to the old garage.

"California? In a forty-eight Woody? Well, you've come to the right man, I tell you. I have a forty-eight pickup truck, and it hums like a top on a clear Sunday morning. Yes, sir. You know, if you took this thing to one of those dealerships out on the main highway they'd just stare at an old Woody like it was a German tank from Word War Two." Tom walked to the front of the car, and Joseph followed a step or two behind. Tom unlatched the hood.

"Just about how I found it the last time I worked on her!" Tom smiled.

"Well, I think it's been sitting in my father's garage at home for about a year. I don't think anyone's driven it for a while." Joseph looked at the engine.

"Nope. I know it hasn't. Your dad asked me to disconnect the battery about a year ago, when he was getting a bit sicker. He didn't want to run it down, he said." Tom answered.

"That sounds like him. He was always worried about his vehicles, just like you, Paul..." Joseph turned toward his son, but Paul wasn't there.

"I think your young stallion took off after those two pretty phillies in the store." Tom pointed.

"That sounds like him." Joseph shook his head.

"Or any other male about his age, I guess." Tom pulled the caps off of the battery.

"Well, I think I spent an hour or two in that same store, doing the same thing. They all wore dresses back then, though. Now they wear jeans." Joseph shook his head.

"Yep. Things change. Like your oil, by the way." Tom looked into the garage.

"My oil?"

"Yeah. Oil's a little dark. Hey, Billy! We got any more Quaker State back there?" Tom called.

"Yeah, another couple cases." A voice from inside replied. Joseph heard a metallic bang, then the sounds of someone cursing.

"Hey, watch it, Billy!" Tom scolded.

"Damn. Dropped the big wrench on my fingers!"

"Well, let's not scare the customers off." Tom smiled at

Joseph.

"Hah! I grew up in this old garage. I've heard worse than that!" Joseph smiled. He didn't want to admit that he had dropped a wrench on his own hand, and foot and arm. Joseph considered that he probably did the same thing at the same workbench Billy was using!

"Well, it's okay that it's you, but Billy's gotta learn." Tom kneeled in front of the car and slid under the bumper.

"The gaskets look tight. Your dad changed them about the time he shoved this old thing into the garage. Changed the hoses and belts, too. Yep, I can see. He did." Tom scratched at something vaguely metallic.

"What's that?" Joseph asked.

"Just checking the brake pads. He changed them, too. Looks like he put a few hours of work into this thing." Tom said. Joseph was repulsed when he noticed a squirt of brown liquid flying from under the car toward a bush nearby.

"What'ya think about driving it around the block and letting me know how the transmission and engine feels?" Joseph asked.

"I guess I could, but I have to tell you that I rebuilt the transmission myself last year. Did it shift poorly, or something?" Tom slid out from under the car.

"No, actually I was surprised at how smooth and tight it was." Joseph shook his head.

"Was it hard starting?" Tom started wiping his hands

again.

"No, considering it sat in the garage for a year. Hey, wait a minute. Did you say you disconnected the battery a year ago?" Joseph was puzzled. He didn't remember reconnecting it. Tom leaned in, under the hood.

"Yep. It looks like it was re-connected recently, I'd say." Tom answered.

"Huh. I don't think my mother did it. She's never liked touching cars.

"Well, it's back together, so it really doesn't matter, does it?" Tom said. Joseph could swear that Tom was sending a message that this line of talk was over. Tom had tilted his head forward and was staring at Joseph. He was no longer smiling. Joseph changed the subject.

"So, about the engine. I guess that's the biggest concern." Joseph asked.

"It sounded pretty strong when you pulled in here. I can check the timing and replace the spark plugs, if you want." Tom offered.

"Sure, I guess that would be fine. I noticed a little bluish smoke. I'm worried about oil burning." Joseph pointed to the rear of the car.

"If it didn't do that I wouldn't drive it!" Tom replied.

"What? Why not?" Joseph was concerned.

"Forty-eight Chevys are known for oil burning. There's an old joke about these cars. When you pull into a service station, the old mechanics used to ask if they could fill the oil and check the gas!" Tom chuckled.

"Fill the oil?" Joseph wasn't amused.

"Yeah, like the opposite of what you'd say normally nowadays." Tom's smile evaporated.

"Yeah. I get it." Joseph nodded.

"Listen, Mister Marino. I know this car. It'll get you there. It won't be as fancy as a nineteen-seventy-one Chevy, with automatic transmission, air conditioning, and some newfangled nice radio, but it'll get you there." Tom turned from looking at Joseph to studying his fingernails.

"Well, I appreciate it, Tom. Why don't you go ahead and check the timing and the other things." Joseph handed him the key.

"Sure. Can do." Tom refused the key.

"What?" Joseph asked.

"Nah. Your dad kept a spare key here, just in case. I'll use that one, and let you take it with you when you go." Tom smiled.

"Great...thanks." Joseph wasn't so sure about this check-up anymore. There was something about how familiar Tom was about the car that worried Joseph. He couldn't put his finger on what it was, though.

"Why don't you get a pop next door, and I'll take care of everything!" Tom pointed at the store.

"Sure..." Joseph slowly stepped away. Every few steps

he stopped and watched Tom as he worked on the car. What bothered Joseph was how Tom always managed to be looking at him every time he stopped.

"Hey, Dad! If we have time, can we get a ham and cheese sandwich? They have some good food here!" Paul interrupted Joseph's worry.

"Huh? Sure...sounds good." Joseph answered as he entered the store.

Chapter 25

"So, Mister Marino, I'd say you're ready to go!" Tom smiled and offered a hand to shake. Joseph looked down and noticed that they were clean, in a relative way.

"The timing?" Joseph asked. He extended his hand to shake.

"Right on the money. New plugs, too. I had Billy do most of the work, but I checked it all myself. Billy left a couple of quarts of oil for you in the back, for the first couple hundred miles!" Tom smiled.

"Thanks. I was thinking. Are there any other - how shall I say this - unusual quirks or things about driving this car that I should know about?" Joseph decided to get an expert opinion.

"Unusual? For a forty-eight Chevy, no. For someone used to sixties models, plenty!" Tom stepped to the car.

"Such as...?" Joseph asked.

"Well, you probably'll have to get used to the steering. And watch how loose the steering is. It seems pretty tight now, but only a couple of days on the road will tell for sure." Tom offered.

"Anything else?"

"Well, there is the speed issue. Pushing past sixty m.p.h. can be real hard on that engine." Tom raised his eyebrows and pointed toward the hood.

"Sixty? You're kidding! You're saying I should stay in the fifties? How can you possibly drive across the U.S.A. on the interstates at fifty five?"

"Simple. Avoid the interstates. Besides, there'll be plenty of holes in that system still." Tom looked up the street and watched an ambulance drive quickly by.

"Man, there goes the time. We'll be driving for three weeks!" Paul grumbled.

"No, Paul, you're wrong. It'll just slow us down a day or two." Joseph replied in a caustic voice and with a harsh, swinging gesture of his arm. He was frustrated. He hadn't counted on the speed limitation. Of course, he should have known that. His father had never driven it over sixty that he knew of.

"Hey. I was just saying that, not telling you!" Paul walked off.

"I see you're gonna be riding all the way across the

country with a surly teen as a shotgun guard on old Kit Carson, Mister Marino." Tom shook his head and spat.

"Yeah. I think dealing with the car will be easier." Joseph shook his head.

"I know that fixing a forty-eight Chevy is easier, even if parts are hard to find!" Tom chuckled.

"Yeah, I suppose so." Joseph mumbled.

"Hah! Yep!" Tom nodded.

"So, how much do I owe you?" Joseph reached into his back pocket for his wallet.

"Well, it comes to twenty seven fifty." Tom pulled a piece of paper off of the clipboard he was carrying. He reached into his pocket and pulled out two keys.

"Seems a bit steep..." Joseph was surprised.

"New plugs. Oil change. I checked it all over." Tom stopped smiling.

"I guess..." Joseph handed Tom three bills. Tom's smile returned. He handed Joseph the receipt and the two keys.

"Well, thanks for letting me say good-bye to Old Kit!" Tom said.

"Hey, you knew we called him 'Kit Carson'? It dawned on Joseph.

"Sure. Your dad called him that all the time!" Tom walked back into the garage.

Joseph waved good-bye and returned to the Woody.

Paul was already there, and sitting in the driver's seat. He had both hands on the steering wheel, and was staring straight ahead. Joseph cleared his throat.

"Listen, Paul. I'm worried about getting this thing across the country. Cut me a little slack, will you?" Joseph stood outside the driver's door.

"Can you cut me some slack, Dad? You were pretty quick to jump down my throat there." Paul replied. Joseph squeezed hard on the piece of paper that Tom had given him. He decided that this was not the time, and not the place, to go head to head.

"Yeah, sure. Now, move over so we can get going." Joseph said. His teeth were clenched.

"I'll drive." Paul announced.

"No, I don't think so. You have no license. This morning when I called our insurance agent he only put me on the policy for this car." Joseph took a deep breath, and wished that Anne were there.

"It's only three miles, Dad. It won't hurt." Paul was not moving.

"I don't care if it's three feet. You're not driving it." Joseph was having a hard time restraining himself.

"It's my car, Dad." Paul said in an arrogant tone. Joseph turned away and mouthed what he wanted to say, which he knew Anne would not like, then turned back.

"I have the key." Joseph replied.

"Looks like we have a standoff." Paul looked at his father. There was something in Paul's look, or in the way he said things, that gave him an idea. Joseph wondered if Paul could actually do it, either to start the car or to drive it. He decided to call his bluff. Besides, maybe Paul hadn't even brought his learner's permit form, so he could drive with an adult present.

"Okay, Paul. We'll do it your way this time. Here's the key. Now, when the police officer stops you, what license will you show him?" Joseph thought this could be the deciding moment. He was surprised when Paul reached up and pulled the driver's side visor down.

"I have my permit right here. Give me the key and we'll get going. Remember, Dad, we're running late." Paul stuck his hand out. Joseph paused a moment, wanting to slap that hand away, but decided to hand over the key instead.

"There you go, Paul. Let's go." Joseph grumbled as he walked around the front of the car. He watched as Paul, a big smile on his face, inserted the key and turned it. Nothing happened. The smile was no longer as strong.

"Did they mess something up, Dad?" Paul asked.

"You tell me. You're the expert." Joseph said sarcastically as he opened the front passenger side door and sat down. His door was still open. Joseph noticed a slight hissing sound inside the car. He rolled his eyes as he imagined Paul making another one of his stupid, meaningless noises.

"Come on, Dad. You could just show me how to do this. Yeah, you know more about it than I do. It's not like our car." Paul said.

"Would you stop making that hissing sound?" Joseph asked.

"I'm not making any hissing noises." Paul said emphatically.

"Right. Sure. Is the car out of gear?" Joseph asked.

"Huh?"

"I said, is it out of gear?" Joseph repeated.

"How do I know if it's out of gear?" Paul asked.

"What position is the lever on the column in?" Joseph just stared out the front of the car. He turned as he heard the sound of footsteps.

"Is there a problem, Mister Marino?" It was Tom.

"No, Tom. It's just that young Paul here wants to drive Kit Carson home, but can't figure out how to start it." Joseph smiled.

"Oh, that's easy, Paul. Here..." Tom opened the driver's door. Joseph turned to watch.

"You don't have to do this, Tom." Joseph said, angrily. He hoped the mechanic would pick up on the hidden message of 'back off'. Tom looked over at Joseph for a long moment, and then turned toward Paul.

"No problem, Mister Marino. Here, Paul. See that little

button-like thing on the floor?" Tom pointed. Joseph felt his face getting red.

"Sure." Paul nodded.

"Turn the key and press on that. That's a floor starter." Tom pulled back, away from the car.

"What about the gear, like my Dad said?" Paul asked.

"When it's in the position it's in now, it's okay. See it, on the side of the steering column?" Tom pointed and nodded.

"Yes. I get it!" Paul turned the key then pushed on the starter. The car roared to life. Joseph pulled his door closed, using the noise of the engine to whisper a few choice comments to Tom. The door was a bit difficult to shut. The door didn't quite fit the frame.

"Pull up on it when you close it." Paul advised. Joseph turned and stared at his son.

"And suddenly you're an expert?" Joseph asked.

"I'm the one who's been using that door so far." Paul answered as he adjusted the rear-view mirror.

Joseph pulled up and the door shut. He tightened his lips and didn't say what he was thinking.

"Well, let's see if you can get this thing home. First gear." Joseph pointed to the steering column.

"First gear? How do I do that?"

"Listen, Paul. I don't feel like teaching you how to drive a car with a column-mounted manual three speed transmission the afternoon before we leave here." Joseph tried to soften his tone, hoping that would help the situation.

"You never feel like teaching me anything, anywhere." Paul snapped.

"Come on, Paul. That's garbage. Look at how tough this trip has been. I had to bury my father this week, remember? Can you give ME a break this time?" Joseph worked hard to control his volume. He turned to look at his son.

Paul slowly turned and looked at his father. He lifted his hand and grabbed the key. With a flick of his wrist he turned off the motor.

"Okay. Later, then. Listen, Dad. I want to be able to say I helped drive this thin across the United States. All I want is for you to show me enough to drive it a few miles. Can you help me?" Paul asked, in a polite tone that surprised Joseph.

"We can do that, son." Joseph softened as he nodded. Paul handed the keys over to his father.

"Let's go home." Paul got out of the car.

Chapter 26

Joseph, with his right hand up on the edge of the large garage door, took one last, long look into the old garage he had spent so many hours in as a child. The old wooden structure looked forlorn and lost now, with the Woody out of it.

It was missing more than the Woody, though. He looked over toward the now-cluttered tool bench. That part of the garage looked so wrong. The tools used to be neatly lined up on the wall. Now only a few remained. Joseph had packed many of the tools into the Woody. He'd left an assortment of what he thought his mother would need to manage around the house.

There was one more thing missing. His father should be standing there, working on some old car part or broken clock. He closed his eyes for a second, trying to remember the old shirt his father seemed to always wear when he worked in the garage. It was a red and gray plaid woodsman shirt. For decades his father had worn it, and his mother had patched it, sometimes putting a patch on top of a patch. The shirt, too, was gone now.

Joseph turned and watched for a moment as Anne, Paul and Sarah worked with his mother to finish the loading of the cars for the long trips home. It was strange to think of 'cars', as in there was more than one. He hated the idea of Anne and Sarah driving to Boston and flying home without him. It had been a hard night as he had tried to come to an understanding with Anne about what would probably be a weeklong separation.

He shook his head as he turned back to look deep inside the home of his childhood bicycle, the place where he had fixed his red wagon, and the place where he had experienced some of the most difficult moments in his relationship with his father. The old garage.

"I may never see you again, old garage. Who knows what will happen? It may sound strange to do this, but I want to say thanks for protecting my bike, and so many tools that I needed over the years. I'm sorry about the big old dent from when I threw the hammer in frustration back in my junior year in high school." Joseph squinted as he tried to make out the gash in the ceiling that he had created.

What'ya say, Dad?" Paul asked.

"Huh? Oh, nothing. Just saying good-bye to my old garage. I have a lot of memories in here!" Joseph smiled.

"Looks like a lot of stuff, too!" Paul commented.

"Well, most of it belonged to my father. I guess this is his 'museum of Paul Marino's life'." Joseph swung his arm around in a grand sweeping gesture.

"So, what now? Who's gonna clean it out? What'll happen to his stuff?" Paul asked.

"Well, I sorted out a lot of the tools your grandmother might need. She's going to have a rummage sale for a lot of the rest of the stuff. I cleaned up what I could of the junk." Joseph looked over at the pile next to the side door.

"You know, Dad, please don't leave me a lot of crap to go through after you're gone." Paul trailed off, the volume dropping with each word. His facial expressions betrayed his fear of dealing with his own father's passing. Joseph saw it. He knew exactly what his son was thinking. There seems to come a time in every young person's life when they have to consider their own father's death, and it isn't a pleasant experience. Joseph remembered when he felt that way. It was as he left high school to go to college. In fact, it was right where he was standing. Joseph knew there was nothing he could say, and nothing he could do to soften the blow. He had to try, though.

"Don't worry, Paul. I'll work on it. Somehow I'll help you clean up my garage stuff. You won't do it alone." Joseph reached over and rubbed his son's hair.

"You'll help me clean up your garage stuff after you're gone? How will that work?" Paul asked.

"Hey, gimme a break! I'm making this up as I go along! I need some time to figure it out!" Joseph smiled.

"Well, I hope you have a long time to figure it out." Paul smiled.

"Me, too. Maybe it's simple. I'll write something in my will to have someone come over and help you clean it up." Joseph nodded.

"Just don't leave my son a car. It's been a real hassle, Dad." Paul said in a quiet voice.

"We'll figure it out, Paul. I'm not that upset about it anymore. I think your mother figured out years ago that I get over things after a while. I may get angry at first, but I can work things through."

"Yeah, you sure can get angry." Paul's eyebrows went

up.

"Well, I hope you don't remember me only for that, son." Joseph grabbed Paul's shoulder and squeezed.

"I'll try to remember the other things, too." Paul smiled.

"Good. There's something one can learn from just about everything. Remember and learn. Maybe someday this talk here will help you with some other situation in your life." Joseph pointed into the garage.

"Learn from a garage full of junk?" Paul frowned and pointed.

"Oh, yes. I learned something cleaning out my father's garage. Each item has a memory. Each item represented something in his life that was important to him. I realized that some of the stuff I threw out was meaningless to me, but I could tell he enjoyed having those things near him for some strange reason or another. I realized that, ultimately, we only share our daily thoughts and feelings with ourselves." Joseph waxed philosophical.

"What do you think he would say if he were able to see what you threw out?" Paul asked.

"What would he say? Hmm. I don't know. Maybe he would have cried over something or another that I threw out. I was wondering why he kept a lot of the stuff in here. Someday you'll have to look through my things; you'll probably think I was crazy for keeping some of the things that I did. But remember I had a reason for everything, even if the reason was emotional. Sometimes, I think, I keep things as a security blanket." Joseph nodded, as if he had discovered something important about himself.

Paul looked up at his father. Joseph smiled.

"You, too? I've done that all my life, Dad." Paul asked.

"Me, too." Joseph nodded.

"Well, at least now maybe I understand why that old stick with some words carved on it is hung over the door into the house." Paul nodded.

"So, you never knew about that, huh? I put that there the night we moved in. Maybe it has come alive now that you've shared Chocolate Chip Creek with your mother and I." Joseph said.

"Nope. I never knew. I just figured my father had some weird hobby. I thought you liked sticks or something." Paul shook his head.

"Well, I do collect flags. That's considered weird in some circles." Joseph smiled.

"Hey, I wanted to ask you. What happened to the rock you said you tied to the end of the stick? You know, because you couldn't reach the rock where you wanted to, you tied a rock to the end of that stick?" Paul gestured.

"Well, I did it because I didn't want anyone to scratch our names out. If it's hard to reach, it's safer. After I scratched the initials I just tossed the stick and rock into the river. It was your mother who ran into the water and got it back. But the stone was gone. We looked for it, but we couldn't tell which one it was. I just told your mother to pick any old stone, but she said that it was important to have the right one. Just any old stone wouldn't do. So, she took only the stick. For years I felt guilty for just tossing that old stick and stone into the creek." Joseph chuckled and shook his head.

"Mom seems to keep all kinds of things like that. I thought she was the only one who did that, until I saw Grandma's house!" Paul pointed over his shoulder.

"Nah. Don't you have any sentimental objects from your old girl friend? What was her name last year? Penny?" Joseph asked.

"Her name was Pam, Dad. I kept one or two things, I guess." Paul moved his leg back and forth, and looked at the ground. He looked nervous, Joseph thought. He decided that he must have pushed a little too hard, considering that the recent girlfriend just broke up with him, so Joseph decided to soothe the wound a bit.

"Then you and I understand a little about each other. That stick was an important memento of my childhood with the girl that grew up to become your mother." Joseph nodded toward Anne. Paul looked over at her and squinted. The sun was reflecting off of the chrome bumper of the rental car.

"Sometimes that scares me, Dad." Paul looked back into the garage.

"Cleaning out a garage?" Joseph smiled.

"No. That I'm like you. You're not perfect, you know." Paul raised his eyebrows and looked at his father.

"Me? Not perfect? Whoa! This is a revelation, to be sure!" Joseph touched the center of his chest with an open hand then smiled.

"I'll say he's not!" Julie, Joseph's mother, said firmly. She walked up and slipped her hand between Joseph's arm and his side.

"Hey, Ma. Come on, you're my mother. You're supposed to think I'm perfect!" Joseph pretended to be emotionally wounded. He rubbed her hand. He was startled to see how wrinkled it had become over the years. A rush of emotion welled up. He remembered enjoying ho soft and smooth her hands were, back in grade school.

"Sorry, son. I have to tell the truth. You're stubborn, you have a real temper sometimes, and you're not the best at finishing a job!" Julie pointed to the stack of boxes just inside the garage door.

"Ma, Dad piled those there!" Joseph protested. Julie put her hand up to her mouth.

"Oh, dear. I think you're right. I guess Joseph and his father are just too much alike sometimes!" She smiled in a sly fashion and looked out the corner of her eye at her grandson. She winked.

"As much as I hate to, Ma, we do have to go. Anne and

Sarah have to make the last flight out of Boston. The sun's getting higher, and time is not stopping for this family."

Joseph looked at his mother's face. A lump grew in his throat.

"No, dear. Time stops for no one." Julie looked right back at her son, and then put her head on his shoulder. Joseph felt the trembling in his throat first, then the tears as they meandered down the wrinkles of his middle-aged face. Finally, he felt his mother's rhythmic sobbing. They held each other for a long time. He rubbed her back slowly. Step by step he walked with her in his arms toward the old car, the Woody.

"Will you call me?" Julie asked her son.

"You know I will, Ma." Joseph whispered.

"He's going to call me every night, Ma." Anne added.

"So he can call me, too." Julie stated firmly. There was a hint of a question mark in her words.

"Every night, Ma. Promise." Joseph kissed his mother on her forehead.

"You'll be safe?" Julie asked.

"You know it!" Joseph opened the driver's side door. Paul walked around toward his side and then stopped by the front fender. He ran back to his grandmother and hugged her. Sarah followed, and then Anne, who held her mother-in-law for a long time. Sarah and Anne got into the rental car; Anne, behind the wheel, started the engine.

Julie walked over to the Woody one last time and put her palm down on the fender as Joseph started the engine.

She was crying; Joseph could easily see the streaks on her face. He felt his own tears start anew. Paul was silent, except for the stupid hissing noise he made every time the two of them got into the car. Joseph shook his head and reached out to touch his mother one more time. He found it tough to speak; he had to clear his throat.

"I love you lots, Ma. I always will."

"How long?" Julie smiled an impish smile. It was a strange contrast to the tears on her cheek.

"How long? Um, I always will, Ma." Joseph was confused. He wondered if he had forgotten something.

"You forgot." Julie faked a terrible frown. She pretended to hug herself, and something from the dark long ago awoke anew inside of Joseph.

"Just as long as Maine lobsters snap at little boys, Ma! I'll love you even longer!" Joseph no longer held in his sobs and tears. He shifted the car into reverse and slowly backed down the driveway to the street. Anne and Sarah, in the rental car, were out on the street waiting.

He stopped for a moment as he shifted into first gear. He just looked at his mother. He started to wonder if it was the last time he'd ever see her, but he quickly pushed that out of his mind. He couldn't handle that thought.

"Joseph!" Julie called out.

"Yeah, Ma?" Joseph had a hard time replying.

"Your father is with you, and Little Paul, in that car."

She seemed to point inside the car.

"And you're in my heart, Ma." Joseph put the car into gear and slowly rolled down the street.

Chapter 27

The Marino family retraced their route from Boston. They left from the little town of Auburn, went through Portland, Maine, and past Saco and Biddeford. They crossed the state line into New Hampshire just above Portsmouth. As much as Joseph wanted to stop at the little store in Portsmouth again, he knew they were on a tight schedule. Anne and Sarah had to get to the airport in Boston before dark.

Massachusetts rolled by, with Newburyport, Wenham and Danvers and Peabody signs marking their progress. Joseph knew they were close when he saw the signs for Revere and Malden. The sun was still up, but he could tell it wouldn't be for long.

The ride had been relatively quiet. Well, at least as quiet as one could expect in a 1948 Chevrolet Woody. Joseph had been pleasantly surprised at how well the car was handling. The steering was tight and the engine ran like a top.

Joseph drove and Paul slept almost all the way. Joseph made a mental note to get Paul into the doctor's office when they got home to have his nose checked. Joseph noticed that his son seemed to make the same hissing sound while he slept. He figured that maybe he had been too hard on his son. Maybe, Joseph thought, Paul wasn't even aware he was making the noise. Joseph had checked the radio. It wasn't making the hissing. The engine wasn't, either. Besides, it was definitely coming from where Paul sat.

Joseph decided there was nothing he could do about it. Paul's hissing was just one of those things. He shook his head and raised his eyebrows. There was always something about a teenager that rubbed him the wrong way. As the traffic got more congested Joseph checked the rear view mirror more often, to make sure Anne and Sarah were still following as they entered the outskirts of Boston. They had an emergency plan, in case they got separated. They would meet at the airline ticket counter an hour before the plane left. It didn't look like they'd need the plan, though. They were hours early, and the roads were clear and open.

An old Narragansett Beer sign made Joseph smile. It wasn't a beer sold in California, he thought. For him, that beer meant Boston College. He was proud to be a Friar, and he wished he could find the time to make a visit to the campus, but the open road called. He was more concerned about the many states he had to visit.

A little congestion consumed an hour of their extra time as they wound their way through the old cow paths of Boston as they headed for the airport, but Joseph was still able to keep sight of Anne and Sarah behind him. He felt a great relief when he saw the official airport entry sign. They'd made it.

Joseph parked the Woody near the car rental return area. He and Paul walked over to the airline ticket counter. They'd have to return their tickets and get a refund. That money would pay for most of the drive home, if they lived a bit frugally. With all business transactions finished the four Marinos headed for the gate.

"I have to admit something, Anne." Joseph looked out the window at the nose of the airplane parked outside. He was fidgeting with his shirt button.

"Joseph, leave the button alone. You've already lost one on this trip. That's the limit, so cut it out. I'll bet I can guess what you're anxious about." Anne reached out and gently pulled Joseph's arm down.

"You think you know me that well?" Joseph smiled weakly. He allowed his arm to fall to his lap.

"Oh, I think so. My understanding really isn't so magical. Look at where we are, and what we're about to do. I'm a little nervous, too, honey." Anne turned toward the airplane.

"I guess you're right. We have a long trip ahead of us." Joseph nodded.

"Trips. We're going on two separate trips, and that makes it more frightening." Anne corrected her husband.

"Yeah. We haven't been apart for a week much during

the last twenty six years." Joseph assed.

"It'll go by quickly, you'll see." Anne smiled.

"I suppose. I feel the same way I felt when I was twelve. Grandma Marino was going to visit a friend in Montreal, in Canada. I wanted to see Canada so much, but she said I wasn't old enough. I had to go to school. Oh, how I wanted to be all grown up, so I could go and see the world!" Joseph smiled and tried to remember the face of the woman he used to call 'noni'. He felt a twinge of sadness; he realized the more years that went by the harder it was to remember her face.

"So, why does this feel the same, here in Boston?" Anne asked.

"Well, I want to wish one week of my life away. Back then I told her that I wished I was twenty-four. She told me never to wish time to be gone, because we only have so much of it. Once it's gone, she used to say, your life is over. I hate to go against my grandmother, but I wish this week was gone." Joseph forced a small smile and looked at Anne.

"I understand how you feel. But just remember how good it will feel at the other end of the week. Wait...you think you can make it in a week?" Anne frowned.

"I will. I've already figured it out," Joseph pulled a map of the United States out of his back pocket, unfolded it and pointed, "Massachusetts, New York, Pennsylvania, Ohio. Indiana will be next. We'll go through Illinois and across Iowa.

After Nebraska and Colorado we'll be really close to home. We'll zip right through Utah and Nevada!" Joseph was happy with the route he'd chosen.

"Colorado? Across the Rockies in that car?" Anne was surprised.

"What do you mean? Of course, Colorado." Joseph looked at the map.

"That's really pushing it there. You know how those roads get there. Is there a way around Colorado?" Anne asked as she leaned over to look at the map.

"Well, the only logical alternative would be Wyoming, or down south through New Mexico and Arizona. Oh, it would have to be Wyoming! No way am I going to go across Arizona in late June with an old car that has no air conditioning!" Joseph shook his head.

"You've got a problem there. You could drive in Arizona at night." Anne offered.

"The lights on that old car aren't really that good, Anne. Maybe Wyoming is the answer. Heck, if it's really hot, I'm thinking Alberta, Canada!" Joseph smiled.

"I think Wyoming is the answer. It's relatively level, and the elevation doesn't get up there like it does in Colorado." Anne nodded.

"I think you're right. We'll do it that way." Joseph stared at the map.

"So, how much time will that take?" Anne pointed at

Wyoming.

"Well, I figure on driving about ten hours every day. From eight in the morning until seven in the evening, with some time off for lunch and things like that. We'll pull into a motel just before dark."

"How fast can you drive the Woody?" Anne asked.

"I think fifty to fifty-five is tops. I guess I'll use fifty as an average speed." Joseph slowly folded the map.

"So, about five hundred miles a day?" Anne asked.

"Yeah, I think that's a good estimate." Joseph nodded.

"And the length of the drive is about three thousand miles?"

"About that."

"So, seven days might be possible. I thought it would take two weeks."

"No, only a week. I figure we'd pull in on the seventh day. That'll give me one extra day, just in case we have a problem. Maybe we'll be early!" Joseph smiled as he reached out and squeezed his wife's arm.

"As long as you don't push it to hard and get into a problem." Anne frowned.

"Nah. Seven days. I'm going to just pace it out and get there on time." Joseph pushed the map back into his pocket.

"So, what about your trip tonight? You should get in at what time?" Joseph asked.

"Let's see. We'll probably get in around eleven,

California time. That'll be two in the morning here." Anne looked at her watch.

"Ouch! I hope to out cold in some motel bed in Worcester by then!" Joseph glanced at the plane again. He licked his lips.

"I hope so! Where is your reservation at tonight? You did make a reservation, didn't you?" Anne asked.

"Oh, yeah. We're staying at a Best Western. Here's the number." Joseph pulled a slip of paper out of his pocket and handed it to Anne. She folded it and slipped it into her purse.

"Do you want me to call? I know it will be late here." Anne's eyebrows were high on her forehead.

"Sure. I guess so. Yes. I need to know you're home safely." Joseph nodded and looked at his wife. She was frowning.

"Are you okay? You look a little nervous." Joseph put his left hand on her shoulder.

"I am. We're not so different about this, I think."

"We'll make it. We'll be fine." Joseph smiled, wishing he wasn't trying to convince himself as well. At that moment an announcement came over the loudspeaker system.

"Attention, ladies and gentlemen, American Airlines flight forty eight, from Boston to Los Angeles, nonstop, is now boarding at gate twelve. At this time all ticket holders who need special assistance, and those traveling with small children, are asked to approach the boarding gate."

"Hey, flight forty eight!" Joseph looked up at the speaker and smiled.

"So?" Anne looked confused.

"Well, Paul and I will be on an American 'Drive Forty Eight'!" Joseph shook his head.

"That was bad. Some puns are okay, honey. That one was bad. Just plain bad." Anne smiled. Paul and Sarah walked up from the window.

"Hey, Mom. Better get going. They called your flight!" Paul pointed at the boarding gate.

"That's okay, Paul. The first call is for people with small kids, and those in wheelchairs." Anne looked into her purse.

"That's what I mean, Mom. Sarah will need help...she's a small kid!" Paul bent over, away from his sister. He was lucky. She swung her purse at him and missed.

"Stop calling me a little kid!" Sarah said.

"Come on, guys. Enough." Joseph had to smile. It was both good and bad to see that they were recovering from being in Maine most of the week. They were becoming Californians again. Well, nobody's perfect, he thought. The overhead speaker crackled again.

"Attention, ladies and gentlemen, American Airlines flight forty eight, from Boston to Los Angeles, nonstop, is now boarding all passengers with tickets in rows one through twenty at gate twelve."

"What row are you in?" Joseph leaned over to look at the tickets that Anne had just pulled out of her purse.

"Umm...let's see. Row twenty-one." Anne licked her lips.

"It's going to be alright, honey." Joseph squeezed his wife's hand.

"I know. It's just that I've been dreading this. I hate good-byes at airports." Anne said.

"Well, then, we'll make it a 'see you', not a 'good-bye'!" Joseph forced a smile. He was trying to be strong for Anne.

"As if that'll help anything!" Anne showed a quick, nervous smile.

"I know. We have to be confident, for the kids. Someday they'll fly in to visit us with their kids." Joseph watched Paul and Sarah as they gawked at the airplanes taxiing outside.

"Now there's a strange mental image. Paul, with kids? I can't wait to meet that girl!" Anne smiled a broader smile.

"Or Sarah! She's so quiet!" Joseph studied his daughter. She had so many mannerisms, so many gestures, like Anne. He shook his head.

"So, will we still be in our house? Or will we move into that cabin you've been wanting to build for all these years?" Anne faced her husband.

"Hey, I will, someday. I mean it! I think up in Pine Mountain, where they're building that little retirement town.

That was nice." Joseph smiled as he remembered driving into Pine Mountain to look at property. He had loved how it reminded him of Maine, only without the humidity.

"Another project that won't get done, I think." Anne frowned.

"No, really. This one is it. It will get done. Besides, we need to plan someplace to retire to." Joseph gestured with his hands.

"What's wrong with Santa Ana? Why can't we stay where we are?" Anne asked.

"I think I'd like to get out of the big city. I know there are lots of orange groves around now, but it won't stay that way, Anne. Developers will plow them down and put up more housing tracts." Joseph looked at the ticket counter.

"I suppose you're right." Anne nodded.

"But then our kids will be able to bring their kids to Grandma and Grandpa's cabin in the woods! A little piece of Maine in California!" Joseph smiled.

"That would be nice. So, in Pine Mountain will you build me what you promised to build me at Chocolate Chip Creek?" Anne smiled.

"What I promised to build you? I don't remember. What did I promise?" Joseph frowned.

"Of course you don't remember. You were just pressuring me, and wanted me to say what you wanted to hear. I wouldn't say those three words you wanted to hear so much." Anne continued smiling.

"What three words?" Joseph asked.

"Well, one word had one letter. The next word had four letters. The last word had three letters. Do you remember what they were?" Anne smiled? Joseph shook his head. He vaguely remembered the incident, but it was lost in the long ago days of his teen years. He shook his head.

"You don't remember?" Anne put a pout on her face.

"Sorry. It's hazy. I remember the day, but it's been so long. So, tell me. What did I want you to say?" Joseph asked.

"I'll save that for just before I get on the plane." Anne smiled. Joseph was confused.

"So, what was it I promised?" He asked.

"A stone wall. You promised me that if I married you, you'd build me a stone wall just like the one my father had in front of our old house in Norway." Anne answered.

"You lived in Norway? I married a foreign girl?" Joseph flashed a mock frown.

"Oh, not again with the foreign girl stuff!" Anne shook her head. Joseph loved to tease Anne with the name of her town.

"Ooops, sorry!" Joseph apologized. No one believed him when he smiled and shrugged like that. The airport announcement system came on.

"Attention, ladies and gentlemen, American Airlines

flight forty eight, from Boston to Los Angeles, nonstop, is now boarding at gate twelve. At this time all remaining ticket holders are asked to approach the boarding gate. We'll have the last boarding call in about two minutes."

"Seriously, Joseph. Please. I always wanted a stone wall. Someday?" Anne touched her husband's arm.

"I will, honey. I know how much it means to you. And, you know what, I'll finish it, too!" Joseph nodded. Their eyes met. Their lighthearted banter dissolved.

"Always remember one thing from this trip. Please." Anne's gaze was intense. He noticed that her eyebrows were pointing up, just above her nose.

"I think I know what it is." Joseph whispered as he pulled Anne close.

"Chocolate Chip Creek?" Anne whispered in return. He could tell she was fighting tears. Her body shook ever so slightly.

"Chocolate Chip Creek. Forever." Joseph repeated in a soft tone. They walked over, arm in arm, to the ticket counter.

"Hey, Paul! Sarah! Time to go!" Joseph called out. The two teenagers turned from the window they were standing in front of and walked quickly toward the counter.

"Forever." Anne whispered. The way she did it, Joseph wondered if she were talking to him, or to herself. Anne handed the ticket agent two tickets. The man stamped them, added a piece of paper and pointed to the door that led to the plane.

"Just walk through there and an attendant will seat you. Have a nice flight." The man reached for the tickets of the person behind Anne.

"Well, I guess it's that time." Joseph's throat was swollen. He had a hard time talking.

"I guess." Anne's voice was very quiet.

"Can I have my boarding pass, Mom? I wanna sit down!" Sarah thrust her hand out.

"No, honey! We'll go on in a second." Anne said. She looked up at Joseph.

"Don't worry if you forget to call tonight. I'll call you first thing in the morning, Anne." Joseph saw that Anne was feeling overwhelmed. He knew her looks, and that one was definitely the overwhelmed look. He pulled her close.

"I'll remember. Don't worry." Anne tried to smile, Joseph could tell. He could see that she was being brave.

"I'd like to know you got there okay." Joseph whispered.

"I wish you were coming with me on the plane. Something could happen out there. There are a lot of miles of roads." Anne sobbed. She was definitely crying.

"Nah. Remember, I've got the 'Great American Teen' with me. He can handle anything." Joseph smiled as he looked at Paul.

"That's what I'm afraid of..." Anne whispered.

"No, Anne, come on. It'll be just fine. Really. You've got to believe. We'll be fine. Besides, maybe we can build a new relationship, maybe better than what we have now. It's a chance." Joseph said as he held his wife's shoulder. She stepped back and picked up her little carry-on bag.

"You're right. We've got to get going. It will be just fine." Anne smiled as she wiped the corner of her eye. The announcer spoke up again.

"Last call. Last call to board American flight forty-eight to Los Angeles. Present your boarding passes now, please." Anne stepped forward, hugged Joseph one last time, and walked over to the gate. As soon as she presented the ticket the ticket attendant signaled her to walk down the narrow corridor to their right. Sarah followed.

"Hey Sarah!" Joseph shouted.

"Huh? Yeah, Dad?" She turned around.

"I love you. Never forget!" Joseph was choking up.

"Love you, too!" Sarah waved and moved down the tunnel. Joseph felt a desire to be as carefree as Sarah seemed to be. He noticed that Anne was still standing in the tunnel. Paul walked over and stood by his father.

"Joseph." Anne called in a loud voice.

"Anne?" Joseph asked.

"I..." Anne mouthed, with no sound. She held up her right index finger.

"-love-" She held up four fingers.

"-you." Anne held up three fingers, smiled, and then grabbed on to her bag.

For a moment their eyes met. Joseph silently mouthed the same phrase. Anne smiled. He could see the streaks of tears on her face. He shook his head when he thought of how he hadn't been able to figure that out. Words with one, four and three letters. How simple.

Anne turned and walked off into the darkened tunnel. Joseph's tears flowed slowly.

"Come on, Paul. We've got a long drive to California ahead of us." Joseph whispered.

"Yeah." Paul whispered. Joseph turned and noticed that his son was crying, too. There was no hissing sound coming from him, just silent tears.

"We'll be okay, son." Joseph put his arm around Paul, trying to reassure him.

"Thanks." Paul replied.

Chapter 28

Everything felt unreal. Joey looked around, but he couldn't see any trees. Fog covered everything. He was swimming in the water, and it was cold! He was swimming! He was at the pond! Joey realized where he was, and then he looked down and realized he didn't have his swimming trunks on. He stopped in the water.

A distant sound reached Joey's ear. It was Petey! He was following behind! Joey knew that somehow they had to get to the other side, where their clothes were.

"Petey! I'm over here!" Joey called out. There was no reply. He could see Petey's outline in the dim haze, but Petey wasn't saying anything.

"Petey! Are you okay? What's happened to you?" Joey called out. There was still no reply. He decided to swim over to where Petey was. He reached out with his arm and started pulling water toward him. After it had seemed like he'd been swimming for fifteen minutes Joey looked up at Petey. He was still out there, and not nearby at all.

"Hey, Petey! Stop, will you! What's wrong? Where are you going?" Joey called. There was still no answer.

"Petey!" Joey called again.

The phone rang.

Joey turned and looked around. A phone, he thought? In the middle of a lake? That was wrong.

The phone rang again. Joey reached out in the direction of the sound. He couldn't quite grab the receiver. He opened his eyes wider. A nightstand appeared, with a phone on it. He grabbed the receiver.

"Hello? Petey?" Joey said into the mouthpiece. Joey looked around. The pond had disappeared. There seemed to be a room, with a bed and a table in it, around him.

"Joseph? It's me, Anne! We're home!" The voice said.

"Petey?" Joseph asked.

"No, it's not Petey, honey. Are you awake? Have you been dreaming?" The female voice asked.

"Anne? Huh?" Joseph sat up. It was coming back to him. He was in a motel. Where was the motel? Massachusetts?

"Yes, Joseph, it's Anne. We just walked in the front door. Sarah fell asleep on the couch. She couldn't even make it upstairs!" Anne seemed happy, he thought.

"Anne! Oh, right! You're home! Thank God!" Joseph's mind cleared.

"You're having a hard time waking up!" Anne said.

"Yeah. I was having some strange dream. I was swimming in a pond." Joseph rubbed his head as he straightened his hair. It was hard for him to open his eyes.

"Really? Maybe Thompson Lake?" Anne asked with a chuckle.

"Yeah, where Petey and I used to go fishing and swimming. How did you know?"

"You thought I was Petey! Where else did you two go back then?" Anne chuckled again.

"I guess. It was weird. I didn't have any clothes on, and I couldn't reach Petey. Never mind, it makes no sense." Joseph shook his head. He turned over to check on Paul.

"So, you two must be pretty tired? I see you made it to

Worcester." Anne asked. Joseph noted that he was, indeed, in Worcester. He couldn't remember the name of the town.

"Yeah. That was a long forty miles, believe me."

"So, how's Paul? Is the car doing okay?"

"Paul's out cold. He's snoring a bit, but he's out. By the way, I wanted to tell you that I thought we need to get him in to see Doctor Sheldon. He makes a strange hissing sound sometimes." Joseph lowered his voice.

"Hissing? What do you mean? Sometimes he snores, when his allergies are flaring up. He seemed better in Maine, though." Anne sounded concerned.

"Maybe that's it. We can wait until we get home."

"Well, I'm really tired, honey. I need to get to bed." Anne said.

"Everything okay at the house?" Joseph asked, with a worry in his voice.

"Oh, sure. Everything's where it belongs. The board over the garage window is just where you put it. Conrad took down the flag. I can see the empty pole in the backyard now." Anne answered.

"The flight? How was it?" Joseph mumbled.

"Oh, just fine. We saw one of my favorite movies on the flight! 'West Side Story'! It was great. Even Sarah liked it!" Anne sounded tired, Joseph thought.

"Good. Nice." Joseph found it hard to talk.

"How is the car running? Still okay?" Anne asked.

"Oh, it purred like a kitten. I stopped, but I couldn't find the kitten." Joseph smiled at his own pun.

"Another bad pun. Ugh." Anne grumbled.

"I know, but, hey, it's the middle of the night. It's the best I can do. Anyway, I think we'll be just fine in the Woody, Anne." Joseph reassured his wife.

"We both need some sleep. So, are you going to call me tomorrow night?" Anne asked.

"Uh-huh. Every night, between seven and eight local time. Tonight, about four or five in California." Joseph almost dropped the receiver.

"I'll be expecting it." Anne said.

"Can do." Joseph replied.

"And call your mother. Remember. She's worried."

"Okay. Will do."

"Get back to sleep. I know you're tired when you start using two word sentences!" Anne chuckled again.

"Sleep. Right." Joseph fell back onto the bed.

"Good night, honey." Anne said with a soft voice.

"One four three, Anne."

"One four three?" Anne sounded confused.

"Yep. One four three. Think about it." Joseph said.

"Okay, whatever. Good night. I love -" Anne stopped in mid-sentence.

"You got it, huh?" Joseph smiled.

"I got it! One-four-three to you, too!"

"Hah! That would look great on a bumper sticker! Numbers and letters! 1-4-3-2-U!" Joseph shook his head. He felt pleased with his idea.

"I'll see you soon, Joseph."

"Not soon enough, Anne." Joseph found it hard to say good-bye.

"Go back to sleep and rescue Petey! I really have to go." Anne said.

"Nah. You never get a second shot at the same dream." Joseph lamented.

"Well, good night."

"Or good morning." Joseph reached toward the phone.

Joseph hung up the receiver and went back to sleep.

Chapter 29

Joseph rose before dawn. He was anxious to get underway. The first day of a long drive was always the worst, he thought. You're not used to sitting for so many hours, for one thing. Mostly, though, the road looms long and unknown ahead of you. At least after a day or two you feel like you've accomplished something.

He decided to let Paul sleep as he loaded the car. They had each prepared a suitcase for use along the way, making packing up in the morning a little easier. I a third, and much smaller, bag they kept their toothbrushes and Joseph's shaving kit. He left that in the bathroom for the last walk to the car.

Joseph decided to shave and brush his teeth before waking Paul. That would make for fewer 'collisions' between the two of them. The bathroom would be free for Paul to use when he woke up. As Joseph brushed his teeth he scraped the side of his face with his fingernails. Shaving was always a hassle to Joseph. As his finished a brush stroke on the right side of his mouth an idea dawned in his mind. After a week, he thought, his unshaven face would look like a young beard.

Joseph stepped back from the mirror and imagined his face with a beard. He'd never had one before. His mother had been so strongly anti-beard. She used to say that she always felt a man with a beard was trying to hide something. How ridiculous, Joseph thought. What was bizarre was the habit of scraping cold steel along a freshly awakened face at an unholy hour of the morning. Like right now, he thought. Joseph stood for a minute, and then shrugged. He'd let his beard grow. What a sight that will be, he thought, when he is in the middle of Nevada. A twenty-three year old car with a man whose face looks like a hobo! Joseph smiled. He put the razor back into the toiletry bag.

"Hey, Paul! Time to go!" Joseph called out through the bathroom door. He heard a mumbling and some stirring.

"Huh?" Paul said.

"Time to get up. We're burning daylight, cowboy!"

Joseph did his best to imitate an actor in an old western movie.

"What time is it? It's still dark!" Paul sounded like his nose was stuffy.

"It's five in the morning. I want to be on the road before six." Joseph brought a cupped handful of water to his face, and then picked up a bar of soap. After lathering his hands he covered his face with soap.

"Six? I thought you said we'd be driving from eight to six at night?" Paul said. Joseph heard the covers being pulled across the bed. He knew Paul's pattern. He was trying to climb deeper into the covers.

"On the first day we need to put a little more real estate behind us. I like getting a head start, in case something slows us up later." Joseph rinsed his face. He leaned forward and inspected his beard growth. Well, the first day, he thought, he'd just look like he had a five o'clock shadow. Maybe it will look better tomorrow. Joseph cleaned up the sink and counter, and put his toothbrush away. He left Paul's toothbrush and the toothpaste out on the counter.

"Come on, Dad. We didn't get in until late last night. I need sleep." Paul's voice sounded muffled now. Joseph knew his son had pulled the blanket up over his head. Joseph walked out of the bathroom and switched the room lights on.

"Paul, you can go back to sleep in the car, but we need to get on the road. I mean we have to get going now."

Joseph was a bit firmer in his request. It was more like an order now.

"Just ten more minutes." Paul said through the blanket.

"Paul. Now. Let's move. I've loaded everything into the car except your toothbrush and toothpaste." Joseph kneeled next to the bed and looked underneath; he was trying to see if he'd left anything under there. His mother used to always do that when they'd visit folks. Once that habit had saved him from losing his favorite toy car.

Paul didn't reply.

"Paul, come on. Don't make me get angry. Not on our first day out." Joseph stood up and watched the lump under the blanket that was his son. It didn't move. Paul had gone back to sleep.

There was only one way to get Paul moving, he thought as he grabbed on to the edge of the blanket. Waking a teenager up is a serious problem.

"I'm going to count to three, Paul. One." Joseph started counting in a raised voice. Paul stirred again.

"Wha...?" Paul said.

"I'm counting to three. You need to get up now. Two!"

"Dad! I'm not a little kid." Paul protested as he moved slightly.

"No, you're not. If you were a little kid you'd just get up and stagger into the bathroom. Last chance."

"Last chance for what?" Paul asked.

"Three! This!" Joseph pulled the blanket and sheet off of the bed.

"Hey! It's cold!" Paul tried to grab the blanket but it flew off the bed and landed on the floor.

"An old army trick, son. My first sergeant used to love to do this with his men." Joseph pulled the blanket to the side of the room.

"Alright, already. I'll get up." Paul threw his legs over the side and onto the floor.

"Well, get your teeth brushed and we'll get going. I see you slept in your pants and shirt." Joseph wanted to laugh at how the seams on Paul's clothes were all twisted around. He looked like a tussle-headed waif with ill-fitting clothes. He wanted to laugh, but decided that Paul wouldn't be very receptive to the humor.

"I'm hungry. When do we eat?" Paul stood up and staggered toward the bathroom. He scratched his stomach as he walked.

"Let's get a few miles under our wheels and then we'll stop and eat. Maybe in Springfield." Joseph walked around to the other side of the bed. All that was on that side was a pair of shoes, Paul's tennis shoes.

"Springfield? How far is that?" Paul asked from the bathroom.

"Maybe an hour or so."

"Aw, Dad. Too long."

"Maybe we can stop and get a donut at the store down the road before we leave town." Joseph sighed.

"Well, I'm ready." Paul announced. Joseph turned to look at his son. Paul had tucked one side of his shirt in and one pocket of his pants was pulled completely out.

"Missing anything?" Joseph asked. Paul shook his head as he opened the motel room door.

"Paul? Your shoes?" Paul looked down, and then turned back.

* * * * *

A couple of chocolate covered cake donuts seemed to satisfy Paul. After ten minutes of driving Paul had fallen asleep again. Paul had fallen asleep so quickly that Joseph had to reach over and pull the last third of a donut from Paul's grip. He knew Paul was out because there was no struggle over the donut. If he had been only lightly asleep, Paul would have put up a struggle. Joseph knew this from experience.

Joseph considered turning on the radio, but decided against it. Maybe it was best to let Paul sleep as long as possible, he thought. Tuning in to Joseph's favorites, nineteen forties big band music, would definitely wake a nineteen-seventies teenager. Besides, Joseph thought, he'd have to go back and forth all over the dial to find something worthwhile.

In silence the two Marino men drove through Leicester, Brookfield and Palmer. Joseph noticed the sign for Springfield and looked across at his son. He realized he had a dilemma on his hand. There wasn't much between Springfield and Albany, New York. Joseph considered his choices. Should he wake Paul in Springfield, or let him sleep, hoping he'd sleep all the way to Albany? Joseph looked at his watch. It was about seven exactly. He decided to let Paul sleep. It was only a couple of hours to Albany. As he looked from Paul back to the road, Joseph noticed an old ladder in the middle of the road and swerved to avoid it.

It was at that moment that Joseph noticed the hissing started again. He looked over at Paul, catching a glimpse of him every minute or so as he tried to keep his eyes on the road. Joseph was trying to figure out what Paul was doing that made that noise.

* * * * *

About an hour out of Springfield, in the middle of the Berkshires, Paul woke up. The sun was high in the morning sky. Slowly Paul sat up and rubbed his face.

"Well, good morning, sleepy head. Enjoying the trip?" Joseph looked at his son, then back at the road ahead.

"Huh? Yeah. Good morning. Sleeping in this car isn't exactly a whole lot of fun, Dad." Paul was squinting.

"I suppose not. But at least we've put a hundred miles or more behind us." Joseph looked down at the odometer.

"A hundred miles. Pretty good. Hey, what about Springfield?" Paul looked out the side window as they passed a road sign.

"Oh, you slept through that town! You looked like you were really out, so I just let you sleep. Besides, we still have a couple of donuts left here." Joseph pointed to the white bag sitting on the seat between them.

"Gag me! Those were some pretty crummy donuts, Dad. Any real food around here?" Paul scanned the road ahead.

"I'm sure we can find something, even out here. We just crossed into New York, by the way. If you see someplace to eat, make sure you point it out to me way before we get near it, so I can figure out how to get off the road." Joseph adjusted himself in the seat. A bad spot in the road seemed to start the hissing sound from Paul again.

"Are you okay, Paul?" Joseph turned and looked at his son, then quickly returned to watching the road.

"Yeah, why?" Paul asked.

"Well, son, you've been making a strange hissing sound every now and then. I've been worried." Joseph said in a kindly tone.

"Hissing sound? I thought that the car was doing that."

"Nope. Checked." Joseph answered.

"Hey, look! There's a place to eat! I know because the sign says 'EAT'." Paul laughed as he pointed.

"Pretty original name for a restaurant, huh?" Joseph smiled.

"It's stupid. Why would they put a big sign up that just

308

says 'EAT'? Why not a sign that says the name of the restaurant?" Paul asked.

"Well, since we're not driving on the interstate highways much, we'd better get used to that. I'm sure it's about money, Paul. The sign with 'EAT' on it is a lot cheaper than a sign that says 'LINO'S RISTORANTE ITALIANO'." Joseph smiled.

"I guess so, but it'll work. I'm sure I can find something there I could eat. I'm starved." Paul stated.

"I guess I could use something to drink, and maybe a piece of toast would be good." Joseph slowed the Woody down. He winced as the car hit a small pothole. Paul bounced, hitting his shoulder on the door.

"Oww!" Paul exclaimed. He grabbed his lower leg.

"Bump your head?" Joseph asked.

"No! Something snagged my ankle! It felt like something sharp. No bleeding. I guess that's good." Paul pulled his leg up and inspected his lower leg.

"Something bit your ankle?" Joseph looked down as he slowed to a stop at the red octagonal sign.

"Maybe there was something sharp on the edge of the seat. It wasn't anything. Didn't break the skin." Paul rubbed his ankle.

"Hey! They have home-made lemonade here!" Joseph smiled as he saw a handmade sign in the window. He knew this was the right place to stop.

"Well, I'm ready to get out of this car for a while." Paul

said as Joseph turned into the parking lot. He parked the car by an old tree on the edge of the woods.

* * * * *

"That wasn't bad, Paul. Mom's always used margarine, but sometimes I like real butter on my toast. She says it's too fattening. Every now and then it's kinda nice to have real butter." Joseph smiled as they walked back to the Woody.

"How was the lemonade?" Paul asked as he took the last bite of a piece of muffin.

"Homemade my foot! It was canned. I guess they could claim it was home made because some waitress made it at her house last night. Ugh. Oh, well. That'll be the first thing I make when I get home. Some fresh lemonade. Lots of sugar!" Joseph smiled again. He loved summer; it was lemonade season in the Marino house.

"Speaking of foot, can we see if there's something sharp sticking out from the seat? I'd hate to get stuck again." Paul asked.

"Sure. Here, I'll hold the door open. You look under the seat." Joseph opened the passenger-side door as Paul kneeled to look under the seat.

"Holy crap!" Paul shouted as he jumped back. He took four or five steps away from the car and fidgeted nervously.

"What? What is it?" Joseph looked at his son. He was wringing his hands. Paul had a look on his face that Joseph had never seen before

"Under the seat! Look!" Paul pointed.

"Under the seat?" Joseph repeated. He turned to look into the car.

"Like I said. Look, just don't put your hand in there." Paul was breathing hard.

Joseph leaned over and squinted to see under the seat. Looking back out at him, from two feet away, were two eyes. Two distinctly reptilian eyes.

"Well, well. What'ya know. An old hognose." Joseph smiled.

"It's a hognose rattlesnake? Is it poisonous?" Paul asked.

"Nah. It's just an old hognose. There aren't any poisonous snakes in Maine." Joseph studied the snake from a step further back.

"Maine? How do you know it's from Maine? Maybe we got it in Massachusetts. Maybe it's poisonous. Oh, no! It bit me before we went into the restaurant." Joseph turned toward his son, who was obviously panicking.

"Paul. Slow down. If a poisonous snake had bitten you, you would have felt something by now. That was forty-five minutes ago. Think about it. And remember, it didn't break the skin. You've got a pair of Grandpa's thick wool socks on. Calm down." Joseph stepped over to Paul and put his hand on his shoulder.

"But it bit me!" Paul said. Joseph could tell his son was

on the verge of tears.

"No, it didn't. It didn't break the skin. Besides, like I said, it's an old eastern hognose. I've seen them all my life. He's more scared of you than you are of him. Or maybe it's a 'her'. Anyway, they aren't poisonous." Joseph shook his head.

"But my science book at school last year said poisonous snakes have a funny shaped head. Non-poisonous ones have a smooth head. This one had some strange looking head!" Paul was still agitated.

"Paul! Listen! Why do you think they call them 'hognose'? They have a funny-looking snout!" Joseph was losing his patience.

"They do? You mean, like, it's not poisonous?" Paul asked. He was calming down. Finally, Joseph thought.

"No, not 'like it's not poisonous'. It is 'definitely not poisonous'." Joseph looked into the woods and saw a small stick. He walked over and picked it up, then returned to the car.

"What're you going to do? Are you going to get it out?" Paul stepped away from the car.

"Yep. I did this when I was in high school once. I found a hog in the back of my father's truck." Joseph slowly inserted the stick under the seat.

"Can you get it with that stick?" Paul asked.

"Oh, yeah. You just get a long stick, reach in, like this,

and it should move out from under the seat. Yep. There he is. Or she." Joseph smiled as the snake stuck its head out.

"See what I mean! Look at the head!" Paul stayed away.

"Hognose. Definitely." Joseph eased the stick under the body of the snake and pulled. Slowly the snake's body came out of the car.

"What're you going to do with it?" Paul asked. His voice was calming down.

"I think it would like to hang out in those woods more than under the seat of an old Woody." Joseph said as he carried the snake toward the tree nearby. He put the stick down just after he had made it to the tree. The snake moved slowly toward the high grass.

"Welcome to New York, Mister Hog." Joseph said.

"How the heck did it get into our car?" Paul looked back at the passenger-side door.

"I noticed the door doesn't shut well. Maybe somebody left the door open a bit when the car was in my dad's garage and Mister Hognose just decided to get some shelter from the cold night." Joseph shrugged.

"Maybe." Paul nodded.

"We'll probably never know. Life is like that a lot, Paul. I know that television makes life look like everything can be wrapped up in a half an hour, but the real world is full of what I call 'small mysteries'. Sometimes you go your whole life never knowing the answer to something. This is one of those 'small mysteries', I'm afraid." Joseph watched the last of the snake as it slithered into the grass.

"Well, at least it isn't in our car anymore." Paul commented.

"I'll check the rest of the car to make sure none of his snake friends tagged along." Joseph picked up the stick and walked back to the Woody.

Chapter 30

It was dark as Joseph, Paul and the Woody pulled into the motel that night. They hadn't made it to Cleveland, as far as Joseph had wanted to, but at least they were in Ohio. Joseph was able to park right in front of their room for the night.

"Let's get inside. It's almost seven forty, and I told your mother I'd call every night by eight. Besides, I've gotta go!" Joseph said. Paul just nodded.

"Yeah." He mumbled.

"No protest? I'm sure you're hungry." Joseph stepped out of the car and looked at his son. He was bent over and staring under his seat.

"Well, I'd just like to lie down for a bit." Paul stepped out of the car.

"The snake's gone, son." Joseph had to smile as he

walked up to the door to the room. It had been like this every time they stopped for gas, to go to the bathroom, or for food. Joseph pulled out the motel room key that he had been handed in the office and unlocked the door.

"Yeah, but I'm still creeped out." Paul shook his head as he went into the room. Joseph turned the light on. Both of them stopped and stared at the gaudy decorations that seemed to be everywhere. There were pink flamingos painted on the ceiling. Pictures of women in grass skirts were hanging on every wall. The television had a bamboo box around it, with coconuts hanging from the sides.

Joseph debated how badly he needed to go to the bathroom. If the main room was splattered with pink and coconuts like this he was terrified to find out what the bathroom looked like!

"Whew! Somebody had a party while decorating in here!" Joseph chuckled as he closed the door.

"It looks like a nightmare to me!" Paul added. He walked over and inspected the fake zebra lampshade.

"Well, at least the phone looks normal." Joseph shook his head and walked to the side of the bed. He picked up the receiver and dialed O, for the motel operator. The phone rang, and rang.

"Hello, motel operator." A voice on the other end of the line said

"Hi, this is Joseph Marino in room one twenty three.

You have some unusual room here!" Joseph looked at the cheetah bedspread.

"Oh, you're in the Safari Honeymoon Room! It's one of our most requested rooms! We get a lot of newlyweds that want this room. You're lucky it's the middle of the week. That room's booked for months on Saturdays!" The voice said.

"I can see why!" Joseph shook his head and fought back laughter as he noticed the elephant nose light switch.

"Is everything alright, sir?"

"Oh, just fine. I'm sorry. I've had a long day. Um, how do I place a long distance call to California from here?" Joseph asked, his suppressed laughter ebbing away.

"Just dial nine, to get out of the motel phone system, then dial zero when you hear the regular phone dial tone."

"Great! That'll work. Thanks!"

"You're welcome, sir. Is there anything else?" The voice asked.

"Oh, no. I think we have everything we need here." Joseph hung up and started laughing. He pointed at the opened closet. Paul turned and looked inside, then joined his father in laughter.

"Wow! Where in the world do you think they found bright yellow zebra hangers?" Paul said, with difficulty, as he sat down.

After scanning the entire room, and counting a total of forty-eight different animals, Joseph picked the phone. He had almost forgotten about the call. It was almost eight. He gave his home phone number to the operator and waited as the phone rang.

"Hello?" It was Anne's voice. She sounded stressed, Joseph thought.

"Yes, this is the operator. We have a collect call from Joseph Marino. Will you accept the call?"

"Oh, yes! Please!" Anne sounded relieved.

"Anne? It's me!" Joseph smiled.

"Oh, I'm glad to hear you're alright! Where are you? Cleveland?" Anne asked.

"No, I'm afraid we didn't quite make it that far, honey. We're in a town near there, though. Ashtabula. I wanted to at least get into Ohio. We did."

"How are you doing? How's Paul?" Anne asked.

"We're fine. Except for the snake, and some roughness in the engine in upstate New York. We stopped in a little town and got some gas. That seemed to take care of it. Strange, though. The town was Auburn!" Joseph smiled.

"Auburn! Too weird! A snake?" Anne sounded worried.

"Just an old Maine hognose who wanted to move to New York. At least we know what was causing the hissing! Nothing serious. He's gone." Joseph explained. Paul started laughing from the bathroom.

"Is that Paul? He's laughing?" Anne asked.

"Yeah. He went in to check out the bathroom. We've got one unusual room here, Anne." Joseph looked up as Paul stepped out of the bathroom.

"Hey, Dad! The bathtub's a hippopotamus!" Paul chuckled.

"You don't say! Why is it I'm not surprised?" Joseph laughed.

"What kind of room did you get?" Anne sounded worried.

"Oh, don't worry Anne. It's just some small local place that made one of the rooms up like a cheap pink jungle room for newlyweds." Joseph pointed at the dresser, which had little handmade wooden alligator feet holding it up. Paul sat on the bed and fell back, laughing.

"Wow, if I had known that Paul would like something like this, I would have told the two of you to drive back and forth from L.A. to San Francisco a few times!" Anne chuckled. Paul got up and went to the door. He made a signal that he was going to the car to get something.

"Oh, no. It's been a long day. The pink flamingos on the ceiling are just the comic relief at the end of the day." Joseph smiled again as he caught a glimpse of the curtains on the window. They were made of a material that featured gigantic yellow, red and pink flowers.

"So, have you eaten?" Anne asked.

"We will right after this. There's a hamburger place

next door." Joseph answered.

"Okay." There was a silence. Joseph was tired, and having a hard time keeping his end of the conversation up. His eyes felt heavy.

"I should let you go. It was nice just to hear you're okay, and at the motel." Anne said. Joseph agreed to some extent, but he enjoyed hearing her voice.

"No. It's okay. So, how are things there?" He asked.

"Just fine. Conrad brought your Norwegian flag back, all neatly folded." Anne said.

"Great." Joseph took a deep breath.

"Are you going to call your mother?" Anne asked.

"Oh, no. I forgot. I don't know if I can. Talking to her always drains me. I guess I should." Joseph frowned.

"I can just give her a quick call and tell her where you are. She just wants to know you're okay." Anne offered.

"That would be nice. I'll take you up on the offer this time. Tell her I'll call her directly tomorrow." Joseph was relieved.

"I'll let you go, then, honey. Thank you for calling. I can't tell you how relieved I was to hear your voice."

"One day done. Five to go. We'll get there." Joseph tried to reassure his wife.

"I know. But I'll be able to sleep tonight." Anne said.

"Me, too. By the way, I found the perfect curtains for your kitchen!" Joseph smiled as he looked up at the window.

He noticed Paul coming toward the door.

"I love you." Anne said.

"One-four-three, Anne!" Joseph chuckled. He stood up, anticipating having to open the room door.

"Yeah! One-four-three! Bye!" Anne said.

"I love you, Anne. I'll see you soon!" Joseph hung the phone up. He walked over and let Paul into the room.

"Hey, Dad. I found this envelope under the seat. It's addressed to you." Paul handed it to his father.

"Envelope? What?" Joseph frowned as he took the manila colored object. On the outside was written, in pencil, 'Joseph Marino'. It looked like his father's handwriting.

"Who wrote it, Dad?" Paul asked.

"It looks like my father's handwriting." Joseph replied as he gently opened the envelope. He pulled out a single piece of paper, but stopped before he opened it. He smiled as he thought of his father writing a note. It could only be one page long. He was a man of few words.

"What does it say?" Paul asked. Joseph unfolded the paper and slowly read the note silently. He found it difficult to speak. He opened his mouth, but couldn't say anything. He handed the note to Paul and sat on the edge of the bed. The room didn't seem as comical anymore. Paul studied the paper.

To my son Joseph -

All these years I wanted to say some things, but I never knew how. I figured I'd write them down, that way you'd at least know what I thought of you. I was afraid to write them. You're a college man. I can't write. It's embarrassing. I wrote a few of these little notes and hid them in the car. I hope you got them all, and they are okay with you.

The last thing is I want to tell you how proud I was the day you graduated from that college in Boston. I told all my friends that my son is a college graduate. I guess you know what I mean.

Love, your father,
Paul Marino

"Wow, Dad. Some note. Do you suppose there are others?" Paul gently placed the paper on the nightstand. Joseph sat up and stared at the note.

"I guess so. That's what he said." Joseph turned and rubbed his son's head.

"Huh! I guess we'll have to find them!" Paul looked out the window at the car.

"I guess so. Now I know what my mother said as we drove off." Joseph shook his head.

"What was that?" Paul asked.

"She said something about my father being in the car with us. I guess he is!" Joseph smiled slightly.

"Did he put the snake in there? I found this note where

the snake was." Paula asked.

"Nah. The snake did it on its own. He wanted a ride to Ashtabula so he could live in this room!" Joseph chuckled as he swept his arm around.

"I guess you're right. I haven't seen any snakes in here." Paul smiled.

"Everything else is here, but no snakes!" Joseph laughed.

"Ready to eat?" Paul asked.

"Yep. After I go to the bathroom." Joseph glanced at the bedside table. There it was. A note. His father was trying to reach out in the only way he knew how.

Chapter 31

Joseph rose early on the third day of great journey across America. He noticed that it was not yet five, and the sun hadn't risen yet, as he found his way to the bathroom. He decided to not turn the light on, which would allow Paul to sleep undisturbed. Returning to his bed he noticed that the room door was slightly open. He couldn't remember locking it, but he couldn't believe that he had left it ajar all night. He walked quietly to the door and closed it softly, being careful to not wake Paul. For a moment he stared at the doorknob, wondering if he had just been so tired that he'd forgotten to lock the door. Joseph walked, in pain, around Paul's bed and slipped into his own. His legs ached.

Joseph decided he could catch another hour of sleep before starting the day's drive. He felt sore in his upper arms, from manhandling the Woody's steering, and in his right leg, from pressing on the accelerator. He was trying to keep the same speed each hour. That helped to estimate travel time. As he felt sleep overpower his eyes a sound startled him.

"KNOCK - KNOCK - KNOCK" A loud knock invaded the motel room.

Joseph stared at the dark wall next to his bed. Who, he wondered, was knocking at their door at four forty-five in the morning? Was it their door, or the door to the room next to theirs?

"KNOCK - KNOCK" The knock was definitely at their door.

"Hold on. Just a minute." Joseph reached for his pants, put them on, and slipped his feet into his shoes, without socks. He walked over to the door, looked over at Paul's bed, and wondered why the loud knocking hadn't awakened Paul. He had to smile when he realized that Paul was still a teen-ager. He could sleep through anything! In February, only a few months ago, Joseph had to wake Paul up to tell him that an earthquake had hit Southern California! Joseph nodded. He shouldn't be surprised that Paul was still asleep.

"KNOCK - KNOCK - KNOCK"

"Hey, I'm coming!" Joseph unlocked the door. He was

surprised to see Paul standing on the other side.

"What the heck? What are you doing outside?" Joseph was confused.

"Why'd you lock the door on me?" Paul was upset. He switched on the light. Joseph put his hand in front of his eyes. The sudden burst of light stung his eyes.

"Hey, first things first. It's not even five yet and you've been traipsing around Ohio! Do we need the light?"

"Dad, I was not 'traipsing around Ohio.' I was out looking at the car. Yes, I need the light. I have to get to the bathroom." Paul answered. Joseph noticed grease on his son's arm.

"What happened to your arm?" He asked.

"Nothing. Just some grease, that's all." Paul answered as he stepped into the bathroom.

"What have you been doing with the car? Come on, Paul. Our safety depends on that car." Joseph's stress level was going up.

"I noticed it was running a little rough, so I was just looking at the engine, that's all. Dad, I think that guy back in Maine didn't check anything." Paul started washing his arm.

"Paul, next time you feel like tinkering with the car, or any car that this family owns, please talk to me first?" Joseph's question sounded more like an order.

"I didn't tinker with anything. I just figured that the car should be running better if it had new spark plugs, that's all.

Dad, those plugs are old. Either they didn't change them, or they put old ones in and charged us for new ones."

"But why deal with this at four-thirty in the morning, and why couldn't you talk it over with me?" Joseph was frustrated. Paul had a stubborn, 'I'm right and there is no discussing it', streak in him a mile wide, Joseph thought. He was too much like his grandfather, Joseph lamented.

"You were asleep. I didn't want to wake you up. I couldn't sleep and found myself thinking about how the engine sounded the same after the tune-up as it did before it." Paul dried his arm.

"And you couldn't wait until we got up in an hour?" Joseph snapped.

"Dad, when you get up on a long trip you're anxious to just get in the car and go. I thought this would make it easier. Besides, I figured I'd only be out there for a minute."

"How long were you out there?" Joseph asked.

"Almost an hour, I guess." Paul turned off the bathroom light and headed back to his bed.

"Wait a minute. Did you mess with anything? I need to know." Joseph switched the light back on.

"Dad, all I did was pull the wires off of the plugs, check them, and then replace the wires. The plugs are still in the right place." Paul pulled the sheet and blanket over himself.

"So, you didn't take them out?" Joseph asked.

"Yes, I did. But I put them right back in the same place.

Each wire is on the same plug that it was on before. Can you shut off the light?" Paul turned over.

"I guess we'll find out if that's true in the morning." Joseph turned off the light.

* * * * *

Joseph started the Woody's engine just before six-thirty that morning. It roared to life as it did the day before.

"Well, I guess you were right, Paul. She seems to be running about the same. I'm thinking you're wrong about that mechanic. What was his name?" Joseph said as he closed his door.

"Billy. The guy that owned the shop was Tom. Billy was the guy who worked with him." Paul pulled his door shut, but it wouldn't latch. He tried again.

"What's wrong?"

"The door won't shut. It's, like, not lining up right or something." Paul slammed it again.

"Wait! The more you slam it the worse it's going to get. Think about it. There's something making it do that. We need to figure out what it is." Joseph opened his door and walked around the front of the car. As he stepped in front he noticed a large smear of grease on the grille.

"Hey, Paul. Why is there a blob of grease on the front grille?" Joseph asked as he reached for the handle of the passenger door. Paul wiggled the door up and down. Two children walked to the edge of the sidewalk and watched what was going on in the front seat of the Woody.

"Hey, wait. Hold on. Don't move the door, I said!" Joseph's left hand made contact with the handle just as Paul pushed it out. It slammed into Joseph's knuckles.

"Oh, sorry, Dad!" Paul immediately stopped moving the door.

"Ah! Come on! Damn!" Joseph shouted as he pulled his hand in. One knuckle was bleeding.

"Hey, I said I was sorry."

"Saying sorry doesn't stop the bleeding or the pain! Damn!" Joseph growled. He pulled his handkerchief out and wrapped his left hand.

"Dad, watch the language." Paul said under his breath, watching the children on the sidewalk.

"What? Why don't I just say some foul words and then, later on, apologize? That's the way you do things!" Joseph glared at his son.

"Come on, Dad." Paul got out of the car.

"Let's just get this door fixed and get out of this town! Joseph snapped.

"I tried. It won't shut." Paul answered.

"Well, here's why. The wood's warped, or rotten, near the front bottom corner!" Joseph pointed.

"Oh, man! How do we fix THAT?" Paul squatted down and studied the door.

"We can't. Not here." Joseph pulled open his handkerchief and studied his wound. The bleeding was slower.

"We have to shut the door, Dad." Paul said.

"Paul, I know that. We'll have to tie it shut or something." Joseph turned around and spotted a hardware store across the street.

"With what?" Paul asked.

"There's a hardware store over there. We can find something to use there." Joseph nodded, pointing his head to the other side of the street.

* * * * *

"Do you think the bungee cord will last all the way to California?" Paul asked. The two of them hand wound an elastic rope, called a bungee cord, through the window of the door, and around the back of the front seat. The door was forcibly held against its frame. They were just about to turn on to US route 30, in Wooster, Ohio.

"It has to. That's why we bought two. If one breaks, we can replace it on the road and get to another hardware store." Joseph found it harder to turn the steering wheel now that his left hand was hurting. It was tough holding the wheel with that hand while shifting with his right hand. Miles of Ohio farmland passed as they drove in silence. Near the little town of Van Wert, near the Indiana state line, Paul cleared his throat.

"So, we'll stay on route 30 for a while?" Paul picked up

his map of the United States and unfolded it. Joseph grumbled to himself about how his son didn't even notice how he was injured. Joseph stopped the car at a stop sign. He considered his response. What he actually felt like saying he couldn't. Anne would never forgive him for that. He took a deep breath.

"Yep. Today, Ohio, Indiana, Illinois and, finally, I hope, into Iowa." Joseph settled back as he got up to speed. He decided that this was all that needed to be said. Paul had other plans, however.

"Fort Wayne, Chicago, and then Clinton, Iowa?" Paul asked.

"No, I think we can go around Chicago. I have no desire to drive this thing into Chicago." Joseph watched as fields of corn, mile after long Ohio mile, already growing taller, lined the side of the road. Joseph thought the corn plants looked like people in a New York parade. Joseph unbuttoned the second button on his shirt. Must be getting near noon, he thought.

"Dad?" Paul asked. They were just starting to see signs advertising businesses in Fort Wayne.

"Yeah?" Joseph replied.

"It's feeling really warm in here."

"Huh. I think you're right. Why don't we stop, and I'll check the engine. Hey, look!" Joseph felt the heat coming from in front of his feet. He pointed at a sign.

"Well, check it out. One more down!" Paul smiled.

The sign said, "Welcome to Indiana. The Hoosier State."

"I'm not sure how many more we can get through, but at least we got this far!" Joseph pulled the car over, next to an open farm field, just yards into Indiana.

* * * * *

"Paul! Why? You just had to did you mess with the oil this morning? Now what do we do?" Joseph kicked at a rock by the side of the road. Paul had checked the oil, but had not replaced the oil fill cap properly on the engine. Oil had leaked out all over. Anyone driving by with his or her window down could feel the heat radiating from the engine block.

"Hey, I said I was sorry!" Paul extended his arms.

"Sorry won't fix the car! Have you ever thought about that? You've used that excuse all of your life. Sorry isn't cutting it, son. The real problem is that you just don't think ahead. You think you know everything. Well, let me tell you something. You don't know everything." Joseph walked away, in the direction from which they'd come.

"Yeah, well, you have to act like you know everything when you have a father that just puts you down. Have you ever thought about how you treat me?" Paul shouted.

Joseph stopped, and closed his eyes. He didn't turn around. He was stunned. Those sentences sounded too familiar. It was an echo from a long time ago. The words went right through him like an arrow. He had become his father. How he hated what he had become. A car passed by, then two. Joseph slowly turned around. Joseph put his hand up - his injured hand.

"Okay. Stop. That's enough. You've hurt me enough." Joseph was trembling. He could barely say the words loud enough for Paul to hear.

Joseph looked up and to his right. There was the "Welcome to Indiana" sign. Some welcome, he thought. Then the situation became clear to Joseph. Paul had thrown an insult from one state to another. Joseph was barely inside of Ohio.

Paul nervously moved his foot back and forth. He was looking down, as if he were studying the Indiana soil. Joseph just continued standing in Ohio.

"What're we going to do, Dad?" Paul said in a barely audible voice.

"I think we're going off the deep end here. Let's just take a deep breath and figure out what our options are. Can we try and work together on this?" Joseph offered. Paul looked up.

"I guess so. Maybe we have to." Paul nodded.

"Let's make a deal. Let's each lay out our ideas, and then talk about the problems and advantages of each. What do you say?" Joseph was calming down.

"Sounds good. Do you think we can do it?" Paul

squinted as he looked at his father.

"It will work if each of us decides that getting the Woody back on the road, and us getting home, is more important than making sure that one of us is right and the other one is wrong. Maybe we just have to stop this competition between us. What do you think?" Joseph answered. Paul nodded.

"I think so. Nobody's right if we're stuck here." Paul added.

"Well, let's get out of the sun and try to see what we have to do." Joseph walked back into Indiana and extended his right hand. Paul looked into his father's eyes and then looked away. He grabbed Joseph's hand and shook it.

"So, we need some oil?" Paul asked.

"I would say so." Joseph agreed. The two Marino men walked back to the car and sat down on the front seat. Paul had to remove the bungee cord to get in. He sat with his back to Joseph, and his feet dangling out the side.

"Hey, there was more oil in the back. Maybe we could figure out how much is needed and then add that amount." Paul perked up.

"Yeah, that would solve one problem." Joseph nodded.

"There's another problem?" Paul asked.

"Somehow we have to get the mass of oil off of the engine block. It's like a blanket. It keeps the heat inside when it should radiate out." Joseph explained. Paul looked down, and kicked a rock. Joseph wondered if what he said sounded too authoritative, when the truth was he wasn't sure if this idea was true. Joseph considered that maybe (just maybe, mind you) part of the problem was that he was just an old-fashioned know-it-all. He took a deep breath and watched as a farmer with a tractor started plowing the field next to where they were parked.

"Oh, heck. Paul, I'm just guessing. Listen, it's hard for me to say this. I'm not sure if a thick baked-on oil coating on the side of the engine block would make the engine run hotter. I've just heard that over the years, and I feel it's probably true. Maybe we do only have one problem, son. Maybe it's just a lack of oil, as you say, and that caused friction to build up, which caused more heat." Joseph felt his eyebrows go up.

"I think what you said made sense. I wouldn't want to wear a blanket on a hot day." Paul nodded. Joseph turned and watched the back of his son's head go up and down. He felt a knot well up in his throat.

"My father would know. Lord, how we would lecture me. He'd be angry because I couldn't tell a whosamawich from a thingamabob. Man, I can't imagine what he'd have to say to the both of us, Paul. We'd both get a tongue lashing, that's for sure!" Joseph shook his head.

"Ha! I can't imagine him like that, Dad. He always treated me really nice." Paul chuckled.

"Sure. I think it's so much easier when it's your grandson. You can always send him back to his parents when you're tired! Besides, I think you learn to be a parent as you're in the middle of parenting. I've always hated the idea that by the time you have it all figured out, and by the time you have enough money, they're all grown up." Joseph chuckled, and he noticed how much the two of them sounded alike when they did it, even though they were years apart. Joseph shook his head.

"Maybe you're right. I'll have to remember that when the time comes for me to have kids. Man, that sounds like a nightmare!" Paul exclaimed.

"If it does, then you're not ready. On the other hand, if it doesn't frighten you a bit, you're not ready either." Joseph nodded. Paul turned and faced his father.

"Huh? What did that mean?" He asked.

"It means that you have to be realistic about becoming a parent. It's going to change your life forever, and not all of the changes are good, or ones you can predict. I've seen a lot of kids decide to have a baby thinking it will make them happy, or feel loved. Sometimes all it does is make you feel tired and tied down. I'm a good example, I guess. I always wanted to go to Stockholm, Sweden. It's been postponed until we have a little more money. You had to get your baseball equipment. Sarah wanted piano lessons. There are positives and negatives about parenthood." Joseph watched as the tractor in the field moved closer. As Paul turned around with his mouth open he considered that he may have said the wrong thing. No, he knew he had said the wrong thing. Paul's face said so.

"Is that how you feel?" Paul asked. Joseph closed his eyes, wishing he could pull his words back into his mouth.

"Oh, no, Paul. I said the wrong thing. I was stupid. Believe me, I was just thinking of a lot of teenagers I've seen over the years. You and Sarah are definitely wanted. Sweden can wait. Those canals will still be there. Your mother and I made that choice, and we knew it was one we could live with. So, forget what this loose-tongued over-fifty man said." Joseph waved his hand in the air.

"It's okay. I see what you're saying." Paul said in a reassuring tone. Joseph turned again and looked at the back of his son's head. He was genuinely surprised that Paul had said this.

"Thanks. I needed to hear that, Paul." Joseph said with a quiet voice.

"Hey, I'll go check the oil in the back of the car. Let's see if we have enough." Paul slapped his thigh and stood up, back into the mid-day sunlight.

"Good idea. Thanks. My father would be happy to see that his grandson was a practical, problem solving young man." Joseph responded. He decided a compliment would help about now.

"Oh, I forgot! I think I found another one of your father's notes!" Paul reached back into the car and pulled something from above the passenger-side visor. He handed it to Joseph.

"Oh! I think you're right!" Joseph whispered as he gently opened the envelope, unfolded the paper and read the words scrawled on it.

Son -

I made mistakes when you were a kid, and I feel bad about them. I have to tell you this. One night you yelled at me that I was too hard on you. What I wanted was to make a man out of you. I wanted you to try harder. I guess now I realize that I just made you angry with me. I'm sorry. I was stupid.

Love, your father,

Paul Marino

Joseph let his head rest on the door as he stared out at the blue Indiana sky. The wind caressed his cheek as he wondered if it would rain. This was so unfair, he thought. The relationship he had with his father was becoming so much clearer now, but Paul Marino the Elder was dead. Just then Paul Marino the Younger walked up beside him, holding two cans.

"We have two cans left, Dad. What should we do? Paul asked.

"That's probably enough to get us into Fort Wayne. Then we can get some more." Joseph answered.

He turned quickly to the right as he realized the tractor plowing the adjacent field was getting very close to the car.

He was shocked at how large it was. It stopped only ten or twelve feet away, and then the engine shut down. Joseph squinted and tried to see if the farmer was signaling, or climbing out of the cab. The tractor cab door opened. Joseph opened his own door and stood up next to the car.

"Howdy!" A man with a battered old hat called out. Joseph was amazed at how much the man looked like a picture of a Midwest farmer that he had seen in a geography book. He had overalls, work boots, and a plaid shirt.

"Hello! That's quite a tractor you've got there!" Joseph pointed at the green behemoth near the Woody.

"Yep. She's quite a worker, that's for sure." The man took off his hat, removed a red bandana from his back pocket and wiped his bald head.

"I guess!" Paul smiled.

"So, you boys having some car trouble?" The old man walked up to the Woody, inspecting it carefully.

"Just a bit. My son was checking the oil..." Joseph stopped in mid-sentence.

"He was what?" The old man asked.

"Well, it's simple, really. We lost some oil." Joseph smiled at Paul. Paul nodded.

"I can see. All over the block. Say, what year is this car anyway?" The old man asked.

"Forty-eight. Chevy." Joseph answered.

"I had me one of these once. Wish I'd never given it to

my son. He went and wrecked it!" The old man spat.

"Sorry to hear it..." Joseph shook his head.

* * * * *

The gas station clock said it was almost seven-thirty when Joseph decided to find a pay phone and call Anne. He walked to the fast food restaurant next door. He knew they wouldn't be in the motel room until at least ten. She'd worry.

"Hi, Anne!" Joseph tried to be as cheery as possible.

"You've had me worried! " Anne sounded scared. Joseph could tell she had been crying.

"What do you mean?" Joseph was confused. He had told her he'd call between seven and eight.

"You're a half-hour late! I called the motel you said you'd be at and they'd never heard of you!" Anne sniffled.

"But, Anne. It's only seven-thirty now. I'm on time." Joseph said with a pleading tone.

"Well, last night you called at that time and it was four-thirty here. Tonight it's five-thirty!" Anne was angry.

"Maybe the clocks in western Illinois are..." It suddenly dawned on Joseph that they had crossed a time zone, and he'd forgotten.

"Oh, Anne. I messed up. We're in Central Time now. I should have known. Today was draining and I plum forgot about a time zone change!" Joseph rubbed his head.

"Oh? What's happened?" Anne's tone softened.

"Well, we're not there yet. We were trying for Iowa City.

338

We had some problems, but we're okay. Noting serious. Just with the car." Joseph tried to sound as relaxed as possible.

"Where are you?"

"Just north of here is a town called Dixon, in western Illinois." Joseph looked at the nearest road sign.

"I see it on the map. You're close to Iowa City." Anne said.

"You have a map out?" Joseph chuckled.

"Oh yes. We've been marking your progress. Iowa City isn't far at all!"

"That's easy to say sitting in the kitchen in California!" Joseph smiled.

"So, tell me! What happened?" Anne asked.

"Well, before I tell you the details, I have to let you know that Indiana farmers are decent, good people." Joseph answered.

"Oh?"

"Yep. We wouldn't be in western Illinois if it weren't for a farmer in eastern Indiana. We lost some oil, and he helped us out. Cleaned the old oil of the engine, re-filled the oil, and fed us a great lunch! If a farmer or his wife from Monroeville, Indiana, calls, treat them like royalty!" Joseph smiled.

"Well, they must have been unusual folks!" Anne answered.

"I think that's what's 'usual' in these parts." Joseph looked back at the car. Paul was sitting in the car looking at a magazine.

"I'm glad someone was there to help."

"Well, Paul and I worked the problem a bit ourselves." Joseph watched Paul turn a page.

"Good. It's good to hear you two are getting along." Anne said.

"How about if I spell out the details after I get to the motel?" Joseph asked.

"I guess so. Call me as soon as you get in?" Anne asked.

"You've got it. One-four-three!" Joseph said.

"Ha! One-four three to you, too!" Anne replied.

"Call you soon! On to Iowa City!" Joseph hung up the phone.

Chapter 32

Joseph and Paul had arrived at their motel in Iowa City at almost midnight the night before. Neither had bothered to undress or brush their teeth; they had simply pulled their overnight bags form the car, locked the car doors, opened the motel room door, locked the motel room door, and made their way to the beds.

Joseph had made a quick call to Anne while lying on the bed on his side. He had mumbled a few words that, if he were interrogated in a court of law, he couldn't swear he had said. Anne, he thought, had said that she had called his mother after the first call of the evening, from Illinois. That was the last thing he remembered that night, even if it was a vague memory.

"Dad! Wake up!" Joseph heard a familiar voice. It sounded as if Paul were far away, in a canyon or a cave somewhere. That wasn't possible, he thought. Joseph couldn't understand how he could hear Paul in a cave from a boat in the middle of the ocean.

"Huh?" Joseph mumbled.

"Come on, Dad! You've gotta wake up!" Joseph felt the boat rock violently back and forth.

"Paul. Stop! The boat's moving all over the place!" Joseph called out to his son.

"Dad! You're dreaming! Wake up!" Paul seemed somehow closer.

"Paul? On the ocean? Dreaming?" Joseph asked.

"Dad! Open your eyes! We're in Iowa! We're a million miles from any ocean! We overslept! We're really late!" Paul was calling.

"Overslept? Iowa?" Joseph opened his eyes quickly. He tried to sit up, but felt dizzy. He grabbed on to the headboard and slowly pulled himself into an upright position.

"Dad! It's almost ten in the morning! We were supposed to be halfway across the state by now!" Paul jumped over to the window and opened the blinds. Bright, clear sunlight streamed across the room.

"Oh, no! Ten? You're kidding! Joseph reached for his watch on the nightstand. It was gone.

"What're you looking for?" Paul asked in a panic.

"Watch. My watch." Joseph looked on the floor next to the bed.

"Dad! Wake up! It's on your wrist!" Paul pointed as he headed for the bathroom. Joseph looked at his watch. He had re-set it to Central Time the night before, in Illinois. It definitely indicated two minutes to ten.

"Oh, Lord! What happened to our wakeup call this morning at seven?" Joseph tried to stand up, but couldn't. He felt a bit light-headed.

"Did you ask for one when we checked in?" Paul was busy combing his hair, then brushing his teeth.

"I thought you did, Paul." Joseph scratched his head and rubbed his eyes.

"I thought you were going to do it. What're we going to do, Dad? We're really late!"

"Well, first of all, let's not panic. I'll change tonight's reservation for somewhere in Nebraska. We'll just have to take a half a day longer, that's all." Joseph thought Anne would be proud of him for being so calm. Maybe, he thought, he wasn't panicking because he was just so darned tired. He looked at Paul as he moved back and forth across the room.

"So, Paul. Why the panic?" Joseph asked.

"Dad, yesterday was lousy. I just want to get home.

The sooner we get on the road, the sooner we get home. That's what I figure." Paul shook his head.

"Paul, we're going to be fine. Yesterday was a long, hard day. Today's going to be different. Take it easy." Joseph wondered if something else was bothering him.

"Dad, can we just go?"

"Sure. I guess so. How about breakfast first?" Joseph licked his lips. He had some French toast and bacon in mind, with orange juice on the side.

"Why don't we get going first, and maybe stop in Des Moines to eat?" Paul had his bag by the door. Joseph had to smile at his son's pronunciation of the state capital.

"That's Day-Moy-ns, not Dess Mow-ans." Joseph smiled.

"Dad!" Paul shook his head and looked out the window. Joseph suddenly noticed that Paul seemed cared, not anxious to get home.

"Is there a problem, Paul? You weren't tinkering with the engine again, we're you?" Joseph smiled. He was glad that they had pushed that problem out of the way.

"No, just looking at it." Paul kept staring out the window. Joseph's smile evaporated

"But you didn't touch anything, I mean besides the hood?" Joseph asked.

"Just the hood. It's supposed to rain today and I wanted to see how the windshield wipers worked. Are you ready to go?" Paul turned to look at his father.

"Rain? How did you know that?" Joseph stood up and tucked his shirt in. He ran his hand through his thinning hair as he walked toward the bathroom.

"Can you wait and go somewhere on the road?" Paul asked. Joseph stopped in the bathroom doorway and turned around.

"Now, son, when nature calls, there's gotta be a darned good reason to put your fingers in your ears and ignore the call. So, you want to tell me what's going on, or should we just play this game for a while longer?" Joseph asked. He wiped his face with both of his hands, trying to scrape the sleep away. His fingers were finding coarse resistance. His beard had become quite stubbly.

"I didn't do it, Dad. Really.' Paul started.

"Okay, what is it that you didn't do?" Joseph asked.

"I really didn't insult his stupid motorcycle. Really." Paul stammered. Joseph didn't know how to respond. Well, here's a fine mess, he thought. Joseph wondered if Paul had insulted a police officer.

"So, someone thinks you insulted his motorcycle. Who?" Joseph turned and went into the bathroom. He heard a low rumble from in front of the motel room. He turned on the water, and looked into the mirror. He thought about how good a splash of cold water would feel. He cupped his hands then lowered them into the water stream.

"Them." Paul answered.

"Them? Did you say 'them'"? Joseph let the water drain from his cupped hands. He stared into the mirror. The data from the situation started connecting in Joseph's mind. The data included loud motorcycles, plus Paul's use of the word 'them', plus Paul's admission of an 'insult', plus the fact they were in a roadside motel. Only one conclusion fit the situation, and it wasn't a pretty one. A motorcycle gang! Joseph turned around quickly.

"You insulted a motorcycle gang?" Joseph shouted. Paul nodded. Joseph closed his eyes.

"Of all the careless things to do! Paul! Think! Those grizzly characters just don't mix with a loud-mouthed teenager!" Joseph shut his mouth, even though he wanted to say more.

"How did I know? He was insulting our car! He said it was a rot-infested lumberyard on wheels! Can you believe that?" Paul shook his head.

"No, I can't, Paul. I can't believe you even bothered to listen to that. Just smile and walk off!" Joseph was almost shouting.

"Dad! I didn't do anything!" Paul gestured with his arms.

"So why are you in here looking scared?" Joseph pointed at his son's nervous leg movement.

"Listen. All I said was that it wasn't any uglier than their motorcycles. What's wrong with that? Then this guy said he was going to go back, get a couple of his buddies and come back."

"Paul! Think about it! These are people who are LOOKING for a reason to fight. ANY reason at all will do!" Joseph walked over to the window. There were three motorcycles, and one of them had a girl in a bathing suit top sitting on the back. She wasn't a girl, Joseph realized. She dressed like a teenager, but had the wrinkles of a fifty-year-old. Joseph winced.

"How was I supposed to know?" Paul's voice was shaking.

"Okay, the problem is here, right outside of our room. We have to deal with it. I have an idea. You'll have to follow my lead, understand?" Joseph stared at his son.

"What is it?" Paul asked.

"I have no time to explain. They haven't seen you in here. You're just going to have to play along, no matter how strange what I say sounds. Do you get it?" Joseph reached for the handle to the door.

"But I don't know what..." Paul was interrupted.

"Paul! Can you just do as you are told for once? Or do you want to go out there and deal with them?" Joseph gestured toward the door. Paul's eyes widened.

"I'll just have to go along with it."

"Okay. Now, stay behind the door and don't make a

sound. No matter what I say, just STAY there. Understand?" Joseph showed him where to stand. Paul nodded.

"Okay. Now, get behind the door as I open it." Joseph directed. Paul went into the corner, behind the door.

"Good. Now, only come out of the room when I say the phrase 'looks like rain today', then go right to the car, hide down in the foot area in front of the seat and put that old blanket in the back seat over you. Got it?" Joseph opened the door as Paul nodded again.

* * * * *

"Howdy, boys! Oh, and a young lady! Sorry, ma'am!" Joseph said in his best country bumpkin voice. He bowed toward the woman on the back of the bike. He smiled politely at her, but was unable to continue after she smiled back. He counted three teeth. He switched the suitcase he was carrying from his right hand to his left.

"Well, geezer, where the blue blazes is that mouthy boy of yours? I suppose you've got him around here?" The fattest, ugliest biker asked as he pointed at Joseph's room. Joseph thought the fat old biker had the stringiest, dirtiest beard he'd ever seen.

"My boy? What? My son's a police officer back home in Maine." Joseph looked back at the room and shook his head.

"Police?" The fat man's eyebrows went up. Joseph

nodded.

"Oh, yeah. But if you mean that scrawny, no-account kid that I caught messing with my car, he ran off in that direction. Caught him trying to steal my car battery. Stupid teenager. These no-account kids will steal you blind, I'm telling you." Joseph shook his fist in the direction he pointed.

"Battery? What are you talking about?" The fat man walked toward Joseph.

"Yep. These kids think they can steal off of other people's vehicles. The sell the stuff for their drugs, I think!" Joseph shook his head.

"That boy needin' a beatin, that's fer sure!" The fat man looked angry.

"Oh, yeah." Joseph nodded.

"Take a peek into my room, if you need to. Just me, traveling to a retired police convention." Joseph lied, then smiled and turned

"If there's a spineless, worthless, stupid, mealy-mouthed piece of garbage teenager in that room, come on out and take a poke at my eye. Free!" Joseph held his breath. Here's your big chance, son, he thought. He turned and winked at the old man with the stringy beard.

"I tell you, Roy. This old guy's right. No decent, manly, self-respecting teenager would be able to stand that!" The lady with three teeth said to the other man, in the back

"Well, I'll have a quick look inside, to be sure." The fat

biker said.

"Oh, that's okay! Just make sure you stay away from my corn snake. I let him loose in motel rooms when I travel. He likes his freedom. " Joseph replied. Paul had better not move, Joseph thought. Joseph watched the fat man, who was looking a bit jittery as he stepped up to the motel room door.

"You never know what he's going to do." Joseph whispered.

"What?" The fat man shook his head.

"Corn snake. Be careful. His name's Satan!" Joseph pointed at the room.

"Satan?" The fat man asked.

"Oh, yeah. I swear he's possessed!" Joseph reached back into his pocket and pulled out his handkerchief.

"Old man, you're just messed up" The fat man waved his hand. Joseph winced. Hey, fifty-one isn't old, he thought. He kept smiling, trying to keep up appearances. Joseph started picking his teeth, just for effect.

"Come on, Freddy; let's get out of here. The kid headed over to Coralville. Let's ride in that direction and see if we can spot him." The woman on the motorcycle said as she shook her head. The fat man, and his skinny friend who just stood and stared, stepped on to their bikes. One other man, who had stayed in the back, sitting on his bike, just shook his head and spat.

"We're gonna get that kid!" The fat man said as he

started his engine.

"Hey, I'm okay with that!" She replied with a lisp.

"Slim?" The fat man turned to his skinny sidekick.

"Let's ride that direction and see if we can pick up the varmint." He smiled.

"What about you, Wolf?"

"Let's just get moving!" The last biker shook his head and started rolling. The motorcycles and their riders moved off and went around the building. The sound of their engines faded in the distance. Joseph turned toward the motel room.

"Looks like rain today!" Joseph smiled.

* * * * *

"Whoa, Paul!" Joseph grabbed his son as he ran by toward the car.

"What?" Paul looked around quickly.

"Change in plans. Relax. They're not coming back. Come back into the room for a second." Joseph gestured.

"You did it, Dad! But that was kinda tough on me!" Paul asked.

"It was funny, though." Joseph looked out the window and grinned.

"I figured it out as soon as you started talking, Dad. They bought it hook, line and sinker! I wouldn't have believed it if I hadn't heard it myself!" Paul shook his head.

"They're really softies, actually. I heard this trick from

an old sergeant right after World War Two. Tell somebody that a snake is in something. I'm amazed that it worked so well, frankly!" Joseph walked over to the bathroom.

"Where are you going?" Paul asked.

"Nature's still calling, Paul." Joseph grimaced.

* * * * *

"Dad! You shaved!" Paul exclaimed as the two Marino men settled into their seats in the Woody. Joseph checked his motel receipt, and then inserted the keys into the ignition.

"Yep. Last thing I did before we checked out. The best deterrent to a man growing a beard is for him to see a beard on a fat biker that looks like it needs a razor!" Joseph smiled as he turned the key.

* * * * *

The rain started just west of Des Moines. Joseph switched on the windshield wipers, and Paul was surprised at their sound.

"What the heck? What's the strange sucking sound, Dad?" Paul asked.

"Don't worry, it's not a snake! Back in the forties windshield wipers were powered by a vacuum tube from the motor. The engine's vacuum powered the blades back and forth." Joseph explained.

"Weird!" Paul shook his head.

"Wait until you see what happens when we have to go uphill!" Joseph smiled.

"Uphill? What?" Paul asked.

"The vacuum loses power as the car goes up a hill. The wipers slow down. Sometimes, if the hill is long and steep, they stop altogether." Joseph described the situation.

"No way! That's tough when you're driving in someplace really hilly like California!" Paul shook his head.

"Or most other places! Cars have come a long way, son." Joseph nodded, thinking of his Camaro back home.

A minute later they started up a hill and, as Joseph explained, the wipers lost power. Joseph smiled, and felt like a prophet. He looked at his son, who seemed amazed.

"Welcome to my world, Paul!" Joseph said.

* * * * *

The sun was just going down as they pulled into the little motel in the middle of what appeared to be nowhere. They had arrived earlier than what Joseph had expected, but that was okay to him. They were in the middle of Nebraska. They were nearing the one hundredth parallel, where the climate turns from mostly humid to mostly dry. Joseph smiled as he thought of one page of his U.S. geography lecture notes. Here he was, on the real location of the material on page thirty-six. He frowned as he realized he hadn't brought a camera along. A slide would help in class, he thought.

"Hey, Dad. What're those little black dots all over the parking lot and sidewalk?" Paul sat up and squinted as they turned into the little drive in front of the quaint little motel office.

"I don't really know." Joseph shrugged.

"Dad! They're moving!" Paul grimaced.

"No, maybe your eyes are just tired." Joseph squinted. He swallowed hard when he came to realize that the little black dots were, indeed, moving!

"Yes, they are! Look! One of those things jumped! Man, I'm closing my window!" Paul said loudly as he pointed. He turned to start rolling his window up. Joseph decided that was, indeed, a great idea. A moment later there were dozens of black insects hopping all over the hood of the car.

"Dad! That's disgusting! Let's get out of here!" Paul sat back, trying to get as far away from the bugs as possible.

"I already paid for the room, Paul! I can't afford to throw this away!" Joseph winced at the sight and thought of so many members of the insect world being on his car.

"Oh, man, there'd better not be any in the room, or I'm sleeping in the car! What the heck are they?" Paul asked.

"I think they're grasshoppers or crickets or something." Joseph guessed.

"They don't bite, do they?" Paul asked, his voice trembling.

"I don't think so. I think it looks worse than it really is."

Joseph added.

"I don't know, Dad. It looks pretty bad!" Paul coughed. Joseph felt a strong impulse to keep his mouth every tightly closed.

"Let's make a run for the office."

"You first, Dad." Paul closed his eyes.

Joseph slowly pulled the door handle, and then opened the door quickly. He closed his eyes as he stepped out with force.

CRUNCH.

Joseph gagged as he tried to close his nose, and even his ears. He discovered he didn't have enough muscles in those places. He squinted to look out, and discovered that the insects weren't jumping much higher than his knees. He turned and looked at the car. He had parked next to a bush, and the insects were jumping from the bush on to the car.

"Paul! Get out and move toward me. They're only as high as your knee."

"But they're all over the hood!"

"Because we're next to a bush." Joseph was frustrated. He stepped quickly toward the office, hoping it was clear of these invaders. He discovered that there were few of these things inside.

"Howdy, friend! Welcome to the Platteland Corn Field Motel!" A man in a plaid woodsman shirt said from behind a counter that had twenty or thirty flyswatters lying all over it.

"Hi! I'm Joseph Marino. I think we have a reservation?" Joseph stepped up to the counter.

"Oh, sure! I've been waiting for you and the missus!" The man smiled. Joseph noticed he had, maybe, seven or eight teeth. Ten at the tops.

"Um, it's for my son and me." Just then the door slammed, and Paul walked up. Joseph turned and pointed.

"Oh, sure. That's hunky-dory, too." The man reached beneath the counter and pulled out a card. Joseph noticed the man was missing the two fingers on the left side of his left hand.

"Hey, mister. What are all those little black bugs?" Paul asked as he stared outside.

"Oh, those? Those are the summer crickets! They'll be gone in a few days. Not to worry." The man pointed to a few blank lines on the card.

"You want information on my car?" Joseph asked.

"Oh, sure. We just like to know which cars belong in our parking area and which ones don't."

"Okay. Hey, Paul, can you see what the license numbers are on the Woody?" Joseph was filling in his address.

"You got a Woody?" The old man asked.

"Huh? Uh, yes. A Chevy. Nineteen forty-eight." Joseph wrote down his home phone number.

"It's three one nine five two seven, Dad." Paul

answered.

"What's that, Paul?" Joseph asked.

"The license plate. Three one nine five two seven." Paul repeated.

"So, how's she been running?" The clerk asked as he handed Joseph the key to their room.

"Just fine. Where is our room? Close by?" Joseph asked.

"Oh, sure. Just a couple of doors down. Here, I'll show you!"

Chapter 33

As soon as they had settled in, Joseph sat down on the edge of the bed and picked up the phone. He dialed the long distance operator and asked to make a call, charging it to his home phone. He gave his mother's phone number in Maine to the woman on the line. The phone rang. He heard a familiar voice answer.

"Hello?" Julie Marino said.

"Hi, Ma, it's Joseph!" He said, trying to sound upbeat. Actually he was just plain tired.

"Joseph! Good to hear from you! Anne's been telling me about all your adventures driving across the country! Are you home now?"

"Uh, no. We're in the middle of Nebraska right now. Everything's been just fine." Joseph stretched the truth.

"I'm so relieved to hear that! So, have you met Johnny Carson yet?"

"Johnny Carson? Met him? What do you mean?" Joseph was confused.

"Anne told me last night that Johnny Carson is from Nebraska. I just figured you'd see him there. I watch his 'Tonight Show' every night! I was so excited to think you might see him!" Julie said. Joseph considered how to deal with her. Should he tell her that the 'Tonight Show was filmed in Southern California and that Johnny grew up in Nebraska but has lived for years in California? Should he say he had seen him? Joseph shrugged. There was no point in lying, and there was no point in being mean either. Joseph decided what to say.

"That's nice, Ma, but no, I haven't seen him. We've been busy driving"

"Oh, I see. How is Paul doing? Is he having fun? Does he get to eat at McDonald's every day like he said he wanted to?"

"Um, he's fine. We eat there a lot, I guess." Joseph answered.

"So, how is the motel room?" Julie asked.

"Just fine. There are a lot of crickets around here, though. Paul's been a little upset about that, but they won't hurt anything." Joseph replied

"Crickets? Oh, no! They're good luck in China, you

know." Julie offered.

"In China, huh? You don't say?" Joseph just kept chatting with his mother for a few minutes longer, and then he felt his eyes getting heavier as his body begged for sleep.

"Joseph? Are you there? Can you hear me?" Julie was worried.

"Huh? Oh, yeah, Ma. I'm just really tired, that's all." Joseph said.

"I should let you get some rest. I'm sorry, son, but I was so glad to hear your voice. You've been so busy, but it's nice to know my son is safe." Julie sounded apologetic.

"It's okay, Ma. I think I need to get some sleep."

"I'll just say goodnight and you can do that! A traveler needs his sleep!" Julie said.

"Thanks, Ma. I love you. Please believe me, I do." Joseph was sincere.

"I know, son. I love you, too. Good night!"

"Good night, Ma." Joseph pushed the receiver buttons down and dialed zero again. He placed a collect call to Anne, in California. The phone rang.

"Hello?" Sarah answered the call.

"Sarah! Hi! It's Dad!" Joseph was happy to hear her voice.

"Oh, hi! Can you call back in about fifteen minutes? Lisa's going to call. That boy Michael told her that he likes me!" Sarah was full of energy. Joseph could tell.

"Michael? Is he the one that used to come by our house on his bike a year or two ago?" Joseph asked.

"Dad! That was when we were little kids, like three years ago or something! He's practically in high school!" Sarah sounded disappointed in her father's lack in the area of the perception of time. Joseph smiled.

"Oh, sorry! Sometimes we old people lose track of that sort of thing." Joseph chuckled.

"Do you think I could go out with him if he asks?" Sarah sounded scared.

"Um, well, I'd have to talk to your mother about that one, honey." Joseph felt caught without a clue as to what to say.

"She's right here. You can talk to her now and ask her!" Sarah offered.

"What about your call?" Joseph asked.

"Oh, it can wait. Lisa always calls back whenever the phone is busy anyway!" Joseph heard the muffled sound of a phone receiver being handed over. He shook his head as he considered how teenagers seemed to always take the path that served their immediate interest best.

"Hi, honey!" Anne sounded happy.

"Well, hi! I guess I'd better speed up this trip somehow! If I take too long Sarah will be married to this Michael character!" Joseph chuckled.

"I think there's more dreaming than reality. I'm glad

that you got through. The phone's been busy non-stop today. Lisa, Julie and Laura called. Oh, and that girl that moved to Bakersfield phoned Sarah three times just this afternoon! What was her name? Oh, yes, Jenny. Oh, Joseph, the drama!" Joseph could hear a chuckle in Anne's voice.

"Maybe I need to slow the drive down somehow! I think missing this would be a good thing!" Joseph laughed.

"I wouldn't like that, honey." Anne sounded more serious.

"I know. I'm sorry. I was just teasing." Joseph apologized.

"Well, it will be over soon. So, I presume the dating is out of the question?" Anne asked.

"Let me guess. Sarah is standing right next to you and she won't wait for an answer." Joseph smiled.

"You understand." Anne said cryptically, but the message was clear to Joseph.

"Well, our policy is that a teen has to have a driver's license to be able to date."

"I agree. I'll tell her." Anne concurred.

"Are you going to tell her now? Should I just wait?" Joseph asked.

"I don't think so. All of us need to come to an internalization of the concept that immediate gratification is not always possible." Joseph's eyebrows went up. He had to smile. He recognized what Anne was doing. It was an old family trick. Through the years they would use language that was way over the level of understanding of their children. That kept their conversations private. He caught the hint.

"So, how is your garden? Any worse for having been left by itself?"

"Oh, no! Vicky from down the street came over and watered it. I dug out a few weeds, but now it looks fine." Anne always perked up when she talked about her garden.

"Mom! What about the dating?" Joseph heard Sarah in the background.

"When your father and I finish our conversation, we'll discuss it, dear." Anne answered.

"So, how's Paul?" Anne asked.

"You're asking about my ugly, disgusting brother in some other state when I need to know about dating?" Joseph heard Sarah walk away.

"So, the storm has passed?" Joseph asked.

"Well, it's the eye of the storm." Anne chuckled again.

"Well, getting back to your question, Paul is fine. He's sitting in front of the motel window, watching the crickets." Joseph said.

"They don't even have television in Nebraska? Is it THAT boring there?" Anne asked.

"No, that's not it," Joseph laughed, "but I've never seen so many crickets in my whole life!"

"Crickets? Do you mean those little black bugs?" Anne

asked.

"Yes. I guess they're having an infestation." Joseph answered.

"Ugh. Disgusting."

"They're not so bad, as long as they stay out of the room." Joseph said.

"Well, are they?"

"Oh, yes. Just keep the door shut and you're fine!" He reassured Anne.

"So, how was today?" Anne asked. Joseph took a deep breath.

"Let me put it this way. The day started out with us being bugged by a gang, and ended with us being ganged up on by a bunch of bugs!"

"A gang?" Anne sounded worried.

"Not much of one. Really!" Joseph assured her.

"Well, I'd better get off of this phone. Sarah will be back in a minute. She was staring at me. Time for a talk." Anne whispered.

"I guess so! Well, one-four-three!" Joseph said.

"Hee-hee! How long will this new way of communicating last?" Anne asked.

"Not much longer. It sounds too much like a road number!" Joseph smiled.

"Well, sleep well. I love you!"

"I love you, too, Anne." Joseph said good-bye and

hung up the phone.

* * * * *

Paul broke away from watching the crickets just long enough to give something to his father.

"Hey, Dad. I found the owner's manual to some other car and a bunch of other papers under the seat tonight. Maybe you'll find it interesting." Paul said as he handed his father a large manila envelope. Joseph opened it and went through the papers.

"Oh! Another note from my father!" Joseph pulled an old yellowed envelope out of the larger one.

"What's this one say?" Paul asked without taking his eyes off of the crickets.

"Let me see. Boy, those crickets must be mighty interesting!" Joseph smiled.

"No, not the crickets. The guy who runs the motel office is trying to sweep them up! How weird!" Paul pointed. Joseph walked over to the window.

"With two brooms in each hand? Every time he sweeps, they just move out of the way! Bizarre!" Joseph shook his head.

"Hey, Dad, look! He noticed our car!" Paul and Joseph watched as the clerk dropped the brooms and went over to inspect the Woody.

"Disgusting! He's running his hand over it, and the

crickets are jumping over the hand! He's just standing there, looking at the grille, with crickets all over his head!" Joseph grimaced.

"Dad, this guy is really out there. Weird." Paul shook his head.

"Well, as long as he doesn't bother the car, or us." Joseph went back to the bed and picked up the note from his father. The words really hit him hard emotionally.

Son-

Have you found all five notes I left you? In here you'll find a few things I wanted you to have. My Social Security Card, my Army papers, and my birth certificate.

I also left you a little something in the 1935 owner's manual. That's Babe Ruth's autograph. I kept this for years. I met him one day in a parking lot in Boston. I asked him to sign an autograph for me. I didn't have any paper, so I handed him this owner's manual, from my truck. I drove it that day to Boston to get some parts. He said he'd sign it on the page that was his baseball number. It'll be easier to find the autograph if you remember what his number was.

You probably don't remember that trip. You went with me, but you decided to go talk to some girls while I waited at the train station for the parts. Well, the Babe stepped off the train a few minutes after you left.

By the way, I never told you one other thing. You picked a good wife, son. I'm proud of you. Annie is OK.

Love, your father,
Paul Marino

"I remember that trip! I went along! I was seventeen! We went to get parts! He never told me about Babe Ruth! There's the autograph!" Joseph shook his head.

"Babe Ruth? No way!" Paul walked quickly to the bed to see the signature. Joseph handed the manual to Paul for his inspection.

Joseph stared at his father's signature. It reminded him of how much he missed his dad. Now these little notes will forever be his memorials, at least in Joseph's mind.

Chapter 34

Joseph had a hard time sleeping during their Nebraska night. He kept waking up because of the fear that the crickets had found their way into the room somehow. Of course, there were only one or two, but there's something about the fear of insects that keeps many men awake all night. Joseph turned and looked at the clock. Four ten in the morning.

"Paul?" Joseph whispered. He decided he just wanted to get out of that motel. If Paul were awake, he'd suggest they leave.

"Yeah?" Paul answered very clearly.

"Can't sleep either?" Joseph asked.

"I fall asleep, then I find myself waking up wondering if the crickets are all over me. I just feel like they're all over me." Paul sat up.

"What do you say we just get dressed and get out of here?" Joseph reached to turn on the light.

"You won't get an argument out of me. A little while ago I woke up thinking that someone was looking into our room through the gap in the curtains." Paul added.

"Just kinda creeped out by this place, huh?" Joseph asked as he pulled his pants on. He had looked down the leg openings to make sure there would be nothing traveling with him today/

"'Kinda' isn't the word. 'Really' is the right word." Paul shook his head. Joseph noticed that Paul, too, checked the leg openings.

"How much do you have to pack?" Joseph asked.

"Are you kidding? I took nothing out of my bag last night except a clean pair of underwear and my toothbrush. I don't want crickets jumping into my bag." Paul grumbled. Joseph smiled.

"That's all I unpacked, too. Oh, and a clean pair of socks." Joseph said.

"Well, then, let's start Kit Carson up and get on the way!" Paul grabbed for his overnight bag.

"Let's do it." Joseph nodded as he, grabbed his own overnight bag. The two Marinos opened the door, and they didn't care if the crickets checked into the room. It didn't matter anymore. They were checking out.

There was someone sitting on the ground and leaning back against the outside wall of the room. It as the motel clerk. He was asleep.

"What the heck?" Joseph asked. Paul shook his head and shrugged. Joseph returned the gesture.

"Maybe someone WAS looking into our room, Dad." Paul said. Joseph shook his head again.

"I'd say this is one unusual motel clerk, Paul."

"You think so?" Paul said sarcastically as he shook his head. Joseph stepped close to the man's extended right leg.

"Excuse me? Sir?" Joseph tapped the toe of his left shoe against the clerk's right boot. The man didn't move. Paul looked at his father.

"Is he alright?" He asked.

"Sir? We'd like to check out?" Joseph tried again, only louder.

"Huh?" The man stirred a bit.

"Are you awake? We'd like to check out. Is that okay?" Joseph asked.

"Awake? Check out?" The man started rubbing his eyes. He seemed to realize where he was, and what was going on. He stood up quickly, though unsteadily, and brushed a dozen or so crickets off of his clothes.

"Yes. We've decided to head on down the road. We

wanted to make sure we had someone to hand the key to."
Joseph handed the man the metal key with the plastic
diamond-shaped tag attached to it.

"Hey! You two are the folks with the Woody, aren't
you?" The man seemed more awake by the minute.

"Uh, yes. That's our car. Why?" Joseph asked. Paul
stepped back from the clerk.

"Well, I have two hundred dollars in this here pocket
that you can have if you'll sell me that there car!" The clerk
reached into his pocket and tried to pull out the money.

"What? Two hundred dollars?" Paul shook his head.

"Yeah. Hold on." The man pulled out an opened
Snickers bar and brushed a few crickets off of it. He stuffed it
in his mouth. Paul turned his head and spat. Joseph just
closed his eyes in disgust.

"We're not selling, sir. This car has a lot of emotional
importance to us." Joseph extended the room key again.

"But you don't understand. It does to me, too, and this
here's all the money I have in the world." The clerk waved the
money.

"What? Why would our car, from Maine, have any
importance to you, here in Nebraska?" Joseph asked.

"I practically grew up in the back of one of them Woody
cars it was an older type, but it was a Woody car! My parents
went from farm to farm, working where they could. Me and my
brother used to sleep in the back!" The man nodded. He

pushed the money at Joseph. Joseph shook his head and wondered if he was having another one of his strange dreams.

"I'm sorry, but we can't sell this car. We do have to go."

"Gee wilikers. I was hopin' to make a deal." The man slowly returned his money, and then took the motel room key.

"Sorry. Maybe another Woody will come by another time." Joseph smiled.

"Yes, sure!" Paul nodded along with his father.

Joseph opened the driver's side door, Paul slid across, and then Joseph sat behind the wheel. They had decided not to mess with the bungee cord on the other side. It took maybe a minute to undo it, get in and re-connect it. Every minute counts when you are dealing with crickets.

* * * * *

Joseph studied the map, following a thin red line across the map, a red line that headed straight to Scottsbluff. Joseph had pulled off the road when he saw the sign indicating a junction with U.S. Route 92, and the town of Scottsbluff. They'd been driving about two and a half hours. Joseph nodded with a feeling of understanding and started to fold the map up again.

"Well, Paul, this is where we leave U.S. Route 30. The way into Wyoming is along Route Ninety-Two." Joseph said in a matter-of-fact tone.

"Will we be able to eat there? I'm starving." Paul

mumbled. Joseph turned to look at his son. He had slumped down, and was using a blanket as a pillow. It was leaning against the other door, the broken door. Paul had his Boston Red Sox baseball hat pulled down low over his eyes.

"Paul, you can't lean against the door. It's only secured by a cheap bungee cord. It could break, and you'd tumble into the street. Come on. Move over." Joseph neatly tucked his map up into the visor over his head.

"It's not going to break, Dad. I know what I'm doing." Paul didn't move.

"Paul, I don't want to butt heads with you. I'm tired. You're tired. How about you just move into the back seat and sleep there." Joseph felt a bit more agitated.

"It's too crowded back there, with all of our junk. Dad, can we just drive?"

"Paul, now I'm getting angry. It's not safe! You have to move!"

"Crap, Dad! Okay! Here. Are you happy?" Paul slid toward the middle.

"Even though your language stinks, not to mention your attitude, I'm going to try to reason with you, Paul. I'm not going to yell. Listen, I know we're tired. We've had problems every day, but we'll make more problems for ourselves if we don't think ahead. The more tired you get the more there's a chance of an accident or a problem developing. We have to be more careful." Joseph said in a monotone voice.

"Yeah. Whatever. Look, I moved. Can we go now?"

Joseph stared at his son. He felt his hands shaking. He fought the urge to slap Paul.

"Yeah. We'll go." Joseph said through clenched teeth. He shifted into gear and turned onto Route 92.

Joseph navigated the Woody through Lewellen, Lisco and Broadwater easily enough, but he noticed that it was getting more and more difficult to get up to speed. If he could squeeze fifty miles an hour out of the old car he was doing well. Joseph remembered that they were gaining altitude.

"We're not in Scottsbluff yet?" Paul sat up, pushed his hat back and squinted out of the front window.

"Give me a break, Paul. This old car's working really hard. We're going uphill now, and gaining elevation." Joseph literally and purposely bit his tongue, though lightly, as a reminder to not explode. Paul offered so many reasons why he could and should explode in anger.

"But we're not in the mountains yet." Paul said.

"But the air is a little thinner, and a lot drier now." Joseph answered. About an hour later, they pulled into downtown Scottsbluff.

"Let me know if you find a place to eat, Paul." Joseph said as he scanned both sides of the street.

"How about that little place next to that gas station on the right?" Paul pointed.

"You mean the one that says 'EAT'?" Joseph asked.

"Yeah. That one."

"I'm not sure." Joseph stopped in front of the little diner, and looked inside.

"Come on, Dad. What can you do to a hamburger?" Paul insisted.

"Okay. We'll try it." Joseph turned right at the intersection and steered the Woody into the parking lot next to the little diner. Joseph wondered if Paul was being surly because he was not being allowed to have input in the decision-making. Joseph shook his head as he remembered how it had been a joint decision that morning to leave the 'cricket motel'. Joseph decided to just go along with Paul's decisions for a while, as long as they aren't safety issues.

As they waited for their order Joseph decided to try to start a light conversation with Paul.

"We're now closer to home than to Maine, in case you haven't thought of it, Paul. Not much more. Wyoming is definitely in the west! Wyoming is in twenty miles or so!" Joseph stroked his arm as he looked out the window.

"Yeah. I think I've had it with this trip. This was a stupid idea. If we had flown back with Mom and Sarah I would be playing baseball with my friends instead of picking crickets out of my clothes!" Paul said.

"Paul, you'll have plenty of chances to play baseball. Someday you can tell your friends about the summer you drove across the country with your father. I look back at the

things I did with my father and I regret I didn't do more."
Joseph tried to reach out with his right arm to touch his son.
Paul pulled back.

"Dad, the car's slowing down. When we get up there in
Wyoming we'll be going about twelve miles an hour. We'll run
out of gas in the middle of nowhere."

"That's not true. We'll be fine. Look at what we've
gotten through already." Joseph smiled as the waitress
delivered their orders, then read her name badge. He looked
down at his plate.

"Um, Margie, what is this? I ordered a cheeseburger."
Joseph pointed.

"That's a cheeseburger, sir." Margie adjusted her hair
clips.

"The bun looks like pancakes." Joseph frowned.

"They are. We're out of buns. Junior here got the last
one." Margie gestured at Paul.

"How about a couple of pieces of bread instead?"

"We're out." Margie snapped her gum. Joseph opened
the "bun" up. Inside was a hamburger patty and, on top of it,
something that appeared to be cheese soup.

"Cheese soup? Cheese dip?" Joseph pointed at the
yellow substance.

"One of those. Hey, it's what you ordered. Look, here
on the menu: 'we reserve the right to substitute ingredients if
our usual ingredients are not available. You understood that,

sir."

Joseph stared at the woman standing above him. He didn't know what to say or do.

"Do you have two heels of a loaf of bread? I'd take those instead." Joseph was trying to make this work.

"Heels? What's a 'heel of a loaf of bread'?" Margie asked.

"The end pieces, which have a crust on the outside." Joseph tried to smile.

"I'll see what I can find." Margie shook her head and walked away.

"So, how's the cheeseburger?" Joseph pointed as he asked Paul, who just finished chewing a bite.

"Okay. The cheese soup stuff is pretty good." Paul took another bite. Margie re-appeared at their table.

"Here you are, sir. I found two end pieces. Sorry about the syrup on them." Margie tossed the bread on to Joseph's plate.

"It's okay. I can use the syrup on the pancakes." Joseph mumbled.

"What's that?" Margie asked, frowning.

"Oh, nothing. I was just commenting about how nice it is that I got pancakes and syrup with my cheeseburger." Joseph flashed a smile quickly.

"Sure. No extra charge." Margie left.

"Gee, I wonder if I should leave a big tip?" Joseph

whispered as he re-assembled his cheese/syrup/pancake hamburger.

* * * * *

After leaving the diner, Joseph pulled the Woody into a gas station about two blocks away. It was time for some gas and a check of the oil. Paul spoke up as they pulled into the station

"Dad, I've been thinking. If we adjust how much gasoline squirts into the carburetor, and if we open up the air filter, this old car will do a lot better as we go uphill into Wyoming. My friends back home do this to their cars all the time."

"Paul, we had this experience with the Camaro, remember? I spent two days putting in a new one. We don't have that luxury out here." Joseph offered a different perspective.

"Dad, I know what I did wrong. Look, you can watch. If it makes things worse then you can undo it." Paul sat up.

"I don't know. Maybe we could ask the mechanic here." Joseph pointed.

"Okay, but he'll agree with me." Paul sat back again.

"Can I help you sir?" A station attendant approached Joseph's window.

"Yes. Can we get twelve gallons?"

"Ethyl?" The man asked.

"No, regular, please." Joseph reached into his back pocket for his wallet.

"Nice car! What is it?" The man asked.

"A nineteen forty-eight Woody. Chevy." Joseph answered.

"You drove it all the way here from Maine?" The attendant asked. Joseph nodded. The attendant whistled. Paul leaned over near his father.

"You know anything about carburetors?" He asked.

"Yeah. I rebuild them all the time here. Why? You need one?" The man asked.

"No, but I wonder if making the mixture more lean would help our performance going uphill into Wyoming. What do you think?"

"Lean, no. Maybe if it were richer, I suppose. More gasoline. I gots to go pump the gas" The attendant answered and then gestured toward the back of the car.

"Oh, sorry." Paul said. He looked at his father.

"I'm not so sure, Paul." Joseph knew what the question would be. The attendant returned.

"That'll be five dollars, sir."

"Thanks. That should get us to Laramie." Joseph commented.

"Laramie? Or Fort Laramie?" The attendant frowned.

"Huh? Laramie. Why?" Joseph looked up.

"You're going the wrong way. This road goes to Fort

Laramie, then on to Montana."

"What?" Joseph exclaimed.

"Yeah. You need to head southwest, on U.S. 85, which forks off just inside the Wyoming line." The attendant pointed.

"How far off are we?" Joseph asked.

"Maybe eighty miles."

"Oh, no! What a mess! That puts us way behind!" Joseph shook his head.

"Dad, we need to get more power now. Think about it. The carburetor." Paul said.

"It sounds risky." Joseph said.

"Dad, it' easy. Just a twist of a screw. We can undo it." Paul explained.

"Okay, here's what we'll do. We'll try it for a couple of hours, and then adjust it back if it isn't helping. Deal?" Joseph asked Paul. He needed more power now, definitely.

"Deal." Paul smiled.

"That'll be five dollars, sir."

* * * * *

Joseph felt much better as he pulled into a gas station in Cheyenne about an hour and a half later. He pulled the Woody up to the pump.

"What can I do for you, sir? Gas? Radiator check?" The attendant asked.

"Five dollars' worth of gas, and an oil check." Joseph

said. He stepped out of the car.

"Are you sure you don't want a radiator check? Your car seems to be running mighty warm." The attendant warned.

"No, it'll be alright. We've been really pushing it the last hour and a half. We made a wrong turn. I messed up." Joseph shook his head.

"Whatever you say." The gas station attendant went to fill the gas tank.

"See, Dad. I told you. We've been doing almost sixty!" Paul smiled.

"Okay, Paul. It's your car. We'll see how it does into Laramie." Joseph was a bit worried, but Paul was definitely less surly. Maybe there was something to this idea of sharing the decision-making, he thought.

"Sir, five dollars, please." The attendant put out his hand.

"Thanks." Joseph signaled for Paul to get back into the car.

* * * * *

"Since it went pretty well through Laramie, we'll keep running it this way to Rawlins. The mountains really pick up along here, so we'll need more power." Joseph said to Paul.

"I think it's a great idea. We should be able to hit at least fifty in the mountains." Paul added.

"We'll see." Joseph felt tired. There were still another hundred or so miles to Rock Springs, where they'd be sleeping later. Too many miles left, Joseph thought.

"What's the next town?" Paul asked as he unfolded his map of Wyoming.

"I think it's called Rock River." Joseph replied.

"I see it. How much further is it?" Paul asked.

"Should be along any time now. Was that a sign that we just passed?" Joseph asked.

"Yeah. I just saw a sign go by." Paul turned around and looked out the back window.

"Dad?" He asked.

"Yeah, Paul?"

"We'd better pull over."

"Why is that?"

"Look in the rear view mirror." Paul sounded scared.

"What is it, a highway patrolman?" Joseph asked as he looked into the mirror. Joseph put his foot heavily on the brake as he noticed a plume of black smoke billowing behind them.

"Hold on!" Joseph shouted.

"What is it?" Paul shouted back.

"A fire! We're on fire!" Joseph started trembling. As the car slowed down the smell of burning oil and metal filled the cab of the Woody. Joseph pulled far off the road and stopped the car.

Joseph threw open the door, grabbed Paul by the shirt collar and pulled him out. He leaned back in and grabbed whatever he could. He threw whatever items he could reach out into the field.

"Dad! The hood!" Paul pointed. Joseph, breathing hard and shaking, looked toward the front of the car. Flames were coming out of the front grille.

"Get back! Run!" Joseph reached into the back seat and threw a few more items out into the field. He then turned and ran, following Paul. About fifty yards away they slowed down, turned and looked at the car. It was fully engulfed in flame. A huge black cloud was invading the blue sky above. A small explosion made Joseph and Paul drop to the ground. They watched from that position as the car was consumed. Joseph watched in horror as the wood panels on the side of the car disintegrated.

After about twenty minutes the flames began to die down. Joseph made a handful of excursions close to the car to retrieve the few meager possessions Joseph was able to throw from the Woody.

"She's gone. I can't believe it!" Joseph said. He repeated himself numerous times. He just stared at the car as it turned into a warped, mangled, broken and blackened hulk.

"What happened?" Paul asked.

"I don't know. Something in the engine compartment caught fire. That's all I know!" Joseph continued to stare. He was shaking his head.

After about twenty minutes or so a highway patrol car and a fire truck pulled up. The fire truck immediately started spraying the hulk of the old Woody. Joseph watched in strange fascination as they doused what was left of the flames.

"Sir?" A voice called.

"Huh?" Joseph answered. He was still staring at the car.

"Sir? I'm Officer Martin; I'm a Wyoming state trooper." The voice seemed calm and friendly, Joseph thought.

"Yeah? What happened?" Joseph mumbled.

"Are you alright, sir?" The trooper touched Joseph's arm. Joseph turned to face the police officer.

"I guess so." Time seemed somehow warped. Everything was moving in slow motion, but everything happened so quickly.

"Were you and the boy the only two in the car?"

"Paul? Where's Paul?" Joseph looked around.

"If it's your son, he's alright. He's over by the police car. Sir, was anyone else in there?" The officer pointed.

"Uh, no. Just Paul and I. What happened?" Joseph felt like crying.

"That's what I need to ask you, sir. The car's totaled." The officer said as Joseph turned once again toward the car.

"Totaled?" Joseph started crying.

"Yes, I'm afraid. No doubt about it. Are you feeling alright?"

"It happened so fast! What went wrong?" Joseph shook his head.

"Your son seems to think you had a minor error in the carburetor. The fire people tell me that it looks like gas sprayed all over the hot exhaust." The trooper commented.

"Carburetor?" Joseph looked at the trooper.

"Yes, sir."

"Paul! What did you do?" Joseph shouted and kicked the dirt.

"Let's go sit down, sir. I think you need to get out of the wind and get some rest.

Chapter 35

Joseph felt unable to do anything more than just lie on the bed and stare at the ceiling. Helpless was the only way to describe the way he was feeling. Well, maybe one could add the word "dread". He looked at his watch. It was almost seven o'clock. He had told Anne that he would be calling by six her time. That meant seven o'clock in Laramie, Wyoming.

How in the world could Joseph possible explain what happened? He dreaded calling her tonight. At one point he had worked up the courage. He had grabbed the phone more than once. Three or four times he had decided to just call and get it over with. Each time he pulled his hand back. Each time he had to think through some new perspective on what happened. One question remained unsolved, though. Was the car fire an accident, or did Paul damage the car and that was what did it? Anne would be stressed enough, he thought, without having to wonder if Paul and he were fighting over the incident.

Finally Joseph decided that he would just call it an accident and not worry Anne about the ramifications. The 'relationship troubles between Joseph and Paul' questions could be dealt with later. He knew she would bring that up.

There was a knock at the motel door. Joseph turned around. It appeared that Paul was still in the bathroom. There was another knock.

"Hold on. I'm coming." Joseph walked over to the door and opened it. A Wyoming state trooper was at the door, carrying a small box.

"Mister Marino?" The man asked.

"Yes?"

"I have a box of the few things we were able to salvage from the car. We thought you might want them." The man extended his arms; Joseph took the box.

"I appreciate it." Joseph tried to smile.

"We'll mail a copy of the report to you in California. I expect we'll report it as a 'vehicle malfunction'." The man explained.

"Did anyone figure out what caused the fire?" Joseph asked.

"The firemen said there was evidence of gasoline spraying all over the exhaust from the carburetor. It appears your carburetor either lost a part, or broke, or something. Was it recently serviced?" The trooper asked.

"Yeah, a while back. I don't remember where, but it was back in Nebraska." Joseph shook his head. He found his memory quite lacking for some reason.

"Well, it was either that or the carburetor just gave out, we think. Hey, I've got to get back on patrol. Will you guys be all right? Have you arranged transportation back to California?"

"Yeah. We rented a car. Joseph pointed at a recent model Chevrolet.

"Great. That'll get you there." The trooper extended his hand to shake.

"Thanks, officer. I can't tell you how happy I was to see that officer at the scene." Joseph said.

"That was me. Martin."

"You? I don't remember." Joseph was worried.

"That's okay. I found you wandering in that field. I had to follow you for quite a bit, and you only stopped because I grabbed your arm. You were pretty dazed, but don't worry. We see that all the time. You'll be fine." The state trooper smiled.

"Well, thanks. I won't forget this." Joseph smiled.

"Get some rest. Well, gotta get back on the road." The trooper walked toward his squad car.

Joseph closed the door and put the box down on the end of the bed. He opened the top and started pulling things out. It was a strange assortment of items. There was a 1935 truck owner's manual, the four letters from Joseph's father, a piece of flowered fabric that Paul had found in the motel in Ohio, the keys to the Woody, some tools, a pair of Paul's tennis shoes, the Chevrolet insignia from the front of the car, and, unbelievably, the bungee cord from the passenger side door!

Joseph quickly reached over for the envelopes containing his father's letters. He counted them, and opened each one.

"Damn! He wrote there would be five letters! I saw only four!" Joseph shook his head. He tossed the letters on the bed.

"What?" Paul poked his head out of the bathroom.

"Nothing. Just absolutely nothing. Just talking to myself." Joseph grumbled.

"Listen, Dad, We're okay. We're not hurt. Do we have to stay mad at each other? Paul asked.

"I think we need to just stay apart as much as possible, Paul. I think I need some space." Joseph grumbled.

"But, Dad..." Paul started.

"Paul. Enough already. I don't know how to talk to you right now without yelling. Is that what you want?" Joseph glared at his son. Paul looked down.

"No."

"Then let's stay out of each other's way." Joseph turned away.

"Did you call Mom?" Paul asked sheepishly. Joseph looked at his watch.

"No. Crap! I'm late." He said. Joseph picked up the phone and dialed the operator, then asked for a collect call to his home.

"Hello?" Anne answered. That was good, Joseph thought. He wasn't able to deal with Sarah and her boyfriend issues.

"I have a collect call from Joseph Marino. Will you accept the charges?" The operator asked.

"Yes, of course!" Anne said in a cheery voice.

"Hi, Anne!" Joseph tried to sound happy.

"Hi! You're there! And you're only a few minutes late!"

"Well, I guess so!" Joseph smiled.

"So, another long drive? You sound really tired." Anne asked.

"You might say that." He answered.

"Well, as the kids say nowadays, you can 'crash' now."

"Oh, you don't want to say that, Anne." Joseph replied.

"Oh, sorry. I guess that's not good to say when you're

driving long distance." Anne said.

"Well, that leads me to the topic of the day."

"What? Something happen?" Anne grew quiet.

"I guess so. There was an accident."

"An accident? Are you hurt? Paul?" Anne sounded panicky.

"Whoa, slow down. We're fine. Only a couple of minor scratches." Joseph reassured his wife.

"Oh? Then what happened?"

"The car is gone. Torched." Joseph answered.

"What? Torched? It caught fire?" Anne asked.

"It caught fire on the road. Burned to a crisp in a field."

"Oh, no! What are you going to do now? Do you want me to pick you up? Do you need money? Oh, my! How is Paul doing about this? Oh, no!" Anne was panicking.

"Slow down, Anne. I have it all under control. I've rented a car and we'll be home around noon the day after tomorrow. We'll drive straight through. Believe me, Anne, we're okay."

"So, how are you and Paul doing about this?" Anne asked the expected question.

"Oh, we're okay. There is some tension, but we'll work through it."

"Tension? What do you mean?" Anne asked.

"Anne, really. We'll be fine. It's not one of those 'rest of your life' feuds. We'll work through it." Joseph said.

"I hope so." Anne answered.

"I promise. We'll find a way to understand each other again." Joseph assured his wife.

PART THREE

The Stones

Epilogue

"So, Tim, do you understand why I say it wasn't an accident like you're thinking?" Paul asked as he brushed back his graying hair with his right hand. He lifted the old carburetor into the light.

"Yeah, I guess so. I was thinking it was like you wrecked his car or something. I hate to put it this way, Paul, but, in a way, both of you wrecked the old Woody back in Wyoming." Tim answered.

"Yep. We both own that one." Paul said as stared at a box on the pile of discards near the garage.

"I'm glad you see it that way. I was afraid you'd misunderstand what I meant. You didn't do it on purpose, you just didn't know what you were doing." Tim expanded on his insight.

"But I had the blind stubbornness to keep pestering!" Paul replied.

"I guess Joseph, I mean your dad, did, too." Tim nodded.

"Oh, that's an understatement! Where do you think I learned it? He was the 'master of stubborn'." Paul looked back at Tim.

"Well, let me get the door." Tim said as he reached for

the wooden garage door. He strained but the door wouldn't come down.

"Push to the right as you pull it down, Tim. It's a little off." Paul suggested. Tim tried again, using Paul's advice. The door moved down easily.

"Just like your grandfather's garage door!" Tim observed.

"Huh? What?" Paul stepped closer to the debris that had been thrown out. He was interested in the old cardboard box.

"Just like your grandfather's garage door, back in Maine. You said your father had to push it to one side to get it to close."

"I guess you're right. Huh!" Paul smiled.

"What're you thinking about? You seem kind of lost." Tim asked.

"This box. I hadn't noticed it before." Paul pointed to the top of the pile.

"Probably because I put it there. I couldn't imagine it had any value to you. It's just some old junk." Tim moved closer to Paul.

"Just like that stone you were looking for is just some old rock?" Paul reached for the box. He grabbed the open box top and pulled it toward himself. It slid down an old flowered curtain.

"I guess you've got a point. It must have sounded

pretty strange to you." Tim blushed.

"Oh, it did! This cloth, look at it!" Paul pointed.

"Yeah? Just an old rag, I guess, that used to be something else."

"Oh, it was something else. It was part of a curtain in a motel in Ohio!" Paul lifted the box. Tim pulled the curtain out of the debris pile.

"The curtains looked like THAT? Ugly!" Tim smiled.

"Oh, yes! They were definitely ugly!" Paul nodded as he scanned the rubble once again.

"You guys stole the curtains?" Tim frowned.

"No way! Are you kidding? There was some extra cloth under the bathroom sink and we needed some rags to check the oil in that old Woody. We used pieces of it to wipe the dipstick and our hands. The motel clerk told us to take it; she'd been trying to get the maid to throw it out for a week." Paul pointed at the torn edges of the cloth.

"Hard to believe!" Tim shook his head.

"Yep. It was a pretty low quality place." Paul agreed.

"No, hard to believe that your father would keep it all these years!"

"Or anything else in this pile." Paul nodded.

"Well, guys, we're in the van, waiting to go to dinner." Merrie walked up.

"We just shut the door. I found an interesting box, Merrie." Paul lifted the object up.

"What's in it?" She asked.

"How about we look at it at Edie's over dinner?" Paul suggested.

"Sounds good to me! We're riding with Tim and Shannon and their kids. We decided it would be easier that way." Merrie pointed to the driveway.

"Hmm. That thing looks strangely like an old Chevrolet Woody!" Paul winked at Tim. They started walking to the van.

"I guess so! We got the model with the wood grain station wagon sides." Tim nodded.

"I think you mean with the 'plastic decal that looks like wood grain' sides." Paul chuckled.

"Ha! I guess so. I can't imagine why they use a plastic decal instead of real wood." Tim shook his head.

"Oh, I can explain that. Two words: bungee cord." Paul chuckled again. Paul took a long look at Paul

"I hope you don't mind what I'm going to say, Paul, but so much reminds me of your father." Tim raised his eyebrows.

"You know, maybe twenty years ago that would have bothered me. Heck, maybe thirty years ago I would have hit you! Now? To be frank, in spite of all of his hard-headedness, I miss him more than I can say." Paul said quietly. He looked down into the box he was carrying.

"I do, too." Tim said.

"I know I've missed him every day now for twelve years." Shannon said from the passenger side window.

* * * * *

"It's not the same without Edie." Shannon shook her head. The waitress had just told their party that Edie had retired a week before.

"It sure surprised me, too." Paul added.

"Well, we have a few minutes until our food gets here. So, Paul, what's in the box?" Tim leaned over, trying to see inside the old cardboard container.

"Let's open it up and find out." Paul picked it up off the floor and started to open it.

"Wait! Look at this old mark on the side, Paul!" Tim pointed at the side of the box facing away from Paul. Paul turned the box around.

"I'll be darned! Look at that! I have seen this! It's an old library book box!" Paul exclaimed.

On the side of the box was stamped the words "ROCK RIVER LIBRARY".

"Well, I guess we know when your dad got this!" Tim smiled.

Paul pulled apart the tops of the box and looked inside. His eyebrows went up, high on his forehead.

"Oh, my! I don't believe it!" He said.

"So, show us what you found!" Tim sat forward in his chair. Paul pulled an old owner's manual out first.

"I'll bet you know what you'll find on page three, Tim!"

Paul handed it to Tim.

"Page three?" Tim looked confused.

"Somebody's baseball number?" Paul hinted. Tim's eyebrows went up, and his mouth dropped.

"You're kidding! Babe Ruth? The Yankee player?" Tim gently opened to page three. The yellowed paper held the signature of one of baseball's greatest players.

"Well, also Red Sox. Yep. It should still be there!" Paul looked back into the box.

"Look, Shannon! Joseph's grandfather got one of the most famous major leaguers of all time, Babe Ruth, to autograph this old truck manual back in the thirties! He willed it to Joseph! Now it's here!" Tim handed the book to his wife.

"What? Why would you get a baseball player's autograph in a truck manual?" Shannon asked, obviously confused.

"It was all Joseph's father had to use for the autograph." Tim explained.

"So, there was a woman baseball player in the thirties?" Shannon asked.

"No. His nickname was 'the Bambino'. They shortened it to 'Babe'." Paul helped out.

"Why would a man want to be called 'Babe'?" Shannon shook her head.

"Shan, I think you just don't understand baseball." Tim shook his head.

"Tim! Look! The front Chevy logo from the old Woody! Wow!" Paul grinned as he pulled it out of the box.

"Cool! That's something to hang in the garage!" Tim reached out and touched the back as Paul was looking at the front.

"It's a bit charred on the back, Paul. This was there that day in Wyoming, alright!"

"Oh, yes. I think the metal hood popped when the heat got to a certain temperature. This must have flown off." Paul shook his head.

"It's a heavy piece of metal!" Tim whistled lightly as Paul handed it to him. Paul continued rummaging through the box.

"Here are the four letters my father found. These are the ones my grandfather wrote to him. They're a bit yellowed now that they're more than thirty five years old." Paul opened one, then read it silently.

"Like the letters your mother left your father, Paul?" Shannon asked. Paul looked at the young woman and nodded.

"A lot like that. I wonder if these were what she got the idea from." Paul held a letter up.

"I think about those letters all the time. They were beautiful." Shannon whispered. Paul looked at her and nodded.

"It's like some sort of time capsule." Tim shook his

head.

"You know, this one hurts the most for me." Paul looked away.

"Why? What do you mean?" Tim asked.

"There were five letters. We only found four before the Woody burned. I could tell that wounded my father more than he could say. I think that was the main reason we had such tension between us for so long." Paul closed his eyes.

"Why? Just some old letters?" Shannon asked.

"No, Shannon. My father wanted his father's love more than anything else on this planet. I saw that when we went back to my grandfather's funeral. My father was never quite the same after that. These letters were all he had to show that his father loved him." Paul shook his head.

"I get it. You blame yourself because each one was as precious as gold to your father, and you felt guilty for burning one up." Tim pointed at Paul. Paul nodded.

"Oh, yes. That's it exactly. If I hadn't been so stubborn about tinkering with that carburetor!" Paul frowned and looked like he would cry.

"Paul, remember, your father owned a part of that car burning. He burned the letter up, too." Tim leaned over and looked into Paul's eyes. Paul took a deep breath.

"I'll work on believing that. Remember, I had only a few months with him after my mother died. That's not much time to heal an old wound." Paul shook his head.

"But you did get through to him, Paul. I saw it. He lit up when he talked about how great it was to see your kids. He told me probably four or five times about how the two of you had hugged by that stone wall we built. It meant the world to him that you came to see them back then. And I know your mother was very happy to see the two of you. I don't think you knew it then, but she was having a minor attack on the porch when you and your dad hugged. She wouldn't come in. She said she'd rather die on the porch, with the last image in her life of her son and husband embracing. I was on the porch with Merrie and the kids that day." Shannon looked at Merrie. Merrie nodded.

"Shannon's right. I'd forgotten that part, but that's what the view was like from the porch that day, Paul." Merrie said.

"Thanks. I guess sometimes it's good to get a different view." Paul reached back into the box. His hand felt a piece of paper at the bottom. No, it was more like an envelope.

"Something else?" Merrie asked her husband.

"There seems to be an envelope at the bottom." Paul frowned.

"Pull it out!" Tim said. Paul was finally able to get a hold of it. He pulled it from the box. It was a pink envelope.

"Oh, my gosh! One of your mother's pink envelopes!" Shannon put her hand in front of her mouth.

"But it has my father's handwriting on it!" Paul sat back and stared. He lowered the box to the floor and studied the outside of the envelope. He put his hand in front of his mouth.

"Are you okay, honey?" Merrie touched her husband's arm. Paul just nodded.

"It's sealed. He left it in here on purpose." Paul whispered.

"Do you want me to open it?" Merrie offered. Paul shook his head, indicating 'no'. He gently separated the flap from the envelope, and then pulled the paper from the pouch inside.

Dear Paul,

This afternoon you left with your wife and two little ones. I realized that I may never be able to say all that I'd like to say to you, so I decided to write you a letter, just like my father did for me. Today I told you that we had a lot of things to work out, but there is one thing I want to make sure that I work out with you. You know what it is: the Woody incident.

I realize now that I held this grudge for a long time. I know you lost a car, but I lost one letter from my father. We both had loss from that incident in Wyoming. But the biggest loss was of the years of our lives. Yours and mine. I know I did this, son. Can you forgive me?

I wanted my dad to love me so much, and he was so distant.

These letters mean everything to me now. But I realize

they are worthless if I sacrifice my relationship with the man who comes after me, my only son. I guessed that you need your dad as much as I needed mine. Maybe it's like how your son and daughter need you. When you look into their eyes, and when you see their need, like what I saw in your eyes years ago, hug them and I will be there. Then I will hug you. I know your mother feels the same.

I'm sorry if this letter reaches you when you've cleaned up my stupid, cluttered garage. I hope I was able to send some help somehow, like I promised back in Maine! I put this letter in this box knowing you'd reminisce about our trip there. Do me a favor, if I am gone when you find this. Your mother and I promised to meet on Chocolate Chip Creek in Heaven. Make the journey to Chocolate Chip Creek with your children someday. We'll see you there. We'd love to see them!

I'd love to see you. Eat some cookies there, son. One more thing: my love for you is stronger than I can ever say, even than a burned out 1948 Chevrolet Woody!

You made us so happy today when you visited. I know now that I can die in peace, whenever that day comes. My son hugged me!

I love you...ALWAYS!

Dad

THE END

www.ingramcontent.com/pod-product-compliance
Lightning Source LLC
LaVergne TN
LVHW051222080426
835513LV00016B/1362